Pentecost–Today?

By the same author:

Australian Christian Life
D. Martyn Lloyd-Jones: The First Forty Years
D. Martyn Lloyd-Jones: The Fight of Faith
          (the two-volume authorised biography)
The Forgotten Spurgeon
Jonathan Edwards: A New Biography
The Life of Arthur W. Pink
The Life of John Murray
The Puritan Hope: Revival and the Interpretation
    of Prophecy
Revival and Revivalism: The Making and Marring of
    American Evangelicalism 1750–1858
Spurgeon v. Hyper-Calvinism: The Battle for Gospel
    Preaching

Pentecost – Today?

*The Biblical Basis
for Understanding Revival*

Iain H. Murray

THE BANNER OF TRUTH TRUST

THE BANNER OF TRUTH TRUST
3 Murrayfield Road, Edinburgh EH12 6EL
P.O.Box 621, Carlisle, Pennsylvania 17013, USA

*

© Iain H. Murray 1998
First published 1998
ISBN 0 85151 752 8

*

Unless otherwise indicated, all Scripture quotations
are taken from the New King James Version
© 1982 by Thomas Nelson, Inc.

*

Typeset in 11/13 pt Baskerville at
The Spartan Press Ltd,
Lymington, Hants
Printed and bound in Great Britain by
The Bath Press

FOR OUR GRANDCHILDREN

and in the expectation that
'a people yet to be created may praise the Lord'
Psalm 102:18

Contents

I

How Do We
Understand 'Revival'?

*'I would advise you, my brother, not to talk too much about a "revival".
You will wear out the very word.'*[1]
Theodore Cuyler

It would appear that the advice with which Dr Cuyler of
New York cautioned fellow ministers over a hundred years
ago was not widely received. 'Revival' continued to be one of
the most popular words in evangelical vocabulary. Referring
to the need of 'real revival', Wilbur M. Smith wrote in 1937:
'Our religious papers are talking about it, ministers are
speaking of it from their pulpits, young people at Bible
Conferences are encouraged to pray and labor for a great
advance in the Church of Christ.'[2] Similar discussion of the
theme has continued intermittently to the present time,
sometimes with confident predictions that revival is at hand.
Yet, despite so much being said and written, there remains no
clear and common understanding of the much-used word. In
part this is because, like many terms, 'revival' has changed in
meaning over the course of time. It has stood variously for an
outpouring of the Holy Spirit, for any time of religious
excitement, or simply for a series of special meetings. Few

[1] Theodore L. Cuyler, *How To Be a Pastor* (London: Nisbet, 1891), p. 92.
[2] W. M. Smith, *The Glorious Revival under King Hezekiah* (Grand Rapids: Zondervan, 1937), p. 5.

words in contemporary Christian use have come to represent such a varied collection of ideas.

A Caution over Terminology

In view of this confusion in terminology, it is understandable that some would argue for the disuse of the word altogether. After all, 'revival' as a noun is not to be found in the Bible. Further, as the word is sometimes identified with what has been discredited we may be better without it. 'We are tired of religious revivals', William Sperry, Dean of Harvard Divinity School, complained over fifty years ago.[1] So a case can be made for ending the present confusion by dropping the word altogether. Perhaps, as Cuyler feared might happen, it has become worn out.

Certainly it is not a matter of principle that the term should be retained. It is the *thing itself*, not the word, which matters. It should also be recognised that if we continue to speak of 'revival' we must not allow the sound of the word to determine our understanding of its meaning. 'Revival' in English usage commonly suggests the recovery of life when it is in decay and therefore – if that is taken to be the essence of the meaning – revival only occurs where there has been a preceding decline in churches. Such a sequence has many times been the case; an awakening has followed a period of decadence. But to suppose that the word *demands* that assumption would be to fix a meaning which is contrary to facts. The phenomenon has sometimes been found at the very *start* of the life of churches, as with David Brainerd among the Indians at Crossweeksung, New Jersey, in 1745; with Methodist missionaries in the Pacific in the nineteenth century; indeed in the book of the Acts of the Apostles itself. We must not therefore think of revival only in terms of the alternative to decline and suppose that the history of the church is to be divided into one or other of these two

[1] W. L. Sperry, *Religion in America* (New York, 1946), quoted by William G. McLoughlin, *Modern Revivalism: Charles G. Finney to Billy Graham* (New York: Ronald Press, 1959), p. 462.

conditions. Where such thinking is adopted real mistakes are going to follow as I hope to show in later pages.

'But', it may be asked, 'is it not always a Christian duty to be revived and, if that is not the case, is not the prevalence of declension the only conclusion to be drawn where there is no revival?' The implication of the question is that revival stands for the spiritual health which should always be normative in the church. Rightly understood, however, revival and spiritual health are not to be taken as identical. The mistake has probably arisen in part from the occasional terminology of our English versions of the Old Testament. It has been popular to make a link between the *phenomenon* which we call revival and the same word, in verb form, which appears, for instance, in Psalm 85:6, 'Will You not revive us again, That Your people may rejoice in You?' But the verb here translated 'revive' is a word of broad meaning and conveys the general idea of 'to live'. Only in a few other instances of the many where the same Hebrew word is used by Old Testament writers is it translated in the King James and in the New King James Version by 'revive' (*Ezra* 9:8–9; *Isa.* 57:15; *Hos.* 6:2; and *Hab.* 3:2). These texts do not provide a biblical basis for the meaning of revival. For that we must go elsewhere. In using the word 'revive' the translators of our 1611 version intended no connection with the phenomenon which we call revival. We can be sure of that for the simple reason that the word 'revival', in the conventional sense which it came to possess, was unknown to them. Not until the time of Cotton Mather (1663–1728) did it begin to come into currency in the English language.[1]

---

[1] The actual word was used before Mather, for Mather himself quotes Henry Vane speaking in 1662 of 'a speedy and sudden revival of his [Christ's] cause' in *The Great Works of Christ in America (Magnalia Christi Americana)* (1702; repr. Edinburgh: Banner of Truth, 1979), vol. 1, p. 137. But the popularisation of what was to be the conventional sense of the word belonged to the eighteenth century. By the 1740s Jonathan Edwards could treat the word 'revival' as synonymous with the older terms, 'effusion' or 'outpouring' of the Spirit, e.g., in his *Humble Attempt*, 1748 (see *Works of Jonathan Edwards*, repr. Edinburgh: Banner of Truth, 1974, vol. 2, pp. 309–10).

I accept, then, that the actual *word* 'revival', like many other theological terms, is not of biblical origin and we must not therefore allow inferences from the English word to control our understanding. Scripture itself must do that. Even with these reservations, however, it is arguable that there are advantages in retaining the word. Merely to change it for another would not be to end the current confusion because the disagreement which exists is actually over the phenomenon itself. The basic issue, as already said, is how the thing itself is to be understood. Past usage can help us here. The churches of the English-speaking world have many records of times when there has been sudden and remarkable success for the gospel in the world. In connection with those times 'revival' has been part of Christian vocabulary since the 1740s. The phenomenon and word long went together and, if for no other reason, we need to know how the word was originally used in order to understand the published records correctly. This will not only make history more meaningful, it can, more importantly, draw attention to the theology upon which the term was based. By simply dropping the word we might lose more than we could gain from any modern substitute which has no historical roots.

Irrespective of how revival is defined, evangelical Christians are all agreed that it has to do with the person and work of the Holy Spirit. This provides us with a still more important caution at the outset. Humility of mind is a pre-condition for an approach to this subject. The finite can only grasp a small part of the infinite. 'For we were born yesterday, and know nothing, Because our days on earth are a shadow . . . Behold, God is great, and we do not know Him' (*Job* 8:9; 36:26).

Christ has warned us that we, who cannot even understand the mystery of how the wind blows, ought not to be surprised that we cannot fathom the work of the Spirit (*John* 3:7–8). At every point his work runs far beyond our comprehension: his creative power in the womb of Mary; his inerrant commitment of the Word of God to writing through human instrumentality; his agency in regeneration; his mode of dwelling in the spirits and bodies of Christians; his future work in raising those same bodies from the grave – an understanding of all these things is largely hidden from us. As Robert Traill, one of the Puritans, wrote: 'The operation of the Spirit in believers, the communion of the Holy Ghost, is a great mystery. He works more on them than they feel or know; and they feel more than they can express in words; and they express more than any who have not received "the same Spirit of faith" (*2 Cor.* 4:13) can understand.'[1]

Those who have seen great revivals have been the first to say how there was so much which left them amazed and conscious of mystery. In reviewing his life Theodore Cuyler wrote:

After a long pastoral experience and frequent labours in revivals I confess that there is much that is utterly mysterious in regard to them. Our God is sovereign. He often seems to withhold His converting power at the very time when, according to *our* calculations, we ought to expect it. I have had many disappointments of this kind. On the other hand, several copious showers of heavenly blessings have descended when we were not expecting them.[2]

In an address on 'Revivals of Religion,' Dr W. W. Patton made the same point. Revivals, he believed, 'have a place of special honour and power under the dispensation of the Holy Spirit.' But he warned: 'Doubtless, also, they have their law, in the mind of God, though no one has yet succeeded in definitely stating it, or bringing them under fixed conditions of time and circumstance.'[3]

If we could understand revivals they would not be the astonishing things which they are. ' "My thoughts are not your thoughts, nor are your ways My ways," says the Lord. "For as the heavens are higher than the earth, So are My ways higher than your ways, And My thoughts than your thoughts" ' (*Isa.*

---

[1] *The Works of Robert Traill* (repr. Edinburgh: Banner of Truth, 1975), vol. 2, p. 44.
[2] Cuyler, *How To Be a Pastor*, p. 88.
[3] *History of the Sixth General Conference of the Evangelical Alliance, Held in New York, 1873*, eds. Philip Schaff and S. Irenaeus Prime (New York: Harper, 1874), p. 355.

55:8–9). Patton's caution is right. Andrew Murray, who had experience of revival in South Africa, gave similar warning when he wrote: 'We must beware of laying down fixed rules. God's gifts and love are larger than our hearts.'[1] There are matters here which are beyond us and will ever be beyond us. Yet this is not to say that we should be resigned to the difficulties arising out of the current confusion of thought. Difficulty does not lessen responsibility. In 1 Peter 1:12–13 the apostle says that the great things foretold by the prophets and now announced through preachers 'by the Holy Spirit sent from heaven' are 'things which angels desire to look into'. But though the subject exceeds even the grasp of angels, the command follows, 'Therefore gird up the loins of your mind'. Our thoughts are not to be left hanging loose like clothes impeding one who must run. We must earnestly desire to understand.

It is noteworthy that there are more books describing revivals than there are those which deal with their biblical basis. That may be because to read about revivals is more pleasant, and initially, perhaps, more inspiring, than undergoing the struggle to establish a biblical theology which explains and justifies the phenomenon. But in the long run it has to be the latter which is more important. As a recent writer has noted: 'We need to think more about certain questions raised by revivals rather than read more about more revivals. What is revival? The question of definition is fundamental.'[2] And one reason why it is fundamental is that different and conflicting theories inevitably have direct practical consequences in the life of the church. Teaching on any spiritual subject, whether true or false, always has implications for experience, and eminently so on a theme as

[1] A. Murray, *The Spirit of Christ* (London: Nisbet, n.d.), p. 324.
[2] *Reviving Australia: Essays on the History and Experiences of Revival and Revivalism in Australian Christianity*, eds. Mark Hutcheson and Stuart Piggin (Sydney: Centre for the Study of Australian Christianity, Robert Menzies College, 1994), p. 6. The book, however, does not go on to address the question.

important as this one. The priority therefore has to be an examination of current views in order to form a judgement on which of them, if any, can best be justified from Scripture.

It would appear that current differences on revival among those who acknowledge Scripture as the Word of God can be reduced to three schools of interpretation. I will take these up in turn.

Pentecost, Once and For All

This first view affirms that *the whole concept of occasional revivals is not biblical at all.* We should not, it is said, speak of revivals as extraordinary, periodic events because the *whole* age in which we live is that of Pentecost and of 'the last days'. The Old Testament church prayed for revival. God promised that he would revive his people by the outpouring of the Spirit in 'the last days' and these prayers and promises were permanently fulfilled on the day of Pentecost. Then it was that the Holy Spirit was given, and given according to Christ's promise, 'I will pray the Father, and He will give you another Helper, that He may abide with you forever' (*John* 14:16). So the Holy Spirit is part of the church's *present* inheritance. Does the Scripture not say, 'If anyone does not have the Spirit of Christ, he is not His' (*Rom.* 8:9) or again, 'By one Spirit we were all baptized into one body' (*1 Cor.* 12:13)? Revival means the presence of the Holy Spirit and because the Spirit is given the need of Christians is *to realise what is already theirs.* Any idea of revival as an outpouring of the Spirit as a future event, to be awaited and prayed for, is therefore, they argue, a serious mistake.

This view has been widely held in reformed churches of the Dutch tradition. One of its spokesmen was the eminent Abraham Kuyper who wrote:

Prayer for another outpouring or baptism of the Holy Spirit is incorrect and empty of real meaning. Such prayer actually denies the Pentecost miracle. For He that came and abides with us can no more come to us.[1]

Frederick D. Bruner takes the same position in his more recent well-known book, *A Theology of the Holy Spirit*. The baptism of the Spirit, he says, belongs exclusively to Pentecost and there can be no 'replicas' of Pentecost, no 'little Pentecosts'.[2]

We shall return later to this view but for the moment I want to proceed to a second and very different understanding.

Revival Conditional upon Obedience

This second view holds that *the presence or absence of revival is conditional upon the obedience of the church and the behaviour of Christians.* It is sometimes added that revival could be permanent and continuous, but it is not, and the reason is because we fail to do what God requires of us. For clarification we can further sub-divide this view:

1. There are those who believe that revival can be secured by intense and prayerful evangelistic effort. They say, God has given us the means to evangelise the world and if only we are faithful, if we witness, and preach, and pray, there is bound to be revival. Charles G. Finney is the best known advocate of this position and it is set out fully in his *Lectures on Revival*. 'A revival,' he argued, 'is as naturally a result of the use of the appropriate means as a crop is of the use of its appropriate means'; and if the right means continued to be employed 'revival would never cease.'[3]

---

[1] A. Kuyper, *The Work of the Holy Spirit* (1900; repr. Grand Rapids: W. B. Eerdmans, 1956), p. 127.

[2] F. D. Bruner, *A Theology of the Holy Spirit* (London: Hodder and Stoughton, 1970), pp. 169–70.

[3] C. G. Finney, *Revivals of Religion, or Lectures on Revival* (1835, repr. Old Tappan, N.J.: Revell, n.d.), pp. 5, 534. Fuller attention to Finney's teaching will be given in Chapter 2 below, and, for greater detail, see my *Revival and Revivalism: The Making and Marring of American Evangelicalism, 1750–1858* (Edinburgh: Banner of Truth, 1994).

2. More common, perhaps, is the opinion of those who put their emphasis, not so much on evangelism, but upon the necessity of repentance and renewed personal holiness as the means of bringing revival. One of the many advocates of this view early in this century was Jonathan Goforth, a missionary in China, who wrote:

If God the Holy Spirit is not glorifying Jesus Christ in the world to-day, as at Pentecost, it is simply we who are to blame. After all, what is revival but simply the Holy Spirit fully controlling the surrendered life? It must always be possible, then, when man yields. The sin of unyieldedness, alone, can keep us from revival . . . Pentecost is yet within our grasp. If revival is being withheld from us it is because some idol remains still enthroned.[1]

A more recent exponent of the same view was the Rev. Duncan Campbell who set it out in his book, *The Price and Power of Revival.* 'How is it,' he asks, 'that revival tarries? Is there any reason why the church today cannot everywhere equal the church at Pentecost?' He believed that 'we have only to regard and observe those laws and limits within which the Holy Spirit acts, and we shall find His glorious power at our disposal.' The essential thing, he taught, is sanctification, 'clean hands and a pure heart' (*Psa.* 24:4) – repentance, submission, consecration. 'A full and complete surrender is the place of blessing, but that also is the price of revival.'[2]

In connection with this emphasis the text most often quoted is 2 Chronicles 7:14: 'If My people who are called by My name will humble themselves, and pray and seek My face, and turn from their wicked ways, then I will hear from heaven, and will forgive their sin, and heal their land.' Thus Campbell, speaking of a revival on the island of Bernera in the Hebrides, said that his hearers should note 'the principle brought into operation', and proceeded to quote the scripture we have just cited. He then continued: 'There was at least *one man* on that

[1] Jonathan Goforth, *By My Spirit,* 3rd ed. (London: Marshall, Morgan & Scott, n.d.), pp. 181, 189.
[2] D. Campbell, *The Price and Power of Revival* (London: Scripture Illustrations, 1956), pp. 40, 53–4.

island who fulfilled the conditions of that one passage of Scripture, and because he fulfilled the conditions, God, being a covenant-keeping God, must be true to his covenant engagements. And God, to vindicate his own honour, had to listen to the prayers of the parish postman who knelt in a barn for a whole day.'[1]

Now let us consider this second position. It must be understood what is *not* the issue here. It is not in question whether God uses means, such as faith in promises, prayer and preaching, in revivals; that ought to be universally agreed. Any idea that in revival Christians cease to act and God simply 'takes over' is the worst kind of fanaticism. 'It is ridiculous,' writes John Owen, 'for a man to say he will do nothing, because the Spirit of God doth all; for where he doth nothing, the Spirit of God doth nothing unless it be merely in the infusion of the first habit or principle of grace [i.e., in regeneration]'.[2] Promises and duties are given to Christians to be acted on. But the issue is whether it is our obedience in the use of means which *produces* revivals; that is to say, whether the relationship between the one and the other is simply one of cause and effect. It obscures the issue merely to say that Finney 'felt that revival could be brought about by the use of human means under the power of the Holy Spirit'.[3]

Neither is the issue whether earnest, prayerful evangelism will, sooner or later, lead to real blessing. All are agreed that there is scriptural warrant for believing that it will. So too it is

[1] *The Nature of a God-Sent Revival*, an address given in Canada (Rare Christian Books: Rt. 2, Box 180, Decatur, TX 76234, n.d.), p. 14.

[2] *Works of John Owen*, ed. W. H. Goold, vol. 3 (repr. London: Banner of Truth, 1967), p. 204. Owen's treatment here is very relevant to the question of how our fulfilment of duties or conditions determines events (see pp. 200–4). He shows that our obedience to promises and duties, and the measure of blessing resulting, is not to be understood without regard to the hidden working of the Spirit in us. For to suppose that all depends on 'obedience performed in our own strength' is to distort the whole nature of gospel grace. See also *Collected Writings of J. H. Thornwell* (repr. Edinburgh: Banner of Truth, 1974), vol. 2, pp. 392–4.

[3] E. E. Cairns, *An Endless Line of Splendor* (Wheaton: Tyndale House, 1986), p. 26.

agreed that a concern for a closer walk with God, for an advance in personal holiness, will ever lead to greater spiritual health. But to say that either one or the other of these endeavours will *ensure* and *guarantee* revival is a different matter. In some instances these things have preceded revival but I believe it is wrong to say that there is any promise that where they exist a revival must follow.

Take the case that makes revival conditional largely on evangelism. This argument is assuming that somewhere in the Bible there is a promise that preaching Christ, accompanied by prayer, will always secure remarkable success: so long as we use the means, there is bound to be such a result. But where has God promised that the scale of his blessing will be in proportion to our endeavours? *Our* activity is not the controlling factor. Two men may preach and pray with equal zeal and faithfulness and yet with very different results. Peter is used to bring in three thousand at Pentecost; Paul, beside the river at Philippi, brings in one woman. Was it because Peter was more eloquent and persuasive? Not at all. The same man may preach the same message in two places, with no apparent effect in the one and a harvest in the other. The explanation for such differences when the gospel is preached lies ultimately with God himself. Thus Scripture teaches: 'I planted, Apollos watered; but God gave the increase. So then neither he who plants is anything, nor he who waters, but God who gives the increase' (*1 Cor.* 3:6–7; *Matt.* 11:25; *Acts* 13:48, etc.). Passion for the souls of men and women is certainly our responsibility, and the doctrine of divine sovereignty is never taught in Scripture to justify inaction, as many texts show (e.g., *Prov.* 24:11–12), but the salvation of souls whether in ones and twos or in hundreds is not finally determined by our efforts.

The evidence of church history is also against the view that revival is conditional upon our conduct. Many who have spent a lifetime in continued labours for the gospel have confessed that at certain periods they saw far more conversions than they did at other times. But, as with Cuyler's testimony, already quoted, these larger blessings did not come because of larger efforts, they came unexpectedly. To quote Cuyler again:

We must bear in mind that God always means to be God. He bestows spiritual blessings when he pleases, how he pleases, and where he pleases. We may labour, we may pray, we may 'plant', but we must not dictate . . . Never, in my whole life, have I arranged any peculiar measures to produce a revival which have been successful.[1]

On his second visit to America in 1740, Whitefield was wonderfully used of God in the Great Awakening. He came to the thirteen colonies another five times but without ever witnessing the same great harvest again. In 1857, early in his London ministry, Spurgeon could say, 'In one year it was my happiness personally to see not less than a thousand who had then been converted'.[2] But after 1859, in more than thirty more years of his mature ministry in London, the statement was never to be repeated. William Chalmers Burns was much used in revival in Scotland in the years 1839–46. Then he went to China, where he died in 1868, and during those last twenty years there was no continuation of the blessing on the same scale.[3] Here were the same men, labouring faithfully with the same means of grace, and yet with different results. The theory that evangelism secures revival is disproved by facts.

What then of the call to repentance and holiness as the way to revival? Again, it has to be said that it does not fit the facts. Whitefield, Spurgeon, and Burns were not less sanctified when their ministries bore less numerical fruit. Many of the godliest servants of Christ never saw what we call a revival. Henry Martyn of India is but one of many examples. In this

[1] Cuyler, *How To Be a Pastor*, pp. 91–2.
[2] *C. H. Spurgeon's Autobiography*, vol. 1 (London: Passmore and Alabaster, 1899), p. 43.
[3] The biography of Burns notes one 'outpouring of the Spirit' in China, but at another period he laboured for seven years 'without seeing one soul brought to Christ', Islay Burns, *Memoir of W. C. Burns* (London: Nisbet, 1870), pp. 510, 553. Goforth is clearly wrong to say of 'this great evangelist' that 'all with whom he came in contact were brought to a saving knowledge of Christ' (*By My Spirit*, p. 59).

connection words once written by Dr Simeon MacPhail are significant. MacPhail believed in revival and was a worker in the great revival of 1859 in Scotland, but this is what he later said on the point we are now considering:

It would be a great error to suppose that all the instruments during a season of Revival are more holy, more devoted, more prayerful, or more richly possessed of the knowledge of God's word than others, or than the same men at other times. Many men, much used at Revival work, are conspicuously less marked in all these respects than very many of their compeers. Some, indeed, of those most prominent fifty years ago were much inferior in character, or in Scripture knowledge to ordinary Christians. Also, of those then so largely blessed many could testify that in later years they were not only better men, but lived much more entirely for God and with God than they did then, and yet the power was not with them as in those flood-times of grace. These are no doubt, in some respects, disconcerting statements; but they are not only true, but exactly what Scripture and Scripture history lead us to expect. Power and holiness are not necessarily combined, as Peter taught from the first (*Acts* 3:12).[1]

Confusing Old and New Testaments

But if our actions do not determine revival what are we to make of such promises as the one given to Solomon in 2 Chronicles 7:14? ('If My people . . . then I will hear . . . and heal their land'). The first thing to say is surely that what is being promised is not revival, for the promise has to be understood, in the first instance, in relation to the time when it was given. It is of Old Testament Israel and her land of which healing is there spoken. The promise cannot be of revival, for revival has to do with the abundant giving of the Holy Spirit and that giving, as Old Testament Scripture made clear, lay in the future. It was in the future for Joel, for Ezekiel and all the prophets: 'It shall come to pass *afterward* that I will pour out My Spirit on all flesh' (*Joel* 2:28; *Ezek.* 47:1–10). The blessing

[1] *Reminiscences of the Revival of '59 and the Sixties* (Aberdeen: University Press, 1910), pp. 14–15.

was to follow Messiah's death (*Zech.* 12:10). The mission of the Spirit had to await the fulfilment of Christ's mediatorial work in his sufferings and glorification. Thus we read: 'The Holy Spirit was not yet given, because Jesus was not yet glorified' (*John* 7:39); 'It is to your advantage that I go away: for if I do not go away, the Helper will not come to you; but if I depart, I will send Him to you' (*John* 16:7).

That the Holy Spirit was active in his influences and gifts in the Old Testament is not, of course, denied by these texts. But to identify the Old Testament level of the Spirit's presence and operations with the remarkable kind and measure which was dependent upon Christ's exaltation and intercession is to miss the glory which belongs to gospel times. As John Owen has shown so clearly in his work on *The Holy Spirit*, Old Testament texts which speak of the outpouring and plentiful communications of the Spirit have 'direct respect unto the times of the gospel . . . Although God gave his Spirit in some measure before, yet he poured him not out until he [Christ] was first anointed with his fulness.'[1] To treat a promise made to Solomon as a text on revival is to apply to the age of 2 Chronicles what was not to be seen in the world until the days of the apostles. Revival cannot be made a part of Old Testament experience without, to use Sinclair Ferguson's words, 'flattening the contours of redemptive history, and . . . undermining the genuine diversity and development from old to new covenants.'[2] 'The Spirit had been active among God's people; but his activity was enigmatic, sporadic, theocratic, selective and in some respects external. The prophets longed for better days.'[3]

But what then is the abiding significance of the instruction and promise given through Solomon? Is it not, simply, that

[1] John Owen, *Works*, vol. 3, p. 114. See also pp. 153–6: 'Jesus Christ bequeathed his Spirit as his great legacy unto his disciples.'
[2] Sinclair B. Ferguson, *The Holy Spirit* (Downers Grove: IVP, 1996), p. 26. He adds, 'Paul's teaching in 2 Corinthians 3 indicates that there is an epochal development from the old to the new precisely in terms of the ministry of the Spirit.'
[3] *Ibid.*, p. 30.

God requires obedience and holiness of life of all who profess
his name and that such obedience will not be unrewarded?
But we cannot transfer the nature of that reward from the Old
Testament to the New. As Thomas M'Crie writes:

> The peculiarity of the divine government of Israel, or, as it is
> commonly called the *Theocracy,* consisted in general in two things: in
> a system of laws which was immediately given unto that people from
> heaven . . . and in the exercise of a peculiar providence in
> supporting and sanctioning that system, by conferring national
> mercies and inflicting national judgments, often in an immediate
> and extraordinary way.[1]

In the New Testament the church of Christ ceases to be
connected in any theocratic manner with any land. Ours is
'the Jerusalem above', 'the heavenly Jerusalem' (*Gal.* 4:26;
Heb. 12:22). Certainly, communities and nations are often
blessed because of the gospel, but that is a very different thing
from making God's promise to Solomon the grounds for
believing that if Christians repent and humble themselves
there will be a national healing and a national revival. Many
thousands of believing Israelites were living obediently to the
gospel in the first century but, far from securing for them the
promise, 'I will heal their land', they saw the utter destruction
of Jerusalem in A.D. 70.

It would appear that the confusion which has arisen over
making 2 Chronicles 7:14 a text on revival has come about
through a failure to recognise the great change in spiritual
privilege which was to follow the coming of Christ. As already
mentioned, the mistake may also be partly due to an
unwarranted dependence on the words 'revive' or 'reviving'
as they occur in the King James Version of the Bible in the Old
Testament. While the phenomenon of revival certainly exists
in Old Testament *prophecy* we cannot introduce the *experience*
into the Old Testament without seriously affecting its meaning. Of course, there are important lessons to be drawn from

[1] *Statement of the Difference between the Profession of the Reformed Church of
Scotland, as Adopted by the Seceders, and the Profession Contained in the New Testimony
and Other Acts,* T. M'Crie (repr. Edinburgh, 1871), p. 131.

God's mighty acts in the Old Testament era but when these are made the basis for interpreting the New Testament teaching we are bound to go wrong. Pentecost inaugurated a new age, a new era in the economy of grace which was impossible before Christ's promise to send the Spirit was fulfilled. Thus we read in Acts 2:33: 'Therefore being exalted to the right hand of God, and having received from the Father the promise of the Holy Spirit, He poured out this which you now see and hear.' W. G. T. Shedd has written:

The whole book of Acts contains frequent allusions and references to the person and work of the Holy Spirit, in a manner and to a degree which are not seen in the four Gospels, showing that immediately after the ascension of Christ a more powerful agency and influence of the third Person began to be experienced in the church. This descent and gift of the gracious operation and influence was directly connected with Christ's presence and intercession in heaven. And this intercession rested for its ground and reason of success, upon that atoning work which he had performed upon earth.[1]

Such was the extent of the change which the work of Christ brought for Christians that his words on the contrast between John the Baptist and the privileges of the humblest member of the kingdom of God were fulfilled, 'he who is least in the kingdom of God is greater than he' (*Luke* 7:28). As David Brown has said, 'The day of Pentecost lifted the Church out of infancy into manhood.'[2] This was the great turning point which brought the transition from nationalism to universalism, and empowered the church, under 'the ministration of the Spirit', to go into all the world and preach the gospel to every creature.

[1] W. G. T. Shedd, *Dogmatic Theology*, vol. 2 (Edinburgh: T. & T. Clark, 1889), p. 377.
[2] David Brown and A. R. Fausset, *Commentary, Critical, Experimental, and Practical*, vol. 6 (London: Collins, n.d.), p. 10. Brown speaks of two extremes to be avoided in stating the difference between the old and new economies: 'The one is that, until the day of Pentecost, the souls of believers were total strangers to the operations of the Spirit . . . But the other extreme – which would reduce the superiority of the one economy to the other, in respect to the Spirit's work, to one of greater *copiousness* and *extension* – is not less to be avoided.'

Revivals are Larger Measures of the Spirit of God

We move on to a third understanding of revival which, I will seek to argue, supplies a more biblical explanation for the phenomenon. This is the view which once prevailed in the English-speaking churches on both sides of the Atlantic and I will refer to it as the 'old-school view'.[1] It rests upon the New Testament doctrine respecting Christ as the exalted head of the church. In the Gospels Jesus appears as the 'Christ' – the 'anointed' – who, for the accomplishment of the work of redemption, received the uninterrupted fullness of the Holy Spirit: 'God giveth not the Spirit by measure unto him' (*John* 3:34, AV). With Christ's redemptive work now completed, believing sinners enter into what belongs to their Saviour; they, too, are now anointed; they are 'Christians'. Pentecost declared that the plenitude of the Spirit was not for Jesus alone. The Holy Spirit is 'poured out on us abundantly through Jesus Christ our Saviour' (*Titus* 3:6).

This third view, then, agrees with the first already stated, namely that at Pentecost the Spirit of God was given once and for all to the church – a giving as final as Calvary itself. But there is a vital difference. Old-school spokesmen believed that, while the Spirit was permanently given, he was not given permanently in the same *measure and degree* as was witnessed at Pentecost. Two things overlapped at Pentecost. The first was the coming of the Spirit which established the *norm* for the whole gospel age – the Spirit was given, never to be removed, and therefore the work of conversion and sanctification in the whole earth is never to cease. But the second thing was the *largeness* of the degree in which the influences of the Spirit were then experienced by the church and by thousands who until that day were ungodly. This was extraordinary and not

---

[1] I have written of this more fully in *The Puritan Hope* (London: Banner of Truth, 1971); and *Jonathan Edwards: A New Biography* (Edinburgh: Banner of Truth, 1987).

continuous. It was not the permanent norm that the whole body of Christians should be 'filled with the Holy Spirit'; not the norm that three thousand should be simultaneously converted; and not the norm that, wherever the church exists, fear should come 'upon every soul' (*Acts* 2:43). So, from Pentecost onward, the work of the Spirit can be viewed in two aspects, the more normal and the extraordinary. These two differ not in essence or kind, but only in degree, so much so that we can never determine with certainty where the normal ends and the extraordinary begins. It should also be noted that by the word 'extraordinary' I do not mean to include what are sometimes called the 'extraordinary' or miraculous gifts of the Spirit, to which I will return later. These gifts were auxiliary to Pentecost rather than integral to it. They existed before Pentecost (e.g., *Matt.* 10:2,8) and, while more lavishly bestowed at the inception of the Pentecostal age, they form no part of the permanent giving of the Spirit to the church as promised in John 14 to 16.[1]

What is the evidence for this distinction between the 'normal' and the 'extraordinary'? Let me offer three lines of proof:

(1) It is clear from the book of Acts that all Christians did not remain permanently 'filled with the Holy Spirit' in the sense of Acts 2:4. Had that been so it would not have been possible to say of the *same* persons again in Acts 4:31, 'and they were all filled with the Holy Spirit'. Here was an element of Pentecost which was clearly repeatable; there was a further giving of what they already possessed. Again, if being 'filled with the Spirit' was uniform in every Christian, what would be the point of the apostles instructing the disciples in Acts 6 to look for a characteristic which all possessed, 'Seek out . . . seven men of good reputation, full of the Holy Spirit'? It must be true, as the *Larger Catechism* of the Westminster Assembly states (Question 182), that, while the Holy Spirit is given to all

[1] See below, Appendix 1, p.197.

Christians, his working is 'not in all persons, nor at all times, in the same measure'.

Against this it is sometimes urged that we cannot speak of different measures of the Holy Spirit. It is asked, Can a believer have all of Christ and only part of the Holy Spirit? Can we believe that the Holy Spirit, in the body of the believer, dwells in a temple which he does not fill? But our knowledge of the mode of the Spirit's indwelling is far too small for us to be ruled by such logic. What is indisputable is that there are differences in the manifest presence of the Spirit of God. Thus Scripture says that the Spirit was present in the Old Testament, while John 7:39 says, 'the Holy Spirit was not yet given'; and Jesus in the upper room said, 'Receive the Holy Spirit,' while, at the same period, he pointed to a future coming of the Spirit, 'You shall receive power when the Holy Spirit has come upon you' (*John* 20:22; *Acts* 1:8). So these various references to the Spirit cannot be taken in an absolute sense.[1] The thought behind the word 'measure' is clearly scriptural. We have to say with the *Westminster Confession*, 'Christ has purchased for believers under the gospel . . . fuller communications of the free Spirit of God'[2]. Yet even the fullness now to be enjoyed by Christians is still only the beginning – 'the firstfruits of the Spirit' (*Rom.* 8:23).

The idea of variation in the 'measure' in which the Spirit is known is commonplace in Puritan writing. Isaac Ambrose, for instance, writes of the Spirit:

At first [i.e., in Old Testament times], he was sent only in drops and dew, but now he was poured out in showers in abundance, 'The

---

[1] The same point is clearer with reference to Christ himself. John Owen writes of 'the full communication of the Spirit unto him . . . yet it was carried on by several degrees and distinctions of time; for, (1.) He was anointed by the Spirit in his incarnation in the womb, *Luke* 1:35. (2.) He was so at his baptism and entrance into his public ministry, *Matt.* 3:16. (3.) He was peculiarly anointed unto his death and sacrifice in that divine act of his whereby he "sanctified himself" thereunto, as *John* 17:19. (4.) He was so at his ascension, when he received of the Father the promise of the Spirit.' *Works*, vol. 4, pp. 392–3.

[2] *Westminster Confession*, xx:1.

Holy Ghost (saith Paul) was shed on us abundantly through Jesus
our Saviour,' *Titus* 3:6. As there are degrees of wind, a breath, a
blast, a stiff gale: so we cannot deny degrees in the Spirit; the apostles
at Christ's resurrection received the Spirit, but now [at Pentecost]
they were filled with the Spirit; then it was but a breath, but now it
was a mighty wind.[1]

(2) The New Testament indicates that while the Spirit it
always present in the church the degrees of his power and
influence remain subject to Christ himself. The plenitude
remains with the head of the body and from his fullness he
gives according to his will. Referring to Peter's use of the word
of God through Joel on the day of Pentecost ('I will pour out of
My Spirit on all flesh'), George Smeaton observed: 'According
to the New Testament quotation, there is a shade of meaning
not to be lost in the words "of my Spirit" (*apo*), distinguishing
between the measure vouchsafed to men and the inexhaustible
fulness in the resources of the fountain.'[2] So the apostolic
churches received repeated givings of the Spirit because there
is always more of him to be given. The church in Jerusalem
received more in Acts 4. Paul prays for the Christians at
Ephesus that they will receive more – that 'the Father of glory
may give to you the Spirit of wisdom and revelation in the
knowledge of Him' (*Eph.* 1:17; or again, 3:16). Thus Bishop
Moule, in commenting on Ephesians 1:17, wrote: 'We are not
to think of the "giving" of the Spirit as of an isolated deposit of
what, once given, is now locally in possession. The first "gift"
is, as it were, the first point in a series of actions, of which each
one may be expressed also as a gift.'[3]

In other words, the church is ever dependent upon Christ,
her ever-living head, for the 'actual influence' of the Holy
Spirit.[4] Thus Paul looked for 'the supply of the Spirit of Jesus

[1] Isaac Ambrose, *Looking unto Jesus,* vol. 2 (Berwick: Richardson, 1816),
p. 209.
[2] *The Doctrine of the Holy Spirit,* 1882 (repr. Edinburgh: Banner of Truth,
1974), p. 28.
[3] H. C. G. Moule, *Epistle to the Ephesians, with Introduction and Notes*
(Cambridge University Press, 1893), p. 58.
[4] See *Westminster Confession,* xvi: 3.

Christ' (*Phil.* 1:19), the genitive being one of possession or origin, 'the Spirit which Jesus Christ has or dispenses'. Similarly, the declining church of Sardis, rebuked with the words, 'you have a name that you are alive, but you are dead,' is to listen to Christ because of what he has authority to give, 'These things says He who has *the seven Spirits* of God'. Whatever the condition of the churches, the plenitude of the Spirit remains with Christ.

So while Pentecost instituted a new era, the work of Christ in bestowing the Spirit did not end then. And the fuller communication of the Spirit which marks the whole age of 'the last days', begun at Pentecost, was not to be constant and unvarying; for, were it so, what purpose could be served by praying for *more* of the Spirit of God as disciples are clearly directed to do? It was in response to the request 'teach us to pray' that Jesus said: 'If you then, being evil, know how to give good gifts to your children: how much more will your heavenly Father give the Holy Spirit to those who ask Him?' (*Luke* 11:13). This promise has no continuing relevance for Christians unless there is always more to be received.[1]

(3) A third line of proof for this understanding comes from church history.

How can the view which sees no justification for occasional revivals offer any convincing explanation for such great and sudden turning points in church history as the Reformation? How are these extraordinary eras to be explained if the Spirit is always uniformly present? John Knox believed he knew the true explanation of the events of his days when he testified, 'God gave his Holy Spirit to simple men in great abundance.'[2]

---

[1] George Smeaton writes: 'No more mischievous and misleading theory could be propounded, nor any more dishonouring to the Holy Spirit, than the principle that because the Spirit was poured out at Pentecost the Church has no need, and no warrant, to pray for effusions of the Spirit of God. On the contrary, the more the Church asks for the Spirit and waits for His communications, the more she receives.' *Doctrine of the Holy Spirit*, p. 255.

[2] *The Works of John Knox*, vol. 1 (Edinburgh, 1846), p. 101.

It was not that at a certain date the reformers realised what they already had and therefore decided to act; it was rather that something had *first* happened *to them*. There was an impulse from the Holy Spirit himself. Robert Fleming interpreted the extraordinary multiplication of Christians which was seen in South-West Scotland in the mid-1620s in exactly the same way. It was, he wrote in 1669, 'a very solemn and extraordinary out-letting of the Spirit'. Likewise James Robe described the revivals at Cambuslang and Kilsyth under the title, *Narratives of the Extraordinary Work of the Spirit of God.*[1]

Witnesses to revivals invariably speak of something being given which was not there before – something much more than a decision on the part of Christians to be more faithful or to make greater efforts. 'Men have felt as if the Lord had breathed upon them. They were first affected with awe and fear – then they were bathed in tears – then filled with a love unspeakable.'[2] The language of James M'Gready, describing the Kentucky awakening, is typical:

The year 1800 exceeds all that our eyes ever beheld on earth. All the blessed displays of Almighty power and grace, all the sweet gales of the divine Spirit, and soul-reviving showers of the blessings of Heaven which we enjoyed before, and which we considered wonderful beyond conception, were like a few scattering drops before a mighty rain.[3]

Edward Griffin says that at the beginning of the revival at Newark, New Jersey, 'The appearance was as if a collection of waters, long suspended over the town, had fallen at once, and deluged the whole place.'[4]

The sheer unexpectedness of such events bears equally against the view that revivals are conditioned by the preceding actions and efforts of Christians. Those who believe that a

[1] James Robe, *Narratives of the Extraordinary Work of the Spirit of God at Cambuslang and Kilsyth* (Glasgow, 1790).

[2] William Gibson, *The Year of Grace, A History of the Ulster Revival of 1859* (Edinburgh: Elliot, 1860), p. 432.

[3] Murray, *Revival and Revivalism*, p. 151.

[4] *Ibid.*, p. 202.

certain line of conduct or prayer *must* secure revival have history against them. Revivals come unheralded. They are, as Edwards witnessed in Northampton in 1735, 'the surprising work of God'. Of the Great Awakening of 1740 it is said that 'it broke upon the slumbering churches like a thunderbolt rushing out of a clear blue sky'.

Records of the cessation of revivals enforce the same lesson. If Christians can secure revivals then surely such Christians as have just experienced a high tide of spiritual life would be best able to preserve the condition which they so prized. But it has not been so. H. Elvet Lewis, one of the observers of the 1904–5 revival in Wales, concluded: 'No amount, no form, of organised effort could produce in 1906 what seemed as natural as a breath of air in the early months of 1905. I have seen, occasionally, an elaborate attempt to make it come: nothing was produced but disaster.' He concluded, 'We are in the presence of an unexplained but impressive mystery.'[1]

The evidence of history thus coincides with the interpretation of Scripture we have sought to give above. Such outpourings of the Spirit as are recorded in the book of Acts have not been uniformly present in the life of the churches in all ages. They have not been the permanent norm, nor were they intended to be. Rather they belong, as Smeaton says, to creative epochs, ushered in by the church's ever-living head: 'When a former awakening has spent its force, when the elements of thought or action previously supplied threaten to become *effete,* a new impulse is commonly communicated by Him who interposes at various stages to make all things new . . . Men look on with awe and wonder when some supply of the Spirit, of which they can neither tell the laws nor estimate the momentum, breaks forth from the kingdom of God and sweeps over a community.'[2]

To summarise, then, this third view: a revival is an

[1] H. Elvet Lewis, *With Christ Among the Miners* (London: Hodder and Stoughton, 1906), pp. 7, 10.
[2] Smeaton, *Doctrine of the Holy Spirit,* pp. 252–3.

outpouring of the Holy Spirit, brought about by the intercession of Christ, resulting in a new degree of life in the churches
and a widespread movement of grace among the unconverted.
It is an extraordinary communication of the Spirit of God, a
superabundance of the Spirit's operations, an enlargement of
his manifest power. In the words of Jonathan Edwards:
'Though there be a more constant influence of the Spirit
attending his ordinances, yet the way in which the greatest
things have been done has been by remarkable effusions, at
special seasons of mercy.'[1] These words are commonly quoted,
but less well-known is the extent to which this older
evangelical understanding was once predominant. It was held
by evangelical Anglicans such as Charles Simeon who wrote
to a friend, 'The work of conversion must be very gradual
among you, unless God pour out his Spirit in a most
extraordinary measure upon you.'[2] Octavius Winslow, a
Congregationalist minister who knew both sides of the
Atlantic, believed:

There is in a work of grace transpiring during an especial
outpouring of the Holy Spirit, a deeper impression of the seal of
the Spirit upon the heart, a clearer and more manifest sense of
pardon and acceptance, than in the normal conversions of ordinary
times. Nor is this difficult to account for. *There is a greater and richer
manifestation of the Holy Spirit.* This is the grand secret. He gives more
of himself.[3]

The same teaching was once uniform in the Scottish
evangelical pulpit. Alexander Moody Stuart, for example,
wrote:

While the Holy Ghost is always present in his church, there are times
when he draws manifestly nearer and puts forth a greater energy of
power. Every believer is conscious in his own soul of changes
corresponding to this; for the Spirit is always with him, abiding in
him, and yet there are times of unusual communion and far more
than ordinary life. And as the Spirit draws near to an individual, so

---

[1] Edwards, *Works*, vol. 1, p. 539.
[2] W. Carus, *Memoir of Charles Simeon*, 2nd ed. (London, 1847), p. 373.
[3] O. Winslow, *The Work of the Holy Spirit*, 1843 (repr. London: Banner of
Truth, 1961), p. 141.

does he draw near to a land, and then religion is revived, spiritual life is revived, spiritual understanding, spiritual worship, spiritual repentance, spiritual obedience.[1]

So too Welsh preachers of the old school spoke of revival in the same terms. In the great revival year 1859–60, the Rev. D. C. Jones reported on 29 February, 1860: 'We have been visited with a larger measure of the Spirit's influences than usual. It came suddenly "like a rushing mighty wind," and that apparently when churches little expected it.' Another wrote, 'I am firmly persuaded that the Almighty is opening the sluices of grace and pouring out streams of blessings on the churches of all denominations.'[2]

Consequences of the Three Views

It is all too easy in controversy to attach consequences to the views of others which the upholders of those views would themselves reject. At the same time it is true, as already noted, that doctrinal beliefs inevitably have a general tendency towards certain consequences in practice, and this is apparent in the three views on revival which we have considered above. As has often been said, 'practice is in danger if theory be falsified.'

The first view is concerned to emphasise the present fulfilment of the Old Testament promise of the Spirit and to affirm that the church of Christ will never again be bereft of his presence. It denies that church history is to be divided into times when the Spirit of God is present and times when he is absent. All this is true and not to believe it is to leave ourselves wide open to many temptations to discouragement. Glorious things belong to the church in all her days! The New Testament never leaves the Christian in the position of believing that all necessary grace and help is not *now* available.

[1] *Lectures on the Revival of Religion, by ministers of the Church of Scotland, given in 1840* (Glasgow, n.d.), p. 79.
[2] Thomas Phillips, *The Welsh Revival, Its Origins and Development,* (repr. Edinburgh: Banner of Truth, 1989), pp. 28–9.

On the contrary we have such promises as: 'God is able to make all grace abound toward you, that you, always having all sufficiency in all things, may have an abundance for every good work' (*2 Cor.* 9:8).

But while this is true it is not the whole truth, and to disallow the expectation of, and prayer for, further and larger givings of the Spirit, tends to leave Christians satisfied with the existing situation and anticipating nothing more than they presently see. If we think only that the Holy Spirit is continuously resident in the church, as if necessarily present and inherent in the means of grace, we can easily begin to forget how urgently we stand in need of the supernatural. Certainly this has often happened in church history. While maintaining the words of the Apostles' Creed, 'I believe in the Holy Spirit', the church has too often settled down into a dull routine in which more attention is given to human plans and gifts and scholarship than to prayer.[1] In such periods it is near forgotten that the Holy Spirit is additional to all Christian activity, additional even to the truth of Scripture, for apostolic Christianity was not 'in word only, but also in power, and in the Holy Spirit' (*1 Thess.* 1:5).

Abraham Kuyper, one of the best known upholders of the first view and opposed to any prayer for any further outpourings of the Spirit, has written that the history of every country 'proves that a satisfactory condition of the Church is highly exceptional and of short duration'.[2] He offers no explanation why this should appear to be contrary to his view of Pentecost as a continuing reality. Elsewhere he has described the awakening which preceded the settlement of Alexander Comrie in the village of Woubrugge in Holland in language which does not readily fit into the viewpoint expressed in his volume on the *Work of the Holy Spirit*. Referring

---

[1] The cause of the first apostasy in the Christian church was, as Owen notes, that 'men grew weary of the conduct and rule of the Holy Spirit, by various ways taking his work out of his hand, leaving him nothing to do in that which they called "the church".' (*Works*, vol. 4, p. 500).

[2] Kuyper, *Holy Spirit*, p. 184.

to the change which came to Woubrugge through a young farmer, Klaas Jansse Poldervaert, Kuyper wrote:

There had been in this village for years and years, as Comrie himself afterwards told, nothing but a dead outward show of religion; there was much orthodoxy and even knowledge leading to historical faith, but the power of the Lord was not manifest, the operation of the Holy Spirit did not show itself. It was the stillness of the tomb . . . He tried by every means to rouse the people from their lethargy, stirred up young and old to abandon their false trust, and never ceased to carry the souls of all around him to the Throne of Divine Mercy in his prayers. Thus he went on for eight years, but without the least shadow of success, till finally, after nine years of quiet waiting, the Lord came down in answer to his petition. So prominent and striking did this work of the Lord then appear, that many came every Sunday from different places in the neighbourhood to witness the outpouring of spiritual blessing. And although the Rev. Mr Blom, minister of the parish at that time, at first began by opposing the movement as throwing his ministry into the shade, still the revival proved so general and so continuous, and maintained such a high character, that he finally gave way, became a partaker of the unspeakable blessing for his own soul, and until his death in 1734, bore public testimony from the pulpit to the great and glorious work of the Lord.

I have called this revival remarkable . . . because it brought to the Cross not a wild and worldly population, but a company of strictly orthodox and outwardly blameless parishioners. It was even more remarkable for the sound character it assumed from the beginning and maintained to the last, as described by Comrie in these terms: 'The work of the Lord in our village was such that all the really converted people, who got the sealing of the Spirit, were constantly moving around the Mediator as their common centre, rejecting everything besides the Surety Himself'.[1]

These words certainly show that an upholder of the first view can believe in revival and this must be acknowledged. Christian opinion may be divided at times only by verbal differences. But it is also true that Comrie himself, who adhered to the third view, could have given a clearer and more consistent theological explanation than Kuyper of what

[1] Kuyper, 'Alexander Comrie: his Life and Work in Holland', in *The Catholic Presbyterian* (London: Nisbet, January 1882), pp. 22–3.

happened at Woubrugge. The first view provides no real biblical understanding for revivals and for that reason it can hardly be said to encourage the expectation of their occurrence.[1]

The second view, as the first, has truth to it. It is right to stress human responsibility. Scripture teaches that diligence will be rewarded and a passive awaiting of future events is no part of Christian duty; witnessing will bear fruit; prayer will be answered. But its mistake is to suppose that the church can only be fruitful, and can only advance *when* we have revival. This second view wants to make the exceptional the normal and it therefore commonly regards all periods when there is no revival as times in which the Spirit of God is being hindered by the church. The absence of revival is treated as 'proof' of barrenness and of God's judgment. Thus, in Finney's words, 'A revival of religion is indispensable to avert the judgment of God from the church'.[2] This kind of reasoning follows inevitably from the thinking upon which it is based. For if we hold that greater obedience will secure revival, then the only conclusion to be reached if there is no revival is that

[1] Kuyper's *Holy Spirit* was first published six years after his articles on Comrie. It appears, as he wrote in his Preface to the English edition, that he was considerably concerned to oppose 'Methodism' and what he regarded as its dangerously subjective tendency. Yet in the last sentence of that Preface (p. xiv), he concluded: 'The Work of the Holy Spirit may not be displaced by the activity of the human spirit.' In 1898 he was to conclude his Stone Lectures at Princeton by speaking of Calvinism 'awaiting the breath of God's Spirit,' and of the alternative possibility: 'Unless God send forth His Spirit, there will be no turn, and fearfully rapid will be the descent of the waters.' (*Calvinism*, Six Stone Lectures, Sovereign Grace Union, London, 1931), p. 298. It is fair to assume that Comrie's belief in the work of the Spirit in revival was the same as that of his friend and fellow-countryman, Hugh Kennedy of Rotterdam, who, in a preface to Robe's *Narratives of the Extraordinary Work of the Spirit of God*, which he wrote in July 1742, forcefully states the then prevailing view: 'The residue of the Spirit is with our God, who, in a way of sovereignty, pours out the Holy Spirit, when, where, upon whomsoever, and in whatever measure and degrees he pleases!' (*Narratives*, p. ix).

[2] Quoted by Arthur Wallis, *In The Day of Thy Power* (1956, repr. City Hill Publishing Co., Mo., 1990). Wallis' book, helpful in some respects, takes the view that revival is conditional upon our obedience.

disobedience continues to prevail. Referring to this consequence, William G. McLoughlin has observed: 'If Finney's
theology was correct then there was no choice but feast or
famine in religion.'[1]

The inevitable tendency of this second view is that, while it
wants to encourage earnest practical endeavours, it will,
sooner or later, produce discouragement. If we suppose that
blessing on the scale of revival is the *only* blessing worth
looking for, and if we pass over the normal out of desire to
see the extraordinary, we are wrong and will be disappointed.

Sometimes Christians who have been through revivals have
fallen into just such disappointment. They were tempted to
think that there could be no real happiness unless times of
revival continued. It was over this point that George Whitefield had to caution his friend William McCulloch, minister of
Cambuslang. In 1749 McCulloch was discouraged because he
no longer saw what they had witnessed in the awakening of
1742. Whitefield's response was to remind him that 1742 was
not the norm for the church: 'I should be glad to hear of a
revival at Cambuslang; but, dear Sir, you have already seen
such things as are seldom seen above once in a century.'[2]
Martyn Lloyd-Jones refers to a very similar instance in the
case of a Welsh minister 'whose whole ministry was ruined' by
his constantly looking back to what he had seen and
experienced in the revival of 1904: 'When the revival
ended . . . he was still expecting the unusual; and it did not
happen. So he became depressed and spent about forty years
of his life in a state of barrenness, unhappiness and useless-
ness.'[3]

This second view also has another tendency. If revival
depends upon *us* then it is more than a possibility that

[1] W. G. McLoughlin, *Modern Revivalism: Charles Grandison Finney to Billy
Graham* p. 149.
[2] *The Works of George Whitefield*, vol. 2 (London, 1771), p. 252.
[3] D. M. Lloyd-Jones, *The Christian Warfare* (Edinburgh: Banner of Truth,
1976), p. 195.

Christians will be eager to *make it* happen.[1] Accordingly all kinds of means may be adopted and, if these produce excitement and crowds, it may even appear *for a time* as though expectations were fulfilled. Probably nothing has done more to demean the whole idea of revival than just such highly publicised efforts and their temporary results.

The third (the old-school) view outlined above confirms that it is closer to Scripture by the better consequences which result from it. I believe that it can be shown to incorporate what is best in the other views while avoiding the dangers which they introduce. The first view so emphasises the finality of Pentecost that prayer for the Holy Spirit becomes unnecessary. The second view so emphasises human responsibility in making the blessing conditional upon us that its real nature is confused. The first view virtually excludes revival, while the second goes to the opposite extreme and treats revival as though it was everything. The historic understanding avoids all these pitfalls. It neither underrates revivals nor exaggerates them. It accepts the permanency of the Spirit's presence and in so doing does not undervalue the 'normal'. It remembers 'Lo, I am with you always', and is therefore not discouraged from continuing in the path of ordinary Christian work. Yet, at the same time, in the words of Dr W. W. Patton, it believes in 'mighty outpourings of the Holy Spirit':

They are to be regarded as glorious additions or supplements to the ordinary workings of spiritual forces; in which God seizes upon a conjuncture of facts and favouring occasions, to work saving results on a large scale and with great rapidity, exalting the faith of his

[1] One of many examples of this kind of thing occurred in Korea in 1909, two years after what was clearly a genuine awakening. In October 1909 the General Council of Evangelical Missions in Seoul followed up a proposal from Arminian Methodists in deciding to ask for a million converts in the coming year. 'All that human zeal could do was done, and all was set to win a million, as decided by the praying committee . . . Statistically the outcome was very disappointing . . . It seemed just that the Holy Spirit would not surrender His prerogatives for a Pentecost to anyone' (J. Edwin Orr, *The Flaming Tongue: The Impact of the Twentieth Century Revivals* (Chicago: Moody, 1973), pp. 170–1. Orr's books provide valuable information on revivals but they do not always possess the discernment shown in this quotation.

people and striking terror into the heart of his foes. In the United States revivals have thus been conspicuously used, at eventful periods, to save the land from prevalent infidelity and worldliness.[1]

A Vital Lesson

We have argued that the difference between the normal and the state of revival is one of degree and measure. It is not a difference in kind. If revival be, in the first place, a larger giving of the Spirit to Christians, it must mean that they receive more of what they already possess.

This fact underlines an important lesson. The authenticity of any alleged revival is to be judged by the *same* tests by which the genuineness of all Christianity is to be tested. The normal mark of true grace consists in spiritual enlightenment producing love to God, reverence and obedience to Scripture, concern to serve Christ, personal holiness, compassion for others and so on. If revivals consist of *more* of what Christians already possess, then these same characteristics of character and conduct will be eminent in every true revival. So it has proved. But where the priority of these things is passed by and other signs are introduced as *proof* of revival, perhaps 'miracles' – tongues, revelations, public confessions of sin, or forms of physical excitement – then mistaken assessments become a near certainty. I am not here discussing what may or may not be present in a revival. The question is where the burden of proof of revival should be laid. If the wrong things are treated as *the* important things then accurate discernment becomes a near impossibility. Things which are not the bedrock of normal Christianity never provide a safe test of the existence of revival, and where revivals have been claimed merely on the basis of unusual phenomena, subsequent events have almost invariably exposed the emptiness of the claim. In any alleged revival the greatest weight in the way of evidence

[1] Address on 'Revivals of Religion' in *History of the Sixth General Conference of the Evangelical Alliance, 1873*, p. 355.

has to be put on those things which are *always* marks of the work of the Spirit. On this subject no writer has superseded the treatment of Jonathan Edwards in his three books: *Distinguishing Marks of a Work of the Spirit of God*; *Thoughts on the Revival of Religion in New England*; and *A Treatise on the Religious Affections*.

When critics of the 1742 revivals in Scotland alleged that they were no genuine work of God, James Robe replied by pointing to the presence of such evidences of the work of the Spirit of God as are to be found always and everywhere where he is at work:

The fruits of it in many are, godly sorrow for sin, universal hatred at it, renouncing their own righteousness, and embracing the righteousness of God by faith in Jesus Christ, embracing Him in all his offices, universal reformation of life, a superlative love to our blessed Redeemer, love to all they see bear his image, love towards all men, even their enemies, earnest desires and prayers for the conversion of all others.[1]

---

[1] Robe, *Narratives of the Extraordinary Work*, p. 57.

2

Charles G. Finney: How Theology Affects Understanding of Revival

'For a long time it was supposed by the Church that a revival was a miracle, an interposition of Divine power. It is only within a few years that ministers generally have supposed revivals were to be promoted by the use of means . . . God has overthrown, generally, the theory that revivals are miracles.'[1]

C. G. Finney

There is no question that it is the name of Charles Grandison Finney which chiefly deserves to be connected with what has become the most popular understanding of revival. William McLoughlin goes too far when he writes: 'The difference between [Jonathan] Edwards and Finney is essentially the difference between the medieval and the modern temper. One saw God as the centre of the universe, the other saw man. One believed that revivals were "prayed down" and the other that they were "worked up".' But his words are not an overstatement when he goes on: 'Finney's revivalism broke the dam maintained by "The Tradition of the Elders" (the title of

---

[1] Finney, *Revivals of Religion*, pp. 12–13.

one of his most pungent sermons) and transformed "the new system" from a minority to a majority religion."[1]

If we are to understand how one man came to command such influence on subsequent history we need to take a closer view of his life and teaching.

A visit to Andover College, Massachusetts, in the year 1831 will introduce Finney to us at the height of his powers. It was the eve of keenly awaited Anniversary meetings at this theological seminary and for the last evening of those special days the speaker anticipated was Dr Justin Edwards. Although Justin Edwards was one of the favourite preachers of New England, the College authorities had reason to be apprehensive; for the local village church had engaged another visitor to preach at the same hour on that same Wednesday evening. Their fears proved justified: a mere thirty persons attended the College chapel to hear the distinguished guest, while the village church was packed with students, alumni and others to hear Charles G. Finney, aged thirty-nine, fair-haired and an impressive six-foot-two in height. One of the absentee theological students who chose the alternative to the College proceedings was E. A. Park. More than fifty-eight years later, when Park wrote of the occasion, he declared he could recall the impression made upon him as distinctly as on the night itself. Finney's sermon, he reported, was on the text, 'One Mediator between God and men, the man Christ Jesus' (*1 Tim.* 2:5). Although an hour and three-quarters in length, it commanded the attention of all, even of those who had gone critically. Park recalled: 'It abounded with sterling argument and startling transitions. It was too earnest to be called theatrical, but in the best sense of the word it was *dramatic*. Some of his rhetorical utterances are indescribable.' As every seat was full, Park sat with five other men on a plank which had been put across chairs in an aisle. Such was the impression of the sermon, he says, that 'The board actually shook beneath us. Every one of the men was trembling with excitement.'[2]

---

[1] *Modern Revivalism: Charles Grandison Finney to Billy Graham*, pp. 11, 66.

[2] Quoted in G. F. Wright, *Charles Grandison Finney* (Boston: Houghton, Mifflin, 1891), pp. 72–4.

It was not only that night that Finney was exciting. He has remained so almost ever since. His *Memoirs* was first published in 1876 and (apart from Augustine's *Confessions*) it is probably the only Christian autobiography which has remained in print for over one hundred and twenty years. It is possible that no man has had such a far-reaching influence on evangelical Christianity in these years as Finney, the 'Father of Modern Revivalism'. His book, *Lectures on Revivals*, has by far outsold every other book on the subject. Dr Billy Graham summarises the general opinion of Finney when he writes: 'Through his Spirit-filled ministry, uncounted thousands came to know Christ in the nineteenth century, resulting in one of the greatest periods of revival in the history of America.'[1]

Life and Teaching

Finney was born in New England in 1792. While he was still a child, his parents moved to the shores of Lake Ontario, in western New York state, and it was here, in the little town of Adams, that Finney was converted to Christ in 1821. He had previously been an unconcerned and frivolous attender at the Presbyterian church in Adams and it was to the surprise of his minister, George W. Gale, that he appeared one Monday evening at an inquiry meeting under strong conviction of sin and wanting to become a Christian. The same week Finney came to peace and assurance. Soon he was helping Gale in the work of the Adams church and, when the local presbytery accepted him as a candidate for the Presbyterian ministry, it was Gale who became his tutor. Finney was ordained in 1824 and almost immediately, it appears, he was used in a series of revivals in parts of Jefferson and St Lawrence Counties. In the October of 1825 he met his former pastor, George Gale, who had now moved to Western in Oneida County. Gale urged Finney to stay with him and it was at this time that Finney first became well known on account of the part he was to play in

[1] Quoted in my *Revival and Revivalism*, p. 298.

what became known as the 'Western revivals'. The majority of those converted under his ministry, wrote Gale:

> were not women and children but strong men, educated men . . .
> Lawyers and judges, men of all professions and conditions of life . . .
> The great secret of his success was that he was a powerful reasoner.
> Though he was a bold and fearless preacher of the Gospel he was a
> man of much prayer, and singleness of purpose. It was to win souls to
> Christ that he labored. His own reputation, or interest, came in for
> no share of his aims, any further than the cause of Christ was to be
> effected. Like Barnabas, he was full of the Holy Spirit, as well as a
> good man, and much people were added to the Lord.[1]

Soon Finney was preaching in the great centres of population on the east coast. Five thousand were said to be converted in a meeting in Philadelphia in 1828, and in 1829 and 1830 his meetings continued to be attended by large crowds in New York City. In the latter place he undertook his first pastorate in 1832 and it was here in 1834 and 1835 that he delivered the twenty-two lectures on revival which became his famous book. In published form they immediately commanded widespread sales. Twelve thousand copies were printed in New York by 1837 and by 1840 a 'thirteenth printing' was published in Britain. A translation into Welsh was published in 1839.[2] Several reasons combined to attract such interest:

1. The subject of revival was then of very general interest throughout the English-speaking world.
2. Word had spread that Finney was himself an experienced preacher in revivals.
3. Finney was saying something which had never been effectively said in print before and which seemed to have great importance for the advance of the kingdom of Christ. He

[1] *Autobiography of George Washington Gale* (Published Privately, New York, 1964), p. 273.
[2] G. M. Rosell & R. A. G. Dupuis, *The Memoirs of Charles G. Finney: The Complete Restored Text* (Grand Rapids: Zondervan, 1989), p. 375n. This is the only unabridged edition of the *Memoirs;* all other printings reproduced the original manuscript in which J. H. Fairchild had omitted or changed about twenty per cent of the text. Because the abridged (Revell) edition is more widely available I generally quote from it in these pages unless otherwise indicated.

argued that 'very few' had previously rightly understood the theology of revival and that 'vast ignorance' persisted among ministers on the subject.[1] People had formerly believed that revivals were like the rain; they could not be produced or organised by any human arrangements. But here was a teacher who believed that it was the church's duty to obtain revivals. If you are a Christian, he said, God 'has placed His Spirit at your disposal'.[2] 'You see why you do not have a revival. It is only because you do not want one. Because you are neither praying for it, nor feeling anxious about it, nor putting forth efforts for it.'[3] 'If the Church will do all her duty, the millennium may come in this country in three years . . . If the Church would do *all her duty*, she would soon complete the triumph of religion in the world.'[4]

Or again, in a reference to the men who had supported him in introducing new measures, Finney wrote: 'If the whole church as a body had gone to work ten years ago, and continued it, as a few individuals, whom I could name, have done, there would not now be an impenitent sinner in the land.'[5]

This teaching caused widespread interest not simply because it was new, and delivered with much authority, but also because it was backed up by the author's repeated appeal to the evidence of success which he had seen in his own ministry. But Finney knew that what he was saying would meet criticism and in *Revivals of Religion* he forewarned his readers of the kind of people who would oppose it:

They are ancient men, men of another age and stamp from what is needed in these days, when the Church and world are rising to new

[1] *Revivals of Religion*, p. 371.
[2] Ibid., p. 134.
[3] Ibid., p. 34.
[4] Ibid., p. 346.
[5] Quoted by Albert Dod, reviewing Finney's *Revivals of Religion*, in *Princeton Theological Essays, Second Series* (New York: Wiley and Putnam, 1847), p. 146. The fact that this quotation does not seem to appear in current editions of Finney's lectures confirms that some revision of the original publication was undertaken after 1835.

thought and action . . . It is dangerous and ridiculous for our theological professors, who are withdrawn from the field of conflict, to be allowed to dictate, in regard to the measures and movements of the Church, as it would be for a general to sit in his bedchamber and attempt to order a battle.[1]

Finney was right in believing there would be controversy, but it did not last many years and, as already observed, significant parts of his teaching came to be accepted as standard evangelical belief. In 1834 he left the Presbyterian Church and became a Congregationalist. The next year he became the Professor of Theology at Oberlin. For a while he combined this post with his New York pastorate but from 1838 his time was divided between Oberlin – where, it is said, he trained some 20,000 students in the course of his life – and itinerant ministry. In 1849–50, and again in 1858, he was in Britain. 'Both these visits,' Frank G. Beardsley asserts, 'were the occasion of extensive revivals.'[2] Another writer adds: 'He was the first man to introduce American revivalistic methods into England and Scotland.'[3] By the time that this 'king of American evangelists' died at the ripe age of eighty-three years it was said that five hundred thousand persons had been converted through his instrumentality.

Possibly the most influential thing which Finney ever did was begun when he had turned seventy years of age. This was the preparation of his autobiography. Edited and abridged by J. H. Fairchild, it was published almost immediately after his death and through its pages untold numbers around the world were to have their thoughts shaped on evangelism and revival .

By the time Finney's *Memoirs* was published in 1876 the controversy in which he had been engaged in earlier years was a thing of the distant past. Most people took the view that it

[1] *Revivals of Religion*, pp. 214–5.
[2] F. G. Beardsley, *History of American Revivals* (New York: American Tract Society, 1904), p. 146.
[3] T. Cuyler, *Recollections of a Long Life, An Autobiography*, (New York: Baker and Taylor, 1902), p. 218.

was no longer of any relevance. The opinion of one New York minister was general: with reference to Finney, Theodore Cuyler believed that, by the 1870s, 'the once bitter controversies between "old school" and "new school" had become quite obsolete.'[1] Yet Finney himself did not appear to think so, for the fact is that a large part of his *Memoirs* is taken up with a defence of the new thinking which he had done so much to introduce in the 1820s and 1830s. Over and over again he tells us of the opposition which he encountered to evangelism and revival, and who was responsible for it. The main culprits were ministers of the Presbyterian Church who still believed what was taught in the Westminster Confession of Faith and the main centre of resistance to change he identified as Princeton Theological Seminary where some of the principal 'ancient men' taught.[2]

It was impossible, Finney believed, to hold what he called 'Princeton theology' *and* be a supporter of evangelism and revival and he tells us why at great length. In brief, the reason was this. Following the Westminster Confession, Princeton believed that man is so fallen that he cannot do anything to make himself a Christian. While holding that it is the duty of preachers to call upon sinners to repent and believe, this old-school teaching taught that for such responses to be saving there needed to be the interposition of the Spirit of God in regeneration. Man is unable of himself to forsake sin and to receive Christ. Finney claimed that this teaching was entirely unscriptural. Instead he held that human depravity is a 'voluntary' condition, that is to say, its continuance depends upon the choice of the human will. Let a man once decide for Christ and he will become a new man. So the evangelist is not simply to preach Christ and to tell men of their duty to believe; he has to help *make* that believing a reality by appointing some outward action to *assist* a change of will. So we read repeatedly in Finney's *Memoirs* of the 'new measures'

[1] Ibid., p. 219.
[2] *Revivals of Religion*, pp. 214–5, 309. Finney does not actually name Princeton in these references but the identification is unmistakable.

with which he directed people 'to make themselves a new heart':

I called upon any who would give their hearts to God, to come forward and take a front seat ['the anxious seat'].[1]

We insisted on immediate submission.[2]

I called upon them to kneel down and then and there commit themselves forever to the Lord.[3]

I called on those only to kneel down who were willing to do what God required of them, and what I presented to them.[4]

I called for those whose minds were made up, to come forward, publicly renounce their sins, and give themselves to Christ.[5]

There were some who regarded controversy on such matters as simply a disagreement over methods but Finney rightly understood that something much more was involved. The fundamental question has to do with whether or not the sin of Adam has ruined *the nature* of all his posterity. The teaching which Finney was consciously opposing asserted that it had; man has inherited a sinful nature from Adam. All the Reformed Confessions taught that sin is not simply a matter of actions which we repeat because we learn them from the example of others. It is rather the result of an evil principle which lies at the centre of a nature which is fallen. Actual sins are only the surface proof of a deeper corruption beneath. Our choices and actions are wrong because our very hearts are wrong. So, on this understanding, for God to deal with our sins would not be enough. It is our *sinfulness* which is the fundamental problem. Finney denied this. He did not believe that men since the Fall are born with a sinful nature. He complained of the Presbyterians that 'they held the doctrine that moral depravity was constitutional, and

[1] *Memoirs of Charles G. Finney* (New York: Revell, n.d.), p. 116.
[2] Ibid., p. 190.
[3] Ibid., p. 255.
[4] Ibid., p. 261.
[5] Ibid., p. 304.

belonged to the very nature; that the will, though free to do evil, was utterly impotent to all good.'[1] To illustrate what he considered to be the injurious effects of such teaching on unbelievers Finney records a conversation which he had on one occasion. A non-Christian, apparently of Presbyterian background, told him:

'The Bible teaches us that God created us with a sinful nature.' I replied, 'Mr. S——, have you a Bible? Will you not turn to a passage that teaches this?' 'Why, there is no need of that,' he says; 'you admit that the Bible teaches it.' 'No,' I said, 'I do not believe that the Bible teaches any such thing.' 'Then,' he continued, 'the Bible teaches that God has imputed Adam's sin to all his posterity; that we inherit the guilt of that sin by nature . . . This is a direct contradiction of my irresistible convictions of right and justice.' 'Yes,' I replied, 'and so it is directly in contradiction of my own.' He began to quote the catechism, as he had done before. 'But,' I replied, 'that is the catechism, not the Bible.' 'Why,' said he, 'you are a Presbyterian minister, are you not? I thought the catechism was good authority for you.' 'No,' I said; 'we are·talking about the Bible now – whether the Bible is true.' 'Oh,' said he, 'if you are going to deny that it is taught in the Bible – why, that is taking such ground as I never knew a Presbyterian minister to take.'[2]

Finney's great argument was that if men have to experience a change of *nature* before they can become Christians, and such a change as only God can effect, then no sinner can be responsible for his unbelief and lack of repentance. The Bible, he asserted, teaches plainly our duty to come to Christ. How can God command us to do what we cannot do? So from the

[1] Ibid., p. 154. He claimed that 'the foundation of the error' propagated by Princeton was 'the dogma that human nature is sinful of itself' (p. 256).

[2] Ibid., p. 125. The catechism to which he referred was of course that of the Westminster Assembly; but here, as elsewhere, Finney presents a mis-statement of the teaching of the catechism. It does not teach that 'God created' anyone with a sinful nature but rather that original sin is the result of man's rebellion against God. Mr S—— had reason to be surprised that Finney would not own a statement of doctrine which he had accepted at his ordination in the Presbyterian ministry. Finney does not offer a biblical argument for human ability: his whole case rests on his assertion that God would be 'an infinite tyrant' if he commanded men to do what they cannot do. For a fuller statement of Presbyterian teaching see Appendix 3 below.

fact of human responsibility – as he understood it – he deduced that men must possess the *ability* to obey. The deduction sounds rational and logical, but it is not scriptural. Finney's opponents did not deny human responsibility. They were even ready to emphasise it. They claimed, however, that the Bible shows that sin has destroyed man's ability to obey God from his heart: 'The natural man does not receive the things of the Spirit of God' (*1 Cor.* 2:14). 'The carnal mind is enmity against God: for it is not subject to the law of God, nor indeed can be' (*Rom.* 8:7). Further they pointed to the ministry of Christ himself for evidence of the need to hold both human responsibility and inability. Jesus said: 'Come to Me, all you who labour and are heavy laden' (*Matt.* 11:28). 'You are not willing to come to Me, that you may have life' (*John* 5:40). 'While you have the light, believe in the light, that you may become sons of light' (*John* 12:36). Such words show the unbeliever's duty and responsibility. But Jesus also said, 'No one can come to Me unless it has been granted to him by My Father' (*John* 6:65). Again, he said that no man can rise above his nature, 'a bad tree bears bad fruit' (*Matt.* 7:17). We bear the nature of our birth: 'That which is born of the flesh is flesh; and that which is born of the Spirit is spirit. Do not marvel that I said to you, "You must be born again" ' (*John* 3:6–7).

There was a great deal said and written on this subject in the 1830s but Finney stuck to his position and it would be fair to say that his arguments were not so much biblical as practical. He believed that evangelism has to involve telling gospel hearers that they are *able* to become Christians at once: they have to be presented with an immediate choice, and to show the sincerity and reality of their choosing Christ let them *do something* to prove it. Hence what became known as the 'altar call', that is, the practice of calling those who would be converted to take some visible action which would clinch the matter. The fact that such novel public actions were calculated to create natural excitement was the opposite, in Finney's mind, to being a drawback: 'God has found it *necessary to take advantage* of the excitability there is in mankind to produce powerful excitements among them before he *can* lead them to obey.'[1]

To oppose this, Finney argued, is to destroy evangelistic preaching. The ministers who disagreed with him, he constantly tells his readers, were useless as evangelists. He carried the practical argument significantly further. If preachers will only do the right thing they will not only secure the conversion of individuals but they will secure revivals. As already said, this was the great message of his *Lectures on Revivals*. Hitherto, he claimed, the churches had supposed that revivals are simply in the hands of God to give or withhold. No wonder revivals are not constant, if we believe that, said Finney! The truth, he claimed, was that the absence of revival is due solely to the church failing to do her duty.

Finney's Case Examined

Finney used two main lines of argument to prove the correctness of his assertions:

1. The Argument from his Experience.
Finney constantly offset the newness of his ideas with assertions that he was sure that they were not his own:

I say that God taught me; and I know it must have been so; for surely I never had obtained these notions from man. And I have often thought that I could say with perfect truth, as Paul said, that I was not taught the Gospel by man, but by the Spirit of Christ himself.[2]

I had no doubt then, nor have I ever had, that God led me by His Spirit, to take the course I did . . . I was divinely directed. [3]

More common than such words is the appeal to the success of his ministry as proof that God owned what he was preaching.

[1] Quoted by Dod, *Princeton Essays*, p. 83.
[2] *Memoirs*, pp. 87-8.
[3] Ibid., p. 222.

The narrative given in his autobiography is very clearly constructed to impress the reader with this fact. 'God,' he writes, 'set his seal to the doctrines that were preached, and to the means that were used to carry forward that great work.'[1] 'After I had preached some time, and the Lord had everywhere added his blessing, I used to say to ministers, whenever they contended with me . . . "Show me the fruits of your ministry".'[2] He frequently follows such statements with reports of how ministers who held Calvinistic beliefs gave them up when they saw how 'the Spirit of God did accompany my labours.'[3]

In this connection Finney omits to say that he had a considerable advantage if immediate visible results were to be made the test of what was scriptural. Under the former preaching the success of the gospel was only judged as people gave steady evidence of changed lives and were subsequently examined for membership of the churches. With Finney's teaching and methods there was now a much quicker and public way of telling converts. If a convert is one who submits and comes to the front, then just how many converts there are on any particular occasion will be apparent for all to see. So the numbers 'converted' made immediate news and figures proving success were now quoted in a way which was new to the evangelical churches.[4] This was not all. If large crowds

[1] Ibid., p. 221.
[2] Ibid., p. 83.
[3] Ibid., pp. 157, 237–8, 259–62.
[4] Speaking of the new type of evangelist, William Mitchell complained: 'He has his own measures, proclaims the number of converts, accomplishes their speedy admission to the church.' 'An Inquiry into the Utility of Modern Evangelists', *Literary and Theological Review*, II (Andover, September, 1835); quoted by McLoughlin, *Modern Revivalism*, p. 126. R. L. Dabney, reflecting on the sensational appeal of the new evangelism, wrote of its promoters: 'They are anxious to exchange strict integrity of conviction and purity of doctrine, and the secret but mighty power of the Holy Spirit through his words, for human *eclat*, numbers, wealth, combination and power. They expect and prepare to convert the world as they built the Pacific railroad, by money and numbers.' *Discussions*, vol. 2 (repr. London: Banner of Truth, 1967), p. 442.

attended preaching services and, for whatever reason, many responded to the evangelist's appeal, then the very numbers responding could be regarded as proof of 'revival'. So there was a visual demonstration, it seemed, of the truth of Finney's teaching and a justification of his claim that revivals could indeed be promoted by the right use of means.

2. *The Barrenness of the Prevailing Orthodoxy.*
This again is another argument from alleged experience. The teaching which Finney was concerned to see overturned could not be of God because it was so useless in obtaining the conversion of souls. So he claimed. This theme runs right through his *Memoirs*. He raised it first in connection with his own conversion at Adams. His narrative gives us the impression that George Gale, the minister of the Presbyterian church, had nothing to do with his conversion and indeed would have been little or no use in aiding anyone's conversion because, holding to the Westminster Confession and being Princeton trained, his theological views were 'such as to cripple his usefulness';[1] 'he did not understand the gospel'.[2] 'The education he had received at Princeton had totally unfitted him for the work of winning souls to Christ.'[3] Under the preachers of that school, Finney asserted, unbelievers are 'almost never converted'.[4] Far from helping in revivals, the prevailing orthodoxy, which he called 'hyper-Calvinism', did the very opposite and created 'the greatest difficulty.'[5] 'I have everywhere found, that the peculiarities of hyper-Calvinism have been a great stumbling-block, both of the church and of the world.'[6] Albert Dod was not going too far when he wrote of Finney: 'He claims, in no guarded terms, the exclusive approbation of God for his doctrines and

[1] *Memoirs: Complete Text*, p. 57.
[2] *Memoirs*, p. 157.
[3] *Memoirs: Complete Text*, p. 510.
[4] Ibid., p. 322. In Finney's abridged *Memoirs* the editor thought it wiser to omit both this statement and the one on Princeton in the previous reference.
[5] *Memoirs*, p. 256.
[6] Ibid., p. 368.

measures. "They (the church) see that the *blessing of God* is with those that are accused of new measures and innovation." [1]

What shall we say to these two great arguments upon which Finney rested his case? On the first, that is the claimed success of his ministry, there is need to say little. That many people may have come to a saving knowledge of Christ under his ministry need not be disputed although the number may have been considerably less than he sometimes supposed. I say 'sometimes' because there were occasions when, in a less-controversial mood, Finney himself conceded that there had been a large fall-away rate from those who had professed to be converts. [2] But whatever the number, we can rejoice that there were true conversions without accepting his claim that it proves the rightness of everything which he said and did. No man ought to appeal to his work as the ground for others to accept his teaching. The best of men may err and build with 'wood, hay, straw' as well as 'gold, silver, precious stones' (*1 Cor.* 3:12). It was a very serious error on the part of Finney to point people to himself rather than to Scripture to justify what he believed was true.

One has to say that Finney's second argument is no less seriously wrong, and here it is an easier matter to prove it to be so. His claim was that the teaching he opposed was a hindrance both to evangelism and to revivals. The facts are against him. Take the case of his allegedly useless pastor at Adams, George Gale. When, in the late 1860s, Finney wrote the manuscript which became his *Memoirs*, Gale was dead.

---

[1] *Princeton Essays*, p. 146.
[2] See my *Revival and Revivalism*, pp. 288–9. Writing in 1835, Dod said: 'Appearances were somewhat in favour of the new measures. At least wherever they were carried, converts were multiplied. But it is now generally understood that the numerous converts of the new measures have been, in most cases, like the morning cloud and the early dew. In some places, not a half, a fifth, or even a tenth part of them remain.' *Princeton Essays*, p. 140.

What Finney did not know was that back in 1853 Gale had written his own autobiography. Finney necessarily remained ignorant of its existence for it was over a century later that it was published, in 1964. Gale's narrative, which runs to 309 pages in its printed form, is at many points in marked disagreement with what is alleged by Finney. Far from being useless and perhaps unconverted, Gale was clearly in the midst of a revival in his church at Adams at the time Finney was converted. The idea that Gale did not understand the gospel in 1821 is absurd. Nor is this simply a case of Gale's memory versus Finney's for the success of the gospel under the ministry of Gale, and others in the same area, is fully corroborated by other sources.

The truth is that when Finney was working on his own autobiography (more than forty-five years after the early 1820s), to have accepted at the outset Gale's usefulness as a preacher would have been to jeopardise the whole case which he was going to present, namely, that Calvinistic belief only promotes barrenness.[1] But there is a more cogent refutation of Finney's appeal to history. It is that the period of the Second Great Awakening, which was a time of many powerful revivals, did not begin when Finney began his ministry in 1824. It began twenty-five years before, in the late 1790s. The readers of Finney's *Memoirs* are told that his ministry constituted the start of a 'new era', and they are led to suppose, as Dr Graham has supposed, that Finney's was the new voice which led to revival times. The truth is that the remarkable age of the Second Great Awakening was drawing near to its close when Finney began and that, despite all his teaching about continuous revival, such an age was not seen

[1] The fact that Gale writes of Finney with esteem and as a one-time friend makes his record the more convincing. Gale says that Finney was far from being an opponent of Calvinism at the outset of his ministry: 'When he was licensed and first labored as a missionary, he was very firm and faithful in bringing out this doctrine' [i.e., of the grace of God] . . . 'His peculiar views, adopted since he went to Oberlin, were no part of his theology at that time, and for a number of years afterward.' *Autobiography of G. W. Gale*, pp. 274, 186.

again in his lifetime.[1] The reason why Finney did not disclose this to his readers of a much later generation was that most of the preaching which had been so used of God, in the years prior to his ministry, was of the very sort that he wished to represent as barren!

The very Seminary at Princeton which he constantly characterised as disabling preachers had been prominently identified with revival since its outset in 1812. Its magazine, the *Biblical Repertory*, gave the common opinion of its professors and students, when looking back on some thirty years, it noted in 1832: 'It has pleased God to make America the theatre of the most glorious revivals that the world has ever witnessed.'[2] Princeton men were leaders in many revivals; a third of the Seminary's students of the first fifty years were to go to mission fields; and there can hardly be a more serious misrepresentation of history than the idea which Finney sought to promote about the institution which thought it necessary to oppose him. Far too much biographical material is currently available on the fragrant and useful ministries of the men on the other side to Finney to make his case even remotely credible.[3]

---

[1] Finney himself accepted this fact. I am not overlooking the awakening of 1857–8 which was powerful but of much shorter duration, and one of the most striking things about its origins is that while revivalism had already become popular in North America it had no part in the beginning of the movement in New York City. See Samuel I. Prime, *The Power of Prayer: the New York Revival of 1858* (repr. Edinburgh: Banner of Truth, 1991), pp. 27–30, 36: 'There were no revivalists; no revival machinery . . . the "anxious seat", and the labor of peregrinating revival-makers were unknown.' Careless assertions about Finney's work in some 'revival' literature convey misleading impressions. Goforth, for instance, links the 1857 revival in New York with Finney and says: 'By 1857, Finney was seeing fifty thousand a week turning to God' (*By My Spirit*, p. 183). This statement is very inaccurate. For Finney in 1857, see *Memoirs of Finney: Complete Text*, p. 562.

[2] 'Sprague on Revivals', *The Biblical Repertory and Theological Review* (Philadelphia: Russell & Martien, 1832), p. 456.

[3] See, for instance, J. W. Alexander, *Life of Archibald Alexander* (1854, repr. Harrisonburg, Va.: Sprinkle, 1991); B. Tyler and Andrew Bonar, *The Life and Labours of Asahel Nettleton*, 1854, (repr. Edinburgh: Banner of Truth, 1975); W. B. Sprague, 'Memoir of Doctor Griffin' in *Life and Sermons of Edward D. Griffin*, 1837 (repr. Edinburgh: Banner of Truth, 1987).

Why the Old School Opposed Finney

1. Finney's so-called 'new measures' were opposed because they confused two different things: an outward act and the new birth. An individual can fall on his knees, raise his hand or walk to the front, but there is nothing in the Bible to say that such actions make, or even contribute to making, a person a Christian. The older evangelical preaching taught the instant responsibility of sinners to obey the gospel in repentance and faith; it did not pass over such texts as, 'God now commands all men everywhere to repent' (*Acts* 17:30), but, at the same time, it knew that the time when hearers of the gospel get grace to obey is not in the hands of men.[1] The new measures, by by-passing that fact, and appointing a physical duty which the unregenerate can perform, represented conversion as something less than it is made in the New Testament. Under old-school preaching it was expected that conviction of sin would show hearers their need of change at the centre of their being – a work of new creation securing a new life and a new moral existence. If no such regeneration is supposed to be necessary then conversion becomes a very much easier matter.

2. This new teaching was thus popularising a dangerously

[1] 'Regeneration differs from conversion. Regeneration is a spiritual change, conversion is a spiritual motion. In regeneration there is a power conferred, conversion is the exercise of that power. In regeneration there is given us a principle to turn, conversion is an actual turning. Conversion is related to regeneration as the effect to the cause . . . In regeneration man is wholly passive; in conversion he is active. Regeneration is the motion of God in the creature; conversion is the motion of the creature to God, by virtue of that first principle.' *Works of Stephen Charnock*, vol. 3 (repr. Edinburgh: Banner of Truth, 1986), pp. 88–9. But because regeneration is a secret work of God in the soul no one is called upon to ascertain its existence before exercising faith and repentance. It is only by the believing acceptance of Christ that the prior work of God can come to be recognised (see, for instance, 1 Thessalonians 1:3–5). Election is first in point of time but not in the believer's conscious experience (*Acts* 13:48). One of the most helpful books ever published in this area is Archibald Alexander's *Thoughts on Religious Experience*, 1844 (repr. London: Banner of Truth, 1967).

superficial view of conversion, arising out of a superficial view
of sin. Man's plight is a great deal more serious than the
representation implied by the new measures. Men, said
Finney, are not converted 'by a change wrought in their
nature by creative power' but by 'yielding to the truth'.[1] In his
view, the Holy Spirit does no more than present the truth,
along with the preacher, and thus regeneration is effected 'by
argument' in which the sinner's will is 'broken down'.[2] The
public appeal for decision was seen as playing an important
part in gaining this end.[3] It was on the basis of this new view of
conversion that Finney told his New York hearers in 1834: 'For
many centuries but little of the real gospel has been
preached.'[4] Princeton's reply was to say with Charles Hodge:
'No more soul-destroying doctrine could well be devised than
the doctrine that sinners can regenerate themselves, and
repent and believe just when they please.'[5]

3. Because the new measures told people that obedience to the
preacher's directions was necessary to becoming a Christian,
compliance with such directions inevitably came to be treated
as a means of assurance that one was now in a state of grace. If
accepting Christ is the same as walking to the front, then all
who have done the latter must be Christians. This was putting

[1] *Revivals of Religion*, p. 377.
[2] Ibid., p. 195. He makes this further extraordinary statement: 'If a person
does not believe that sinners are able to obey their Maker, and really
believes that the Spirit's influences are necessary to make them able, it is
impossible, with these views, to offer acceptable prayer.' For, he alleged,
such prayer would 'insult God' because God would be bound to give his
Spirit as 'a mere matter of common justice' if such was man's condition
(pp. 356–70).
[3] The old school, of course, had no objection to enquirers being counselled
after evangelistic preaching as they sometimes did themselves, but the
primary purpose of the 'altar call', as Dod said, was different: 'Its object is
not simply to collect in one place those who are in a particular state of mind,
that they may be suitably instructed and advised. No, there is supposed to be
some wonder-working power in the person's rising before the congregation
and taking the assigned place.' *Princeton Essays*, p. 122.
[4] Quoted by Dod, *Princeton Essays*, p. 78.
[5] C. Hodge, *Systematic Theology*, vol. 2 (London: Nelson, 1874), p. 277.

assurance of salvation on an entirely new basis, for the older evangelism, in both its Calvinistic and Arminian forms, had insisted that it is the Holy Spirit himself who gives assurance and that no one should assume they have passed from death to life without his witness and a corresponding change of life.

To this it was replied that, supposing a degree of harm was done, was not the fact that some were truly converted sufficient justification for the new measures? The old-school answer was simply to point out that those who were converted in such circumstances did not owe it to the wrong measures but to the grace of God and the truth they heard preached. These converts would have suffered no loss had no new measures been used, but the many who responded to the measures *without being converted* were in a far worse position for in coming forward they did what they were told to do without any result. With some justification they could come to regard conversion as an illusion.

4. The new teaching, by putting its emphasis on the instant action taken by an individual following the evangelist's appeal and not upon a changed life, inevitably lowered standards of membership in evangelical churches and so encouraged an acceptance of worldliness among professing Christians.[1] Speaking of the wrong measures which had been popularised, R. L. Dabney wrote: 'We believe that they are the chief cause, under the prime source, original sin, which has deteriorated

---

[1] A. W. Tozer was one of the few twentieth-century evangelical leaders who spoke out against the danger. Earl Swanson has recorded how as a young minister he heard Tozer preach in Long Beach, California: 'As he came to the conclusion of his message the air was totally electrified. I was accustomed to altar calls and was fully expecting to see a mass movement forward. That surely would have been the case had he chosen to do so. Rather, in his inimitable style and brusque manner he announced, "Don't come down here to the altar and cry about it – go home and live it". With that comment he dismissed the meeting.' James L. Snyder, *In Pursuit of God, The Life of A. W. Tozer* (Camp Hill, Pa.: Christian Publications, 1991), p. 154. Martyn Lloyd-Jones, when asked to be chairman for the Berlin Congress of the Billy Graham Organization in 1966, declined to do so unless the practice of the public appeal was given up by Dr Graham.

the average standard of holy living, principles, and morality, and the church discipline of our religion, until it has nearly lost its practical power over the public conscience.'[1]

The New Testament teaches that the change resulting from the new birth is so great that wherever it occurs a continued living of the old life is impossible: 'whoever sins has neither seen Him nor known Him' (*1 John* 3:6). 'Whatever is born of God overcomes the world' (*1 John* 5:4). Where there is no alienation from sin there is no re-birth. Under the new evangelism this ceased to be recognised and so there grew up many forms of holiness teaching meant to help the numbers of 'unsanctified Christians' now in the churches. Meanwhile the fundamental reason for the existence of so many 'carnal Christians' was largely unrecognised.

5. Finney's teaching that revival should be normal and continuous, not extraordinary and occasional, depended for its success on a change in the *content* of revival. The same word now came to stand for any evangelistic campaign which gathered people together in numbers, and both Finney and his followers encouraged the switch.[2] Finney had charged his opponents with being 'enemies to revivals'. In reply they asserted that the opposite was the case and that it was for the very cause of revivals that they were speaking.[3] They feared that the new teaching was taking the work of the Spirit out of his own hands. 'The influence of the Holy Spirit comes in only by the way,' wrote Dod in his review of Finney's lectures on *Revivals of Religion.*[4] In Wales, John Elias, the Calvinistic Methodist leader, who had preached in many revivals, put his finger on the same point. When the new teaching first

[1] R. L. Dabney, *Discussions*, vol. 3 (repr. Edinburgh: Banner of Truth, 1982), p. 19. See also, vol. 2, 'An Exposition of 1 Corinthians 3:10–15,' pp. 551–74.

[2] The Beardsley quotation given above on Finney's 'extensive revivals' in Britain are a case in point. Finney's visits to Britain saw evangelistic campaigns, not revivals.

[3] See, for instance, *The Life and Labours of Asahel Nettleton*, pp. 348–51.

[4] *Princeton Essays*, p. 82.

crossed the Atlantic, his question was: 'Is there not a want of perceiving the corruption, obstinacy, and spiritual deadness of man, and the consequent necessity of the Almighty Spirit to enlighten and overcome him?'[1] As with brethren in the States, Elias dreaded lest 'the legitimate results of erroneous principles shall be visited upon the ruined churches of our land.'[2]

[1] Letter to Rev. Henry Rees, 2 March 1838: *John Elias, Life, Letters and Essays* (Edinburgh: Banner of Truth, 1973), p. 259.
[2] The words are those of the author of the Preface to *Letters of the Rev. Dr. Beecher and Rev. Mr. Nettleton on the 'New Measures' in Conducting Revivals of Religion* (New York, 1828), p. 103.

3

Our Responsibility and God's Sovereignty

*'The end of our vision is not the starting-point of God's working . . .
It is wisest for us to keep human agency in its own place,
and to aim at reflecting all the glory on the Sovereign Lord.'* [1]
William Gibson, 1860

Probably the most influential argument against the old-school view of revival is the claim that it encourages fatalism and passivity. Because, it is said, if revival is not conditional upon what we do, what room is left for earnest prayer and action? If times of revival are in the hands of God, and belong to the 'secret things' unknown to us (*Deut.* 29:29), then what place can there be for the exercise of such effort as the Scripture requires of Christians? Did Christ not say, 'Ask, and you will receive' (*John* 16:24)? And is not the giving of the Spirit directly connected in Scripture with the obedience of Christians? The apostles declared, 'We are His witnesses to these things, and so also is the Holy Spirit whom God has given to those who obey Him' (*Acts* 5:32). Again, 'You do not have because you do not ask' (*James* 4:2).

From such texts as these it has been argued that the older understanding of revival does not do justice to human responsibility. Rather, it is claimed that its tendency is to encourage complacency and even to lead to the repetition of

[1] Gibson, *Year of Grace*, p. 17.

the sin of those who 'limited the Holy One of Israel' (*Psa.* 78:41).

Presented in this light, the old-school teaching may indeed appear to minimise human responsibility; and, because any teaching which does that cannot be biblical, the alternative case – that revival depends upon us – gains credibility. By way of reply it needs to be shown that what we have said in the previous chapters, rightly understood, does not have any such a consequence. It is true that there have been Christians who have so emphasised God's sovereignty that the impression is given that the church has simply to wait until God acts, as though, when revival comes, duties will be taken out of our hands by divine power. But such an aberration from the truth was never a part of the teaching which I have stated. Those who upheld it knew well that the work of God does not supersede human instrumentality and obligation. Scripture certainly holds us accountable for what we do or fail to do. While God is sovereign, and works all things after the counsel of his own will, yet even responsibility for the salvation of men and women is attributed to us (*Jer.* 23:22; *Ezek.* 33:6; *1 Tim.* 4:16). Such a representative 'old-school' figure as Andrew Bonar, biographer of Robert M'Cheyne, could write in his diary for September 28, 1878:

Yesterday was the anniversary of my ordination; but many interruptions came in my way, so that I had little leisure for the proper use of such a day. To-day I have more time and quiet; and oh! what a review of forty years' ministry. In infinite mercy the Lord has used me for winning souls, but I see to-day with awful fulness that if I had lived *nearer God*, if I had prayed more in the Holy Ghost, instead of winning five I might have got fifty or five hundred year by year. To-day my omissions seem very terrible, as they have sometimes done before; my little improvement of immense advantages and my feeble appreciation of the privilege of being spared so long in the ministry. I have been trying to draw deeper from the fountain of the water of life, but my thirst is soon slaked. To-day this has been much upon my mind, viz., that *just because* I have been filled in some measure, I should be deeply humbled; for that measure of blessing was an incitement to seek more from the Lord, and I was not caring to go on and take more. 2 Kings 13:19: 'Hadst thou smitten five or six times, then thou shouldst have smitten Syria to destruction.'[1]

Major Responsibilities – Conduct, Truth and Faith

Our first response to the argument against the old-school teaching is to deny that it minimised what Scripture says on human responsibility. The Bible makes it plain that the work of God can be stopped and set back by sin. Thus, although it is true that faith is the gift of God, we read, 'He did not do many mighty works there because of their unbelief' (*Matt.* 13:58). Similarly Christians are warned: 'Do not grieve the Holy Spirit of God' (*Eph.* 4:30); 'Do not quench the Spirit' (*1 Thess.* 5:19). However mysterious the fact, the work of God may be hindered or even destroyed by our conduct (*Rom.* 14:20; *Gal.* 5:15).

This truth comes out clearly if we consider three areas where Scripture gives special emphasis to Christian responsibility. The first has to do with *the imperative requirement of obedience to all moral duties*. Moral laxity of every kind, whether it be in the form of pride, impurity, selfishness, contention between brethren or whatever, is ever a sure hindrance to the blessing of God. All duties are vain in the sight of God where the pursuit of holiness is absent; religious activity and prayer are no alternatives to obedience, 'Behold, to obey is better than sacrifice' (*1 Sam.* 15:22). As Abraham Kuyper has written:

Zeal for the church, however pious it may appear to be, is abominable hypocrisy if it goes hand in hand with neglect of spiritual warfare against such enemies of God as lying, uncleanness, self-righteousness, coldheartedness. Some there are who pretend to be faithful watchmen upon Zion's walls but harbor such sins in their own hearts, or overlook them in their children and fellow church members. They are unfaithful.[2]

Blindness to the evil of such worldliness is tragically apparent

---

[1] Andrew A. Bonar, *Diary and Letters,* ed. Marjory Bonar (London: Hodder & Stoughton, 1894), pp. 327–8.
[2] A. Kuyper, *The Practice of Godliness* (Grand Rapids: Baker, 1977), p. 58.

in many professing churches today. The United Reformed
Church in England (which constitutes almost all that is left of
the historic Presbyterian and Congregational denominations)
has recently entertained hopes of a new advance as their
Assembly backed a proposal that the year 1999 be observed
throughout the denomination as 'a year of commitment to
Jesus Christ'. Yet the very same Assembly passed a motion
allowing local congregations to appoint homosexual or lesbian
ministers if they wished, stipulating that 'the fact of an active
homosexual relationship will not in itself be considered
sufficient grounds for rejecting a candidate for training.'[1]

This may be an extreme example but the same antinomian
spirit is widely present in the English-speaking churches on
both sides of the Atlantic. The fear of God has largely
departed. A biographer of A. W. Tozer tells us that, as an
observer on the religious scene, Tozer would often comment
on these two things: 'that there is little sense of sin among the
unsaved; and that the average Christian lives a life so worldly
and careless that it is difficult to distinguish him from the
unconverted man'.[2] It is no wonder that Tozer also thought
that a 'revival' of the kind for which Christians of this kind
were looking would be a calamity from which the United
States might not recover in a hundred years.

A second area of responsibility where unfaithfulness will
blight the work of God has to do with *failure to uphold the truth
as revealed in the Word of God*. Adherence to truth is ever given
in Scripture a high place in the obligations placed upon
Christians. While a special duty lies upon those who teach, all
believers are to be steadfast in maintaining and defending –
even to death – all that God has revealed for our salvation.
Heresy and error are no trivial things according to Scripture.
John Brown of Haddington was surely correct when he
wrote:

[1] *Assembly Hotline*, a broadsheet published by the United Reformed
Church. This motion was passed by 63% to 37%.
[2] David J. Fant, *A. W. Tozer, A Twentieth Century Prophet* (Harrisburg:
Christian Publications, 1964), p. 34.

The scripture represents erroneous persons as 'dogs', 'wolves', 'deceitful workers', 'ministers of Satan', 'deceivers', 'liars', and 'evil men'. Error is false of itself, fathers falsehood upon God, is the 'doctrine of devils', and 'work of the flesh', excluding men from the kingdom of God. It mars the purity, order, union and fellowship of the church, – leads men to blaspheme God, murder souls, and bring forth abominable practices, Matt. 7:15; Phil. 3:2; 2 Cor. 11:13; Rev. 2; Matt. 23; Acts 20:29,30; Matt. 5:19,20 and 15:2; 2 Pet. 2; 1 John 2:22,23 and 4:3; 2 John 9, 10. The *suffering of gross error to be taught* in the church must therefore be *very sinful*. It brings contempt on the oracles and ordinances of God, gives Satan opportunity to employ ordinances and ministers as instruments of rebellion against God. It exalts Satan to an equality with God in the church, the doctrine of one being received as well as the other. It introduces much confusion and destruction to men's souls, and becomes a dreadful plague and source of all manner of immoralities in a nation.[1]

Words such as these sound almost strange in today's climate where there is little concern over doctrinal error and, too often, the hope of revival is entertained while the issue of commitment to Scripture is left unaddressed. Prayer for revival is no substitute for repentance and immediate obedience to the Word of God. Too often dying denominations, faced with declining memberships, have backed calls for 'revival' and looked for the restoration of the brighter conditions of their earlier history. But serious error in the midst is left undisturbed. This was the case among English Methodist leaders in the 1950s. Dr W. E. Sangster, for example, wrote:

If Methodism has lost her true emphasis and passion, both may be

[1] John Brown, *Practical Piety Exemplified and Illustrated in Casuistical Hints* (Glasgow: Bryce, 1783), p. 330. He goes on to say, 'Good men are often too condescending to erroneous teachers'. All the Puritans are strong in their warnings on this subject. Listing people with whom 'Christians must have no intimate, no special communion,' Thomas Brooks names false prophets and false teachers: 'They are not to be given any house-room, 2 John 10,11, nor heart-room, Matt. 24:23,24,26. They are to shun and avoid them, Rom. 16:17. It is not safe for a Christian to hear them, or to have any communion or fellowship with them.' *Works of Thomas Brooks*, vol. 4 (repr. Edinburgh: Banner of Truth, 1980), p. 67.

restored. God will not withhold His grace from a people prostrate before Him . . . the *big* thing is the revival of Methodism.[1]

We do not criticise the denominational loyalty in these words. The fault was rather that such words were unaccompanied by a call to the Methodist churches to return to the Bible and to such fundamental truths as the vicarious sufferings of Christ and the new birth. Instead false teaching went unopposed and open criticism of the Bible continued unchecked. It ought to be no wonder that the hoped-for revival never came. The decline and demise of churches is inevitable where loyalty to Christ fails to include commitment to the upholding of his words. Drawing an example of this from church history, J. C. Ryle wrote: 'When the Saracens invaded the lands where Jerome and Athanasius, Cyprian and Augustine, once wrote and preached, they found bishops and liturgies, I make no question. But I fear they found no preaching of free forgiveness of sins, and so they swept the churches of those lands clean away.'[2]

A third area where Scripture links the health and usefulness of churches with Christian responsibility has to do with *the exercise of faith.* Faith is the mainspring of Christian character and the 'victory which has overcome the world' (*1 John* 5:4). 'Above all, taking the shield of faith' is the New Testament priority (*Eph.* 6:16), because everything else in the life and usefulness of a believer will be found to be in proportion to the strength or weakness of faith. Faith is the grace which honours God by its dependence upon him; and because faith receives all, and attributes nothing to itself, God identifies faith with all that he is himself able to do. Thus to the woman who had suffered an issue of blood for twelve years Jesus says, 'Daughter, your faith has made you well' (*Mark* 5:34) – as though faith were the cause of her health. So close is the

---

[1] Paul Sangster, *Dr Sangster* (London: Epworth Press, 1962), pp. 292–3.
[2] J. C. Ryle, *Home Truths*, First Series, 6th ed. (Ipswich: Hunt, 1860), p. 95. Ryle was one of the few English leaders at the end of the last century who saw the danger of history repeating itself with regard to error quenching the Spirit of God.

conjunction of faith with the action of God that while we read such texts as: 'With God nothing will be impossible' (*Luke* 1:37); and, 'The things which are impossible with men are possible with God' (*Luke* 18:27); *we also read*, 'If you can believe, all things are possible to him who believes' (*Mark* 9:23); 'According to your faith let it be to you' (*Matt.* 9:29); 'Blessed is she who believed, for there will be a fulfillment of those things which were told her from the Lord' (*Luke* 1:45); 'Did I not say to you that if you would believe you would see the glory of God?' (*John* 11:40).

Christians eminent in usefulness and service are described in such words as 'full of faith and the Holy Spirit . . . full of faith and power' (*Acts* 6:5,8); 'full of the Holy Spirit and of faith' (*Acts* 11:24). Conversely, unbelief is represented as departing from God and is set down as the primary cause of all spiritual barrenness: 'If you will not believe, Surely you shall not be established' (*Isa.* 7:9); 'The Lord is with you while you are with Him. If you seek Him, He will be found by you; but if you forsake Him, He will forsake you' (*2 Chron.* 15:2); 'Beware, brethren, lest there be in any of you an evil heart of unbelief in departing from the living God . . . they could not enter in because of unbelief' (*Heb.* 3:12,19).

On this subject the Puritan John Howe commented:

The blessed God has settled this connexion between our faith and his own exerted power. As the extraordinary works of the Spirit were not done but upon the exercise of the extraordinary faith which by the divine constitution was requisite thereunto so that the unbelief which stood in the absence of this faith did sometimes in a sort bind up the power of God (so inviolable had that constitution made that connexion, *Mark* 6:5,6; *Matt.* 17:19,20)[1] – nor also are the works of the Holy Ghost, that are common upon all sincere Christians, done, but upon the intervening exercise of that more common faith . . . We are 'to receive the promise of the Spirit (i.e., the Spirit promised)

[1] Howe's use of 'extraordinary' and 'common' faith distinguishes the faith given to individuals in the apostolic age on particular occasions for the working of a miracle (which the Reformed churches all classified as one of the extraordinary gifts now withdrawn) and the abiding faith which is the possession of all Christians.

through faith', *Gal.* 3:14. Hereby we draw the power of that Almighty Spirit into a consent and co-operation with our spirit. So the great God suffers himself, his own arm and power, to be taken hold of by us. He is engaged when he is trusted; that trust being now in this case not a rash and unwarrantable presuming upon him, but such whereto he has given the invitation and encouragement himself. So that when we reflect upon the promises wherein the gift of the Spirit is conveyed, we may say, 'Remember thy word to thy servant, wherein thou hast caused me to hope,' *Prov.* 1:2,3; *Ezek.* 36:27; *Psa.* 119.

And then surely he will not frustrate the expectation of which he himself has been the Author. He would never have induced those to trust in him whom he intended to disappoint. That free Spirit (which, as the wind, bloweth where it listeth) now permits itself to be brought under bonds, even the bonds of God's own covenant, whereof we now take hold by our faith: so that he will not fail to give forth his influence, so far as shall be necessary for the maintaining a resolution in us of steadfast adherence to God and his service. How express and peremptory are those words, 'This I say (that is, I know what I say, I have full well weighed the matter, and speak not at random), Walk in the Spirit, and ye shall not fulfill the lusts of the flesh!' And so much as this affords great matter of rational delight, though more sensible transports (which are not so needful to us, and in reference whereto the Spirit therefore retains its liberty) be not so frequent.[1] Therefore if we aim at the having our spirits placed and settled in the secret of the Divine Presence, entertained with the delights of it; if we would know and have the sensible proof of that religion which is all life and power, and consequently sweetness and pleasure; our direct way is *believing on the Spirit*. That very trust is his delight, Psalm 147:11. It is his delight to be depended on as a Father by his children . . . And when we thus give him his delight, we shall not long want ours.[2]

The old-school understanding of revival was not formulated in forgetfulness of such vital areas of responsibility. Those who assert the contrary know neither the writings nor the history of the men they criticise. But it is true that a major difference generally exists between the older writers and their critics on

[1] I discuss what Howe calls 'sensible transports' (i.e., a full and felt sense of God's love) below, pp. 123–4.
[2] 'Of Delighting in God,' *Works of John Howe*, vol. 1 (London: Tegg, 1848), pp. 591–2. For greater clarity I have slightly modernised words and punctuation in a few places.

the subject of responsibility. The latter (invariably represent-
ing Arminian or Pelagian views) think that it is by *our acting* on
scriptural promises that blessings are made certain. Thus from
such a promise as, 'he who believes will be saved,' it is deduced
that the personal response is the reason why anyone is saved.
Divine sovereignty does not come into it. God, it is said, has
appointed the condition, we fulfil the condition and the
blessing is made certain whether the case be the conversion of
an individual or the revival of churches.

But the truth is different. God gives promises and duties as
instrumental means to blessing, not as *causes,* for the grace of God
is in the means as well as in the result. God's act does not *follow*
man's, rather the divine and human agency are conjoined so
that we find that what is required of man is also attributed to
God. God gives a new heart (*Ezek.* 36:26) yet he commands,
'Get yourselves a new heart' (*Ezek.* 18:31). The spiritual
resurrection of the sinner is God's work (*Eph.* 2:5), yet we
read, 'Awake, you who sleep, Arise from the dead, And Christ
will give you light' (*Eph.* 5:14). Repentance and faith are both
stated to be God's gifts, and yet both are also represented as
being the duty of sinners, 'Repent . . . and be converted, that
your sins may be blotted out' (*Acts* 3:19). In all these things man
is active, and conscious of his own responsibility, but at the
same time he is dependent upon God 'who works in you both
to will and to do for His good pleasure' (*Phil.* 2:13).[1]

That such a combination of the divine and the human can
exist without overthrowing our responsibility is clearly taught
in Scripture but nowhere explained. The mystery indeed lies

[1] For a treatment of this important text, see Appendix 2 below. Finney
represented the old school as believing 'that there is no connection between
the means and the result' (*Revivals of Religion*, p. 6) and claimed that when we
use the means of grace 'the effect is more certain to follow' than is a crop of
grain from the sowing of a farmer. But the Bible denies that grace operates
through us as do laws of nature (e.g. *1 Cor.* 3:5–7). 'It cannot be too deeply
impressed upon our mind, that the most eminent ministers are but
instruments, and the most excellent preaching but means, and that the
Holy Spirit only can do the work. Surely we are nothing.' *John Elias,*
pp. 329–30.

even deeper for the two agencies – God's and man's – are not only conjoined but the consequence of human action is already predetermined by God and yet man remains responsible. The minds and wills of all men are 'in the hand of the Lord' (*Prov.* 21:1; 19:21; *Ezra* 6:22; *Acts* 4:28), yet, while 'ordering and governing' them 'to his own holy ends', as the Westminster Confession affirms, 'the sinfulness thereof proceedeth only from the creature, and not from God; who, being holy and righteous, neither is nor can be the author or approver of sin.'[1] That both sovereignty *and* responsibility coexist without the one destroying the other is unmistakably clear in the words of Christ concerning Judas. The sin of the betrayer was predetermined by God and yet Judas remained wholly responsible for it: 'The Son of Man goes as it has been determined, but woe to that man by whom He is betrayed!' (*Luke* 22:22). On this subject Spurgeon has said:

Such is the magnificent strategy of heaven, such is the marvellous force of the divine mind, that despite everything, the will of God is done. Some have supposed that when we believe with David, in Psalm 115, that God hath done whatsoever he pleased, we deny free agency, and of necessity moral responsibility also. Nay, but we declare that those who would do so are tinctured with the old captious spirit of him who said, 'Why doth he yet find fault, for who hath resisted his will?' and our only answer is that of Paul, 'Nay , but O man, who art thou that repliest against God?'. Can you understand it, for I cannot, how man is a free agent, a responsible agent, so that his sin is his own wilful sin and lies with him and never with God, and yet at the same time God's purposes are fulfilled, and his will is done even by demons and corrupt men? – I cannot comprehend it: without hesitation I believe it, and rejoice so to do, I never hope to comprehend it. I worship a God I never expect to comprehend.[2]

When it comes to the actions of Christians we have to say with John Owen, 'Our duty is to apply ourselves unto his commands and his work is to enable us to perform them.'[3] Both facts, the

[1] *Westminster Confession of Faith*, v:4.
[2] C. H. Spurgeon, *Metropolitan Tabernacle Pulpit* (London, Passmore & Alabaster), vol. 16, p. 501. Bishop Joseph Hall says: 'It is the greatest praise of God's wisdom that He can turn the sins of man to His own glory.'
[3] Owen, *Works*, vol. 3, p. 204.

believer's activity *and* dependency, are made clear in Scripture but it is the latter that we are most prone to forget. While God has appointed means and promises, such is our spiritual incapacity that if it were not for his enabling grace no good would ever be done by us. To make human action the cause of divine blessing is to overturn the whole nature of salvation. It would be the same as interpreting our Lord's words, 'Daughter, your faith has made you well,' as though he was indeed saying the woman was the author of her own new health.

The Place of Prayer

What we have considered above on the place of means applies very directly to the subject of prayer. It is currently popular in some quarters to treat prayer as the great key to revival. Failure in prayer, it is said, explains the absence of revival; an awakening would be certain if only enough Christians could be brought to pray for it. Two lines of thought support this understanding of the place of prayer:

1. God has promised to hear prayer. Prayer is the appointed means for receiving blessings as many Scriptures show. In Isaiah God promised, 'I will pour water upon him who is thirsty, And floods on the dry ground; I will pour My Spirit on your descendants, And My blessing on your offspring' (*Isa.* 44:3); but for such blessing the church has to ask, 'Concerning the work of My hands, you command Me' (*Isa.* 45:11)[1] In Ezekiel God promised the recovery of the dry bones of the house of Israel but he also directed, 'I will also let the house of Israel inquire of Me to do this for them' (*Ezek.* 36:37). Christ himself connects the giving of the Spirit with prayer (*Luke* 11:13), and it is to prayer that he is referring when he says, 'Your Father who sees in secret will reward you openly' (*Matt.* 6:6).

[1] For a defence of the KJV and NKJV translation of these words see Edward J. Young, *The Book of Isaiah*, vol. 3 (Grand Rapids: Eerdmans, 1972), p. 205.

2. History shows that it is when earnest prayer is multiplied that revivals occur.

In looking at the first of these two arguments we must say that it is true, yet it is not the whole truth. More needs to be said about the nature of effective prayer. There is something missing in the view that 'more prayer' is the answer. Years ago A. W. Tozer pointed out that there has in fact been a great deal of prayer for revival in this century: 'If one-tenth of one per cent of the prayers made in any American city on any Sabbath day were answered, the world would see its greatest revival come with the speed of light.'[1] Yet, he says, 'we go on at a pretty dying rate' and asks, 'Can someone tell us the answer?'.

The 'answer' surely has to do with how God comes into effective prayer. The pattern prayer, which Jesus has given us, begins with the reminder that the starting point for prayer has to do with how we think about God: 'In this manner, therefore, pray: *Our Father* in heaven . . .' Prayer is communion with God and in addressing him we are to begin with the name which assures us of his love. We are to think of him, and speak to him, as 'our Father' (*Matt.* 6:9).

Prayer, then, is not in the first place an agency to meet our needs. Nor is it the exercise of a duty in which we remind God of what he may be unwilling to give. So concerned is Christ to disabuse the minds of the disciples of any such thought that he assures them, 'I do not say to you that I shall pray the Father for you; for the Father Himself loves you' (*John* 16:26,27; cf. *Rom.* 8:32). Nor, again, is prayer an exercise which requires the use of many words, or the engagement of many people, before God will begin to listen. The idea dishonours him. 'When you pray, do not use vain repetitions as the heathen do . . . For your Father knows the things you have need of before you ask Him' (*Matt.* 6:7–8).

Prayer has to begin with the recognition of what God is in relation to his people. 'Our Father' comes first and always

[1] Snyder, *In Pursuit of God*, p. 151.

first. Further, the activity of prayer, as with other duties already considered, is altogether too high for us left to ourselves. We cannot pray to order. God's own agency is involved in all effective prayer.[1] It is the ascended Christ who pours out 'the Spirit of grace and supplication' (*Zech.* 12:10). The Holy Spirit is engaged in true praying. He inspires prayer by giving us confidence in God's love so that 'we cry out, "Abba, Father"' (*Rom.* 8:15); he illuminates promises, strengthens faith and gives expectancy. In one sense everything gained in prayer is attributed to us; it is faith which 'obtains promises'; 'the effective, fervent prayer of a righteous man avails much' (*Heb.* 11:33; *James* 5:16). William Cowper did not go too far when he wrote:

> *Prayer makes the darkened cloud withdraw,*
> *Prayer climbs the ladder Jacob saw;*
> *Gives exercise to faith and love,*
> *Brings every blessing from above.*

Yet at the same time it is only of prayer 'in the Holy Spirit' of which all this can be said (*Jude* 20; *Eph.* 6:18). In other words, the spirit of prayer does not originate with ourselves; another hymn writer, Joseph Hart, had reason to write:

> *Prayer was appointed to convey*
> *The blessings God designs to give.*

We are back again to the combination of the human and the divine and to the mystery which is involved. Prayer is a voluntary Christian activity and an activity which determines results. Yet effectual prayer has a divine source and it achieves the purpose which God himself intended.

What are we to say then to the second argument that history shows that multiplied prayer always *precedes* God's working in revival? In our opinion the statement is wrong when stated in

---

[1] 'Praying is another thing than men generally take it to be. It is not the exercise of a gift, but of grace; not a piece of task laid on men, but a privilege they are advanced to; not a work to be done in our own strength, but by help from heaven.' Thomas Boston, *Whole Works*, vol. 11 (Aberdeen: King, 1852), p. 69.

that form. James Robe, minister at Kilsyth, Scotland, at the time of the revival of 1742, says that before 'this uncommon dispensation of the Spirit that we looked not for', his congregation's 'societies for prayer came gradually to nothing' and were given up.[1] The Rev. Henry Davis, President of Hamilton College, New York, and a participant in the Second Great Awakening which began in 1798, noted: 'I have heard no believers saying that they knew from their freedom or enlargement in prayer, that there was about to be a revival.'[2] A minister who was in the midst of the great Ulster awakening of 1859 wrote: 'I knew that there were always a few (very few I feared) praying persons in the several congregations of the neighbourhood, and there were *always* attempts to keep up prayer meetings in my own; but, up to the very week of the bursting forth of the revival, there appeared no general desire nor felt need for such a thing.'[3]

Such testimonies are significant. Nonetheless there are other accounts of the beginnings of revival which show that such times have been attended by unusual prayer. It is possible, for instance, to see the commencement of the Evangelical Revival in England in the prayer meetings in London which marked the first week in January 1739. Certainly it was a momentous week. The last night of 1738 when Whitefield, the Wesleys, with four other preachers and some sixty other Christians, prayed far into the morning of the New Year, was never forgotten by them. Such was the influence that ensued that Robert Philip, biographer of Whitefield, saw it as 'the cradle of the field preaching' which was about to work such a change in the land. Philip wrote: 'These Pentecostal seasons in private made Whitefield feel through all his soul, that he ought to do everything to win souls, and that he *could* do any thing he might attempt . . . prayer meetings were to Whitefield what the "third heavens" were to Paul: the *finishing school* of his ministerial education. He was as much indebted to them for his unction

---

[1] Robe, *Narratives of Extraordinary Work*, pp. 66–9.
[2] Sprague, *Lectures on Revivals of Religion*, 2nd ed., (New York, 1833), p. 379.
[3] Gibson, *Year of Grace*, p. 8.

and enterprise, as to Pembroke College for his learning.'[1] Yet it has to be observed that Whitefield himself never made that week of January 1739 the starting point. Before that date he wrote to a friend on December 20, 1738: 'Blessed be His holy name! There seems to be a great pouring out of the Spirit in London and we walk in the comfort of the Holy Ghost.'[2]

Instead of putting our hopes in the quantity of prayer, as though that will bring revival, our trust needs to be in the God who is himself the prime mover. Sometimes an unusual spirit of prayer *does* precede revival; to use William Gurnall's words, as 'cocks crow thickest towards the break of day'. But it is neither cocks nor prayer which *causes* the dawn. Brainerd recognised the larger picture when he wrote: 'I saw how God had called out his servants to prayer, and made them wrestle with him, when he designed to bestow any great mercy on his church.'[3]

---

[1] R. Philip, *Life and Times of George Whitefield* (London: Virtue, 1838), p. 76.

[2] *George Whitefield's Letters, For the period 1734–1742* (Edinburgh: Banner of Truth, 1976), p. 491.

[3] Edwards, *Works*, vol. 2, p. 347. On this same point B. M. Palmer has written: 'The scriptural principle is, not that favors are by our importunity wrung from the reluctance of the Divine Being, but that they antedate the prayer in the determinations of his sovereign and gracious will; the true spirit of prayer, which he also imparts, is the sign and pledge of the gift to be conveyed . . . he interposes the prayer of the creature as the channel through which the favor shall descend.' *Theology of Prayer* (repr. Harrisonburg, Va.: Sprinkle Publications, 1980), pp. 140–1. That such thinking does not dampen prayer is well seen in Brainerd, of whom Edwards wrote: 'Among all the many days he spent in secret fasting and prayer, that he gives an account of in his diary, there is scarce an instance of one, but what was either attended or soon followed with apparent success, and with a remarkable blessing, in special incomes and consolations of God's Spirit; and very often before the day was ended.' Edwards, *Works*, vol. 2, p. 456. Daniel Edward, comparing the prayer life of Thomas Chalmers with the prayerlessness of his German contemporary, Schleiermacher, noted: 'It is a fact worthy of study that the stiffest predestinarians, as the Puritans and Covenanters, have been men of most prayer, as it is an anomaly of equal magnitude on the field of common life, which Mosheim records with a moral shake of the head as an insoluble riddle, that, contrary to all the prognostics of ethical science, the countries where the belief in predestination prevailed have been those most eminent for a strict regard to morality and good behaviour.' *British and Foreign Evangelical Review*, vol. 31 (London: Nisbet, 1882), p. 297.

This God-centred view of prayer, as the example of the church in Acts 4:25–30 shows, fuels prayer rather than discouraging it. While not diminishing our responsibility, it sets the God-appointed means in a more biblical and encouraging light than does the view which would make all success depend upon us. The mistake of the latter view is that it draws the wrong lesson from the priority which Scripture gives to prayer. God has chosen to make prayer a *means* of blessing, not so that the fulfilment of his purposes becomes dependent upon us, but rather to help us learn *our* absolute dependence upon him. On this subject John Love wrote:

A believer's encouragement to prayer is not from anything that he expects to work in God by his prayer, but in what he apprehends to be already in God before he begins. He hopes in what God has determined in his own grace to do; and in his prayer he looks for the outbreaking of this. Therefore, in prayer he keeps close by God's promises. A natural man, on the contrary, can pray without a promise; for he thinks to work upon God – to bring him to do what he had no mind to do before.[1]

Such an understanding of prayer, far from leading to resignation or fatalism, engenders a spirit of God-conscious-ness and what a contemporary author calls 'radical prayer'. John Piper writes: 'It is the time for radical prayer and fasting to the end that all our thinking and all our preaching and all our writing and all our social action and missions will have the aroma of God on it and will carry a transforming thrust far beyond anything mere man could do.'[2]

This brings us more directly to the subject of divine sovereignty and the connection with revival.

---

[1] *Memorials of the Rev. John Love*, vol. 2 (Glasgow: Ogle & Son, 1858), pp. 502–3.
[2] J. Piper, *A Hunger for God: Desiring God Through Fasting and Prayer* (Wheaton: Crossway, 1997), p. 165.

Sovereignty and Revival

God is sovereign in the instruments which he takes up to use.

It has often been the case that when God means to draw attention to his truth and power he does so in a way to contradict religious traditions which are bereft of spiritual usefulness. Thus he may call improbable preachers from unlikely places. God moulds his own men for the hour and, like Amos and John the Baptist, they may come from outside the centres of supposed religious leadership and authority. Most of the preachers of the Great Awakening in the Middle States in the 1740s were trained in a school named with disdain by others as the 'Log College'. In England at the same period it was not in the university cities that the gospel began to prevail but often in obscure corners of the land. John Wesley, the only don among the men of the Evangelical Revival, had the pulpits of Oxford shut against him after he preached on the words of Acts 4:31, 'They were all filled with the Holy Spirit', and challenged his peers with the question whether this was true of them. Able men the Methodist preachers often were but by the world's standards they were nobodies. Once again it was shown that 'God has chosen the foolish things of the world to put to shame the wise, and God has chosen the weak things of the world to put to shame the things which are mighty . . . that no flesh should glory in His presence' (*1 Cor.* 1:27–29).

The preachers used in all revivals have always been only *men*, 'earthen vessels', and, forgetting this and esteeming them too highly, their evangelical contemporaries and successors have sometimes accorded to their teaching a degree of authority due to no man.[1] No one has full understanding of Scripture and we should not be surprised that evangelical

---

[1] This is one reason why the emphasis of eminent leaders has been maintained by lesser men who succeeded even when changed church conditions required a different emphasis.

preachers have been used of God in revival whose teaching was in some respects faulty and erroneous. God does not always use individuals in proportion to the correctness of their theological acumen and he imparts different gifts for different situations. Great courage was given to some of the early church fathers who, as John Duncan once said, 'were poor theologians but excellent for burning!' Similarly there have been men used to bring thousands to Christ who could never have written a book of Christian doctrine. Equally, a preacher may live through a revival and yet not have a clear biblical understanding of what he saw. To question some of the views of such men is not to belittle their work. There is more than one way to serve Christ and he has many different places and roles for his servants.

God is sovereign in his purposes in revival.
It is a mistake to suppose that revivals have one sole purpose. Commonly revivals are for a great enlargement of the church and they usher in a new age of evangelism. New agencies also spring into life – missionary societies, Bible and tract societies, and organisations to remedy social sufferings and evils – for which fresh workers are now at hand. No less important are the many young women raised up to prepare the next generation by building godly homes.

But this scenario is not always the case. Sometimes revivals are clearly intended to bring home the elect before their lives are cut short in epidemics or natural disasters. The services of a communion season at Dornoch in the north of Scotland about the year 1831 were long remembered for that reason. A 'heavenly power' had been known in the area for a year or two beforehand and at the fourth table at which the Lord's Supper was served there were sixty young converts from Tarbat, Ross-shire. 'When the service was over the linen cloth was wet with their tears, as though it had been taken out of the sea. Soon afterwards a deadly plague of cholera broke out at Portmahomack and made almost a clean sweep of this crop of young converts. Angus Murray of Dornoch said of them that the

Lord took them away with Him to heaven "soft and warm as they were".[1]

Similarly there have been revivals before mining disasters and, more often, before terrible wars. The major revival in the United States in 1857–8 was soon followed by the conflict which took the lives of some 600,000 men on battlefields across the land. The same thing was seen in Ireland in 1625, in Korea in 1907, in China in the 1930s, in the Congo in the early 1960s, and in Cambodia in the years 1975–9 where it is said that perhaps ninety per cent of the young church of that land 'perished in the Khmer Rouge reign of terror'.[2] Sometimes a definite building up of the church's work was also involved at these dates but it was not always so.

Yet another purpose of revivals appears to be to give special encouragement to the godly before the onset of persecution or other trials. The Scottish church historian, W. M. Hetherington, believed that times of refreshing for the church in Scotland 'were invariably before a time of searching trial, as if to give her a principle of sacred life sufficiently strong to survive the period of suffering'. In that connection he refers to the revivals of 1596 and of the 1620s and, passing to the events of the 1740s, he continued:

Though no direct persecution followed the revivals of Cambuslang and Kilsyth, yet the long dreary domination of Moderatism which immediately followed was more calculated to destroy vital religion in the land than could have been the most relentless persecution; and it seems no very strained conjecture, that these gracious influences were vouchsafed to the Church at that period, to sustain her during her lengthened sojourn in a moral and religious wilderness. Certain it is that the deep and earnest spirit and feeling of vital and personal religion passed not away like a temporary excitement. Not only did many hundreds of the converts of that period continue to exhibit the beauty of holiness throughout the remainder of their lives, proving

[1] Quoted by Murdoch Campbell in *Gleanings of Highland Harvest* (Ross-shire Printing and Publishing, 1964), p. 104. It is a great loss that more detail was not recorded of revivals in the Scottish Highlands.
[2] D. Cormack, *Killing Fields, Living Fields* (Crowborough: Monarch/OMF, 1997), p. 182.

the reality of the great change which they had experienced, but also the very knowledge that such events had taken place continued to operate, silent and unseen, but with mighty efficacy, in the hearts of thousands, constraining them to believe that there was more in true spiritual Christianity than could be expressed in a cold moral harangue.[1]

God is sovereign with regard to the time when revivals begin.

Here again there is no uniformity. Sometimes when unbelief and error enter the churches there is a descent into apostasy for which there is no remedy. Candlesticks are removed and a moral and spiritual wilderness is all that is left. As the Westminster Confession says, some of the purest churches under heaven 'have so degenerated as to become no churches of Christ, but synagogues of Satan.'[2] At other times the descent has been no less real: unbelief, worldliness and error have reached such proportions that Christians have been fearful of worse to come, yet instead there has suddenly been light and blessing and a new day has dawned. For this there can be no explanation other than the sovereignty of divine grace.

The time when revivals begin seems intended by God to show that all the blessings of salvation never come because of human merit or deserving. They come because God delights to magnify his grace in Christ. The sufferings of Calvary are effective to overcome all unworthiness and sin. There are no barriers and no backslidings which sovereign love cannot overcome. The principle set down in Deuteronomy 32:36 is abiding: 'The Lord will judge [i.e., deliver] His people, And have compassion on His servants, When He sees that their power is gone, and there is no one remaining, bond or free.' When in terms of human prospects all is darkness, when nothing is deserved, God often arises in mercy as he did in the city which crucified his own Son.

'God's visiting of us,' Edwards wrote in the 1740s, is 'an

[1] W. M. Hetherington, *History of the Church of Scotland*, vol. 2 (Edinburgh: Johnstone and Hunter, 1852), p. 311.
[2] *Westminster Confession*, xxx:5.

instance of the glorious triumph of free and sovereign grace.'[1] Of the remarkable work of grace which Brainerd saw among North American Indians at the same period, he recorded: 'God began this work among the Indians at a time when I had the least hope, and, to my apprehension, the least rational prospect of success.'[2] It seems to be God's way not to allow the advent of true revival to be known beforehand as though to make impossible the suggestion that it was the result of human preparation. I have already quoted James Robe of Kilsyth who reported that the awakening came at a time when all seemed to grow worse among his people: 'We were going on frowardly in the way of our own heart, when the Lord came to see our ways and to heal them by this uncommon dispensation of his grace; all this has been narrated, that every one may observe the sovereign freedom and riches of grace, in visiting, after this sort, so sinful, degenerate, and ungainable a people.'[3]

Conclusions

1. The sovereignty of God, far from being seen as a discouragement to our efforts, ought to be seen as an eminent reason for hope and expectancy. 'I cannot get along with the doctrine of predestination,' a man once complained to Asahel Nettleton. To which the preacher responded tersely, 'Then get along without it'. Ignoring divine sovereignty may *appear* to give more room for enthusing over human organisation and activity but the truth is that the church has always accomplished most when she has most deeply realised her own helplessness. Dependence upon God is our greatest need; it focuses our attention upon what *he* can do; and it makes his glory a supreme reason for all our concerns: 'Do not disgrace the throne of Your glory' (*Jer.* 14:21); 'Hallowed be Your name' (*Matt.* 6:9).

[1] Quoted by John Piper, *A Hunger For God*, p. 117.
[2] Brainerd's Journal under November, 1745. Edwards' *Works*, vol. 2, p. 399.
[3] Robe, *Narratives of the Extraordinary Work*, pp. 66–8.

Martyn Lloyd-Jones, the foremost advocate of old-school views of revival in the present century, has forcefully argued that with the modern man-centred emphasis on evangelism the churches have forgotten what happened under a different emphasis. 'It is only since the decline of Calvinism,' he believed, 'that revivals have become less and less frequent. The more powerful Calvinism is the more likely you are to have a spiritual revival and re-awakening. It follows of necessity from the doctrine.'[1]

2. Obedience to God is not set down in Scripture as the 'key' to revival. Rather it is normative for all Christian living. The apostles, in affirming that the Holy Spirit is 'given to those who obey Him' (*Acts* 5:32) were not stating a secret of revival. They were affirming something basic to the gospel itself and the fundamental obedience which God demands is 'obedience to the faith' (*Rom.* 16:27; *John* 6:29; *1 John* 3:23 etc.). All for whom such obedience is a reality – as distinct from the Jewish rulers to whom the apostles' words were first spoken – possess the Holy Spirit (*John* 7:38; *Gal.* 3:2). The New Testament knows nothing of a 'higher life', beyond believing in Christ, which is somehow to be obtained.

Confusion of thought may occur at this point because revival – in the classical sense of the term – is sometimes confused with recovery and restoration from backsliding and spiritual declension. To professed Christians or churches in that condition there are plain commands: they are to 'repent and do the first works' (*Rev.* 2:5); 'Therefore be zealous and repent' (*Rev.* 3:19). But the motive presented to such persons is not that without obedience they will not see revival. It is that without it they will be found not to be God's people at all and they will be

[1] D. M. Lloyd-Jones, *The Puritans: Their Origins and Successors* (Edinburgh: Banner of Truth, 1987), p. 211. At the same time he is careful to point out that he does not mean a harsh and cold 'dead Calvinism'. The latter expression, he believed, is a contradiction in terms because 'if your Calvinism appears to be dead it is not Calvinism, it is a philosophy. It is philosophy using Calvinistic terms, it is an intellectualism, and it is not real Calvinism.'

cast out by Christ (*John* 15:6; *Rev.* 2 and 3). This is parallel to the warning of 2 Chronicles 15:2 quoted earlier in this chapter.[1]

In the case of the truly regenerate, the Holy Spirit uses such warnings to prompt their recovery from backsliding. If such recovery involves many people and is powerful, general and sudden, it may indeed be called a revival. A sudden spring may follow a long, cold winter. But there is no *promise* that recovery will always mean such a sudden transition from deadness to conditions of general, outpoured blessing. 'We cannot agree,' wrote James Buchanan, 'that the Church has any sure warrant to expect that the Spirit will be bestowed in every instance, in that particular way.'[2] There may be genuine and gradual return from declension to spiritual health where there is no revival.

3. The claim that the teaching of divine sovereignty interferes with prayer assumes that there is a certain kind of 'praying in faith' for revival which God must answer and which we must not discourage by any other considerations. In support of this various texts concerning effective prayer are quoted. Old-school teaching, on the other hand, while believing that God does give larger influences of the Holy Spirit in answer to prayer, knew no *promise* of an extraordinary giving for any time or circumstances of our own determination. 'Now this is the confidence that we have in Him, that if we ask anything *according to His will*, He hears us' (*1 John* 5:14), and it is not for us to dictate to God what is his will. Critics of this view do not themselves bring forward texts of Scripture which promise the extraordinary, rather they base their confidence either upon contemporary predictions which someone has made or simply upon an impression of their own which they confidently

---

[1] 'Abiding [i.e., continuing] in Christ' is sometimes taught as though the promise of John 15:10, 'If you keep My commandments, you will abide in My love,' belonged to some special inner circle. But 1 John makes clear that the alternative to obedience is not to be a Christian at all (*1 John* 2:3–4; 3:24).

[2] J. Buchanan, *The Office and Work of the Holy Spirit* (1843, repr. London: Banner of Truth, 1966), p. 230.

attribute to the Holy Spirit.[1] Church history is strewn with examples of misplaced hopes of this kind.

But on what basis then did old-school believers encourage earnest prayer for the church and the salvation of the world? They did so in terms of a breadth of petitions for the coming of the kingdom of God, petitions which look ultimately to the coming of Christ himself in glory. Take, for instance, these words of Spurgeon:

> Let the whole militant Church of Christ be blessed; put power into all faithful ministries; convert this country; save it from abounding sin; let all the nations of the earth know the Lord . . . Bring the Church to break down all bonds of nationality, all limits of sects, and may we feel the blessed unity which is the very glory of the Church of Christ; yea, let the whole earth be filled with His glory. Our prayer can never cease until we reach this point: 'Thy Kingdom come, Thy will be done, on earth as it is in heaven.' Nothing less than this can we ask for.[2]

Those who prayed in this way 'for the advancement and enlargement of the kingdom of Christ in the world' (to use Edwards' words) might well include specific prayer for revival but their vision was wider and not simply conditioned by the present. They knew that the measure and time in which prayer is answered lies with God; the petitions of one generation may be fulfilled in another. Brainerd died in 1747 and it was not until the 1790s that the great missionary expansion for which he pleaded began. Spurgeon died in 1892 without seeing any answer to his prayers that God would restore a love of sound doctrine. But Spurgeon's own writings, republished widely after the 1950s, were to be part of the answer.[3] 'For in this the saying is true: "One sows and another reaps"' (*John* 4:37).

[1] I will return below to the question of 'impressions'. See pp. 141, 166–7.

[2] *C. H. Spurgeon's Prayers* (London: Passmore & Alabaster, 1905), pp. 115–6.

[3] See Thomas Goodwin, *The Return of Prayers*, in his *Works*, vol. 3. For Brainerd and 'The International Union and Missionary Vision' see my *Jonathan Edwards, a New Biography*, pp. 291–310. Speaking in 1889 of the prevalent defection from historic Christianity, and the opposition he encountered, Spurgeon said: 'Posterity must be considered . . . For my part, I am quite prepared to be eaten of dogs for the next fifty years; but the more distant future will vindicate me.' *An All-Round Ministry* (repr. Edinburgh: Banner of Truth, 1972), p. 360.

4. If there is anything which more than anything else prepares the way for revival it is the recovery of knowledge and faith in God. All spiritual weakness is ultimately due to poverty of thought about God, and such weakness will persist as long as we suppose that man is the starting point for its resolution. The church's first need is always for objective knowledge and that is why, in God's mercy, a rediscovery of biblical doctrine is the precursor of greater blessing. Too often in the twentieth century there has been faith in 'revival' where there has been little faith in God himself. Thus we have had successive temporary excitements, with very thin biblical content, which have soon come to nothing and even led to the questioning of the whole idea of revival.

Pre-occupation with 'revival' is not the first need. It can even be a symptom that we are not attending to something greater, that is, to know and enjoy God. Scripture never tells the believer that the success of his work for Christ is *the* priority. There is always something wrong when that becomes the consuming interest as Christ warned his disciples when he said: 'Do not rejoice in this, that the spirits are subject to you, but rather rejoice because your names are written in heaven' (*Luke* 10:20). Our first joy is to be in God himself and in his relation to us. And that is a joy for all seasons and all circumstances.

A man such as W. C. Burns understood this when in China he was content to labour quietly far away from the scenes of success and popularity which he had known in his homeland of Scotland. For the most part he sowed what others would reap. That he did not do this in sadness, his biographer noted, is an example 'to every labourer in the Lord's vineyard, teaching us not to live upon the stimulus of a present success, even in the conversion of souls.'[1] The same lesson is well stated by John Colquhoun, a fellow Scot:

The Christian must study, in the faith of God's redeeming love to him, so to love God in Christ, as to be at all times *pleased* with him. In

[1] Islay Burns, *Memoir of Burns*, p. 553.

proportion as he loves his God and Father, he will be pleased with him, with all his perfections, and with *all his will*; and if he be always pleased or delighted with God, he will in the same proportion, be always comfortable, always delighted in his own soul. To be constantly pleased with God in Christ, and with all the will of God is, indeed, a difficult and high attainment; but the believer cannot otherwise become so rooted and grounded in love to him as to attain settled consolation.[1]

[1] John Colquhoun, *A Treatise on Spiritual Comfort*, 2nd ed. (Edinburgh, 1814), p. 404. For a contemporary writer on this theme, see John Piper, *Desiring God* (Sisters, Oregon: Multnomah Books, 1996).

4
The Holy Spirit and Preaching

'Men ablaze are invincible.
The stronghold of Satan is proof against everything but fire.'[1]
Samuel Chadwick

The New Testament shows that the times which saw great ingatherings of people into the kingdom of God were always times when the Word of God was being preached in the power of the Holy Spirit. This was the pattern in Jerusalem, Samaria, Antioch, Iconium, Thessalonica and Corinth[2]. It has been equally true in subsequent history. Before the Reformation, if men preached at all, it was, in Martin Bucer's words, 'frigidly, slovenly, mumbling', and such men knew no revivals. Then when spiritual awakening came it coincided, as in apostolic times, with a change which was seen first in preachers.

The explanation for this connection between preaching and the advance of the gospel is made plain in Scripture. We read that when Christ spoke the people 'were astonished at His teaching, for He taught them as one having authority, and not as the scribes' (*Matt.* 7:28–29). And this was true of his ministry because, as he tells us, 'The Spirit of the Lord is upon

[1] Quoted by Sherwood E. Wirt and K. Beckstom, *Living Quotations for Christians* (New York: Harper Row, 1974), p. 66.
[2] *Acts* 2:40,41; 8:5–8; 11:19–21; 14:1; 17:2–4; 18:4–8.

Me, because He has anointed me to preach' (*Luke* 4:18). The very same thing is what we find in those messengers sent by Jesus to do his work. Peter, 'filled with the Holy Spirit', so spoke to the Jewish leaders that the similarity between him and Christ was recognised: 'when they saw the boldness of Peter and John, and perceived that they were uneducated and untrained men, they marvelled. And they realized that they had been with Jesus' (*Acts* 4:8,13). After the prayer meeting of disciples, recorded in that same chapter, it is said: 'And when they had prayed . . . they were all filled with the Holy Spirit, and they spoke the word of God with boldness.' At Antioch 'a great many people were added to the Lord', and the instrumental cause of that increase was Barnabas, of whom we read that he was 'full of the Holy Spirit' (*Acts* 11:24). It is of Barnabas, again, together with Paul in Iconium, that we read 'they went together to the synagogue of the Jews, and so spoke, that a great multitude both of the Jews and of the Greeks believed' (*Acts* 14:1). The reason for this effectiveness was surely identical to that which explained the later success at Thessalonica and Corinth: 'Our gospel did not come to you in word only, but also in power and in the Holy Spirit' (*1 Thess.* 1:5; *1 Cor.* 2:4).

It was by the same Holy Spirit at the time of the Reformation that preaching was again made powerful. In the Protestant churches of the sixteenth century the sermon was not made central in the worship of God by any human decision; it was the voice of Christ himself, speaking through men by his Spirit, which determined the change. Preaching in itself was not the cause of Reformation success. For, as Calvin said, preaching is 'dead and powerless, if the Lord does not make it efficacious by his Spirit.'[1] It is the work of the Spirit to make hearers conscious of a presence distinct from that of the speaker. 'We cannot receive a single word which is published or preached to us in his name unless his

---

[1] John Calvin, *Commentary on the Epistles of Paul to the Corinthians*, vol. 1 (Edinburgh: Calvin Translation Society, 1848), p. 128.

majesty is there present.'¹ This was the understanding which controlled the Puritan view of gospel proclamation and it was well summarised by William Perkins when he wrote:

The *demonstration* of the Spirit is, when as the minister of the word doth in time of preaching so behave himself that all, even ignorant persons and unbelievers, may judge that it is not so much he that speaketh, as the Spirit of God in him and by him . . . This makes the ministry lively and powerful.²

Eighty years later, near the close of the Puritan era, John Owen was emphasising the same truth:

Preaching in the demonstration of the Spirit, which men so much quarrel about, is nothing less than the evidence in preaching of unction . . . *No man preaches that sermon well to others that doth not first preach it to his own heart*; for, unless he finds the power of it in his own heart, he cannot have any confidence that it will have power in the hearts of others. *It is an easier thing to bring our heads to preach than our hearts to preach.* To bring our hearts to preach is to be transformed into the power of these truths; or to find the power of them, both before, in fashioning our minds and hearts, and in delivering them, that we may have benefit; and to be acted with zeal for God and compassion to the souls of men. A man may preach every day in the week and not have his heart engaged once.³

It follows from this that if times of revival are indeed times when there is a fuller giving of the Holy Spirit then it must be expected that this will be seen pre-eminently in and through the work of gospel preaching. The Holy Spirit is in the world to glorify Christ in the salvation of men and women. This salvation comes by means of the Word of God. 'Faith comes by hearing', and hearing means proclamation: 'How shall they hear without a preacher? And how shall they preach unless they are sent?' (*Rom.* 10:14,15).

¹ Sermon 21 of Calvin's *Sermons on Deuteronomy*, quoted by Pierre Ch. Marcel, *The Relevance of Preaching* (Grand Rapids: Baker, 1963), p. 46.
² *The Art of Prophesying, The Works of William Perkins*, vol. 2 (London, 1617), p. 670.
³ Owen, *Works*, vol. 9, p. 455.

Special Eras of Preaching

As we proceed to look at this, I will first give some evidence that revival times are to be recognised – as they were recognised in the book of Acts – as times when the Spirit of God filled preachers in a marked way. John Knox's testimony on this subject I have already given. Less well remembered is the ministry of his successor, Robert Bruce, which was said by a contemporary to be 'as a great light through the whole land' of Scotland. The explanation for Bruce's influence was 'the extraordinary effusion of the Spirit . . . the power and efficacy of the Spirit most sensibly accompanying the word he preached.'[1] 'Sensibly', here, means evidence plain to the senses of spiritual men and women. John Livingston, one of Bruce's colleagues in the ministry, said of him: 'No man in his time spake with such evidence and power of the Spirit. No man had so many seals of conversion.'[2] Livingston himself was the preacher so remarkably used in the revival at Shotts, near Glasgow, on 21 June 1630. It was, he wrote, 'the one day in all my life wherein I got most of the presence of God in public', and he gives us this observation: 'There is sometime somewhat in preaching that cannot be ascribed either to the matter or expression, and cannot be described what it is, or from whence it comes, but with a sweet violence it pierces into the heart and affections, and comes immediately from the Lord.'[3]

As Livingston indicates, such events as the revival at Shotts were not everyday occurrences in the seventeenth century but the conjunction between the Holy Spirit and powerful preaching was commonplace in Puritan belief. In the latter half of the seventeenth century revivals were no longer seen in Britain and John Owen, writing in 1676, believed that they

---

[1] *Sermons by Robert Bruce, with Collections for his Life by Robert Wodrow*, ed. William Cunningham (Edinburgh: Wodrow Society, 1843), pp. 143,145.

[2] Ibid., p. 142.

[3] *Select Biographies*, ed. W. K. Tweedie, vol. 1 (Edinburgh: Wodrow Society, 1845), pp. 138, 287.

would not be seen again until something first happened to preachers:

When God shall be pleased to give unto the people who are called by his name, in a more abundant manner, 'pastors after his own heart, to feed them with knowledge and understanding'; when he shall revive and increase a holy, humble, zealous, self-denying, powerful ministry, by a more plentiful effusion of his Spirit from above; then, and not until then, may we hope to see the pristine glory and beauty of our religion restored unto its primitive state and condition.[1]

Owen was right but he died in 1683 and more than fifty years were to pass before his words were seen to be true. As we have already noted in the last chapter, on the eve of the new year, 1739, a group of preachers and others met in London for prayer. Of that meeting John Wesley said, 'As we were continuing instant in prayer, the power of God came mightily upon us, insomuch that many cried out for exceeding joy, and many fell to the ground.'[2] Speaking of these same days, Whitefield wrote: 'It was a Pentecost season indeed. Some times whole nights were spent in prayer. Often have we been filled as with new wine. And often have I seen them overwhelmed with the Divine Presence, and crying out, "Will God, indeed, dwell with men upon earth?"'[3]

It was as these eighteenth-century preachers were filled with the Holy Spirit that the same kind of power accompanied their witness as we see recorded in the book of Acts. Those who heard them were constrained to believe that God was there. Minds and consciences were arrested by an authority and boldness for which they could not otherwise account. One hearer of Whitefield reported: 'His words seemed to cut like a sword . . . O with what eloquence, energy and melting tenderness, did Mr Whitefield beseech sinners to be reconciled

---

[1] Owen, *Works*, vol. 7, p. 195. Elsewhere he writes: 'It is not an outward visible ordination by men, – though that be necessary by rule and precept, – but Christ's communication of the Spirit that gives being, life, usefulness, and success, to the ministry.' vol. 3, p. 191.

[2] *Journal of John Wesley*, ed. N. Curnock, vol. 2 (London: Kelly), p. 122.

[3] John Gillies, *Memoirs of the Life of George Whitefield* (London, 1772), p. 34.

to God! When the sermon ended, the people seemed chained to the ground.'[1]

John Newton tells us that when he first heard Whitefield he had already seen in different places 'the great work of revival which God has owned under his hand', but 'one half', he says, 'had not been told me. Never before had I such an idea and foretaste of heaven.' After giving an account of how Whitefield handled the theme of one of his sermons, Newton goes on: 'Something like this was his plan. But the power, the experience, the warmth with which he treated it I can by no means express, though I hope I feel the influence of it. Still, my heart was greatly impressed, and I had little relish either for company or food all day.'[2]

Similar words were used to describe the preaching of all the leaders of the eighteenth-century revival. This is what was said by one of the hearers of Henry Venn of Huddersfield: 'He was such a preacher as I never heard before or since . . . Nobody could help being affected : the most wicked and ill-conditioned men went to hear him, and fell like slaked lime in a moment, even though they were not converted. I could have heard him preach all the night through.'[3]

Daniel Rowland was a contemporary leader among the Welsh Methodists. One man who went to hear him wrote: 'There was a sort of vehement flame transforming and driving away the earthly, dead and careless spirit: and the people drew nigh, as it were, in the cloud, to Christ, and to Moses and Elias, and eternity and its realities rushed into their minds.'[4] Thomas Charles, on his first hearing of Rowland, testified, 'I had such a view of Christ as our high Priest, of his love, compassion, power, and all-sufficiency, as filled my soul with

[1] Henry Venn, quoted by Luke Tyerman, *Life of George Whitefield* (London: Hodder and Stoughton, 1876), vol. 2, pp. 400–1.
[2] Josiah Bull, *John Newton* (London: Religious Tract Society, 1868), pp. 72–3.
[3] Quoted by J. C. Ryle, *Christian Leaders of the Eighteenth Century* (Edinburgh: Banner of Truth, 1978), p. 275.
[4] Christmas Evans, quoted by John Owen, *A Memoir of Daniel Rowland* (London, 1848), p. 153.

astonishment – with joy unspeakable and full of glory. My mind was overwhelmed and overpowered with amazement. The truths exhibited to my view appeared too wonderfully gracious to be believed.' [1]

Before we turn to consider what constitutes powerful preaching, there are one or two negatives which need to be set aside. God sometimes takes up men of outstanding natural gifts; but natural gifts alone cannot be the explanation of the type of preaching which has marked revivals. For one thing, exceptional natural gifts have often been present in the church when there has been no revival. Further, as we noted in the first chapter, the same preachers who have been greatly used in a time of awakening have at other times worked quietly for years with very much less result. The difference has to be more than a question of natural gifts.

Again it has to be said that the power these men saw in revival cannot be identified with the extraordinary gifts which marked the apostolic era. No evangelical preachers in revivals in the three centuries following the Reformation believed that they possessed the *charismata* of the New Testament; on the contrary they constantly disavowed any such claims.[2] Church of England opponents of Wesley and Whitefield claimed that preaching in 'the demonstration of the Spirit' was unique to the long-past age of miraculous gifts. The eighteenth-century awakening proved them wrong. Yet there were false claimants to apostolic power in that century as there are today and we have therefore to consider how the ministry of the Holy Spirit is to be recognised.

It would appear that powerful preaching is made up of two main elements:

---

[1] *The Life of Thomas Charles*, D. E. Jenkins, vol. 1 (Denbigh: Llewelyn Jenkins, 1910), p. 35.
[2] See below, pp. 197–9.

The Power of the Holy Spirit Makes the Truth Plain to Preacher and Hearer

The Holy Spirit is a person. He speaks to persons and he acts, not as some kind of blind force, but as the Spirit of truth and by the Word of God, 'the sword of the Spirit' (*Eph.* 6:17). His is the work which vitalises the truth, making it real to the consciousness of the individual. In this office the Spirit is the teacher of every Christian. Not to be taught by the Spirit, not to have such faith as originates in his light and power, is not to be a Christian at all (*John* 6:45; *1 Cor.* 2: 5; *1 John* 2:20; 4:13; etc.). For this reason a merely nominal Christianity always shows itself by the absence of any thrill in the Word of God – an absence which has too often been a feature of church worship in the twentieth century. In the words of A. W. Tozer:

To the absence of the Spirit may be traced that vague sense of unreality which almost everywhere invests religion in our times. In the average church service the most real thing is the shadowy unreality of everything. The worshipper sits in a state of suspended mentation; a kind of dreamy numbness creeps upon him; he hears words but they do not register, he cannot relate them to anything on his own life-level . . . He is aware of no power, no Presence, no spiritual reality. There is simply nothing in his experience corresponding to the things which he heard from the pulpit or sang in the hymns.[1]

We cannot know how far those who have been taught by the Holy Spirit can share in such conditions. But one thing is sure: the change which revival brings begins with a change of thought about the Word of God. For if it is true that a revival is a fuller giving of the Spirit it must follow that among the first effects of his work will be clearer apprehensions of truth, a more certain knowledge of Christ. At such a time it is not that Christians come to believe new things but the content of their beliefs is now a more vivid reality. The truths of the gospel become invested with such magnitude and importance that

[1] A. W. Tozer, *The Divine Conquest* (London: Marshall, Morgan & Scott, 1964), pp. 90–1.

Christians have expressed themselves as being as surprised as if Christ had risen again before their eyes. Words such as 'amazement' and 'astonishment' have to be used to describe what is felt. A degree of joy, perhaps unseen in the churches for long years, is present again, and there is a hunger for reading and hearing the Word of God exceeding every natural desire.[1]

Such a change, as Owen believed, is generally first experienced by preachers themselves. The Holy Spirit witnesses of Christ to them. They rise to a new level of personal knowledge; their assurance of their own salvation takes on the element of certainty and they speak of the gospel no longer as apologists, or even advocates, but as witnesses to its power. Preaching instead of being simply a duty and a routine again approaches to something like the apostolic ministry of the word. Paul knew a *consciousness* of the enabling of God in preaching – 'Him we preach . . . striving according to His working which works in me mightily' (*Col.* 1:28–29) – and so do men under a larger anointing of the Spirit. It is true that all those sent by Christ to teach are to believe that he is present according to his promise (*Matt.* 28:20), but preaching assumes a different character when that presence is a felt reality in the one who speaks.

It is questionable if there is any powerful preaching without this element. As William Arthur wrote:

The difference, within the soul of man, between merely cherishing an expectation or a belief, and seeing, feeling, thrilling under the

---

[1] Thomas Goodwin wrote on 'the Spirit of wisdom and revelation' (*Eph.* 1:17): 'The Holy Ghost cometh down into a man's heart sometimes in prayer with a beam from heaven; he sees more at once of God, of the glory of God, astounding thoughts of God, enlarged apprehensions of God, many beams meeting in one and falling into the centre of his heart' (*Works*, vol. 1, p. 291). Sibbes, on the same subject, asked, 'What is the reason that illiterate men stand out in their profession [of Christ] to blood, whereas those that have a discursive kind of learning they yield? The reason is this, the knowledge of one is sealed by the Spirit, it is set fast upon the soul, the Spirit brings the knowledge and the soul close together; whereas the knowledge of the other is only a notional swimming knowledge; it is not spiritual' (*Works*, vol. 3 (repr. Edinburgh: Banner of Truth, 1981), p. 463.

impression of a present Friend and Deliverer, makes in his utterance the difference between a tame declaration which disturbs neither prejudice nor indifference, and an overpowering force of speech that bears men's hearts away.[1]

Spurgeon could say: 'I have discerned the special presence of the Lord with me by a consciousness as sure as that by which I know that I live. Jesus has been as real to me, at my side in this pulpit, as though I had beheld Him with my eyes.'[2] Whenever such words can be spoken in truth we should not be surprised at the effects which accompany the preaching.

In revivals the Spirit thus makes clear to many the reality of the power and glory of Jesus Christ. For the first time for some, and in a heightened degree for others, God is a real person and is dealing with them. Testimonies to this effect come from every true revival. Thomas Charles, for instance, writing of what happened in Bala, North Wales, in 1791, reported:

The coming of the Lord amongst us has been with such majesty, glory, and irresistible power, that even his avowed enemies would be glad to hide themselves somewhere. It is an easy and delightful thing to preach the glorious Gospel here in these days . . . Divine truths have their own infinite weight and importance in the minds of the people. Beams of divine light, together with irresistible energy, accompany every truth delivered. It is delightful, indeed, to see how the stoutest heart bended, and the hardest, melted down with fire from God's altar; for the word comes in power and in the Holy Ghost, and is made mighty, through God, to the pulling down of strongholds.[3]

[1] William Arthur, *The Tongue of Fire; or, The True Power of Christianity*, 24th ed. (Belfast: Mullan, 1877), p. 216.
[2] Iain H. Murray, *The Forgotten Spurgeon* (Edinburgh: Banner of Truth, 1973), pp. 41–2. The same thing is surely true in all Spirit-anointed preaching. It is said of William Burns, for instance, 'God was visible to him as he preached; and so he soon became visible also to at least some of his hearers'. *Memoir of Burns*, p. 548. Tozer also argues that the power of the Spirit is seen in his ability to make spiritual things clear to the soul, and he goes on to say, 'In actual experience this is likely to be first felt in a heightened sense of the presence of Christ.'
[3] Jenkins, *Life of Charles*, vol. 2, pp. 90–1.

From the revival of 1859–60 in Scotland comes this account of an open-air service in the industrial town of Dundee:

Just as the sun was beginning to shine out again, and the rain was ceasing, an extraordinary sense of the Divine Presence fell upon the whole assembly. Suddenly the Christians were filled with great joy. Simultaneously many of the anxious found the Lord, and began to break forth in songs of praise . . . The cloud of glory rested there for a season; and no visible signs or miraculous gifts could have added to the blessed consciousness and veritable certainty of the immediate presence and gracious working of God. Till memory fails or the more 'excellent glory' of the unveiled face of Immanuel obliterates the remembrance of faith's brightest visions on earth, it is impossible for us to forget the awful nearness of God at that time, the overpowering sense of blended majesty, love, and holiness, the solemn gladness, and the soft, pure radiance of a Redeemer's face that chased the doubt and sin away from many a soul.[1]

This is surely the first mark both of powerful preaching and of true revival: it is the work of the Holy Spirit vitalising the truth, making God and his Word real to the human heart.

The Power of the Holy Spirit is Evident in the Experience which He gives of the Love of God

Of the things which the Holy Spirit is said to teach, and to give, nothing is more fundamental than an awareness of the love of God. The Holy Spirit is love, and the first of the fruits of the Spirit is love. He is the author of the love described in 1 Corinthians 13; he sheds abroad God's love in our hearts; he provides the strengthening of faith that Christians may know the indwelling of Christ and so, 'being rooted and grounded in love, may be able to comprehend with all the saints what is the width and length and depth and height – to know the love of Christ which passes knowledge . . .' (*Rom.* 5:5; *Eph.* 3:17–19).

Puritan authors all treat love as inseparable from the

[1] John MacPherson, *Life and Labours of Duncan Matheson* (Kilmarnock: Ritchie, n.d.), pp. 127–8.

teaching of the Spirit. 'Where the Spirit dwells,' says Sibbes, 'he begets knowledge, and affection, and love'.[1] 'This Holy Spirit doth, in and by his teaching, breathe into our hearts a holy, divine love unto and complacency in the things we are taught . . . rendering them sweeter unto us than honey.'[2]

Again, therefore, we may argue that if revivals are fuller givings of the Holy Spirit, then love is going to be one of the most prominent features in any preacher who is 'filled with the Spirit'. The evidence of Christian history wholly bears this out. What else can explain Stephen's face shining 'as the face of an angel' and his dying prayer for his murderers (*Acts* 6:15; 7:60)? What but love can explain Paul's ministry and passion that he 'might by all means save some' (*1 Cor.* 9:22)? The love was not their own in the first instance, it was Christ's love in them, as Paul affirms (*2 Cor.* 5:14). Preaching for Paul meant: 'God . . . pleading through us: we implore you on Christ's behalf, be reconciled to God' (*2 Cor.* 5:20). So it has always been.

I have referred already to John Livingston and the revival in Scotland of 1630. Here is an example of the kind of words which men heard who listened to him:

Come, all Christians, and spread forth all your experiences of his love, and declare all that you ever heard or read of it. There is yet an unfound world of love. O angels, that live among the treasure, tell the weight and measure of his love if you can . . . O friends, for Christ's sake, wrestle yourselves in to the royal banquet of love. O strangers, come and taste. O incarnate devils (while you are yet incarnate), come and taste. There is hope, there is hope. I do declare it, a tasting of it can make saints of devils. Suppose ye had seen Christ tempted and carried here and there by the devil. Suppose ye had been with him in the garden, or standing under the cross . . . Suppose he had been asked, Lord, what moveth thee so innocently to suffer all this? He would have answered, Love, love, love to sinners . . . O dear friend, wrap yourself, O wrap yourself in the sea of salvation. O be conquered and led captive by this love. Let it be

[1] Sibbes, *Works*, vol. 3, p. 479.
[2] Owen, *Works*, vol. 4, p. 397.

your delight to be love's prisoners, that so ye may attain the most noble freedom in heaven or in earth.[1]

After a period of comparative coldness, such preaching was heard again in the eighteenth-century awakening on both sides of the Atlantic and it began as God first dealt with preachers on this very subject. They were given an assurance of God's love which made their ministries what they became. One of the biographers of Howell Harris, the man called to evangelise Wales, describes what happened to him in Llangasty church in June 1735 :

The love of God was shed abroad in his heart. Christ had come in previously, but now He began to sup with him; now he received the Spirit of adoption, teaching him to cry Abba Father, and with it a desire to depart and be with Christ.[2]

In Harris's own words: 'Love fell in showers on my soul, so that I could scarcely contain myself. I had no fear, or any doubt of my salvation . . . I felt I was all love – so full of it that I could not ask for more'.[3]

Precisely the same thing was evident in William Grimshaw, the man of whom John Wesley said that 'a few such as him would make a nation tremble; he carries fire wherever he goes'.[4] Henry Venn, another friend of Grimshaw's, said of him: 'His soul, at various times, enjoyed very large manifestations of God's love, that he might not faint; and he drank deep into his Spirit. His cup ran over, and at some seasons his faith was so strong, and hope so abundant, that higher degrees of spiritual delight would have overpowered his mortal frame.'[5]

Charles Wesley first met Grimshaw in 1746 and described

[1] *Select Biographies,* vol. 1, pp. 272–3. 'When three or four of us are meeting together, we should make a fire of love to God, and when we want, fetch kindling from heaven. Christ died for love of us, and rose again to get our love, which he had so dear bought' (p. 284).
[2] R. Bennett, *The Early Life of Howell Harris* (repr. London: Banner of Truth, 1962), p. 27.
[3] Ibid., pp. 30–1.
[4] *Journal of John Wesley,* vol. 4, p. 493n.
[5] Henry Venn, *A Sketch of the Life and Ministry of the late Rev. Mr William Grimshaw* (Leeds: 1763), p. 35.

him in these words, 'His soul was full of triumphant love.'[1] Another who knew him said: 'I have seen him so overpowered with love, that he seemed as though he would have taken wing and fled from the altar to the throne of God.' In 1760 we find Grimshaw ending a letter to Charles Wesley with the words, 'my desire and hope is to love God with all my heart, mind, soul and strength to the last gasp of my life'. Two years later, in January 1762 (a year before his death), he wrote to a Society in Newcastle:

And now, what doth the Lord require of you, between this day and death; this new January, and the new Jerusalem? Only love, and the fruits of love . . . it is your best estate here below, as it will be your best estate above. It is the kingdom of God within you. It is heaven within you everywhere, and thus you are in heaven everywhere. It is heaven on earth, and heaven in heaven. O that you may always be filled with this love, this heaven, this Christ, this God! [2]

Nothing was more characteristic of George Whitefield than this same emphasis. The connection between the anointing of the Spirit and love was one of the themes of his ministry: 'I think it is plain that everyone, before he undertakes to preach the gospel of Christ, ought to be able to say, "The Spirit of the Lord is upon me". . . When it is upon them, the whole world will be set on fire of love . . . I wish well to this poor kingdom – but this will never be until the Spirit of God is poured out on the sons of the prophets.'[3] His own prayer at the very beginning of his ministry was,

> *Unloose my stammering tongue to tell*
> *Thy love immense, unsearchable!*[4]

and his letters and journals show how that prayer was first

[1] J. W. Laycock, *Methodist Heroes in the Great Haworth Round* (Keighley: Rydal Press, 1909), p. 46.
[2] W. Myles, *Life and Writings of William Grimshaw* (London, 1813), pp. 188–9.
[3] *The Revivals of the Eighteenth Century, particularly at Cambuslang*, ed. D. MacFarlan (Edinburgh: Johnstone, n.d.), Appendix, pp. 7–8.
[4] *Whitefield, Works*, vol. 1, p. 19. 'God give me a deep humility, a well-guided zeal, a burning love, and a single eye' (p. 33).

answered in his personal life. We often come across such words as these:

'Night and day Jesus fills me with his love.' 'The love of Christ strikes me quite dumb.' 'I would *leap* my seventy years and fly into his presence.'[1] 'I myself was so overpowered with a sense of God's love, that it almost took away my life'.[2]

This is what made Whitefield the evangelist that he was. He preached the love of God as a great certainty and as the overflowing of his own experience. 'I am persuaded of it,' he would say, 'that we may as well know that God loves us, and we love God, as we may know that the sun shines at noon-day.'[3] Another time, in the course of seeking 'to excite all to come and walk with God,' he included these words in speaking of the believer's joy and prospect of glory: 'I wonder not that a sense of this, when under a more than ordinary irradiation and influx of divine life and love, causes some persons even to faint away, and for a time lose the power of their senses.'[4] Christians who heard Whitefield, and those who have written of him, are all united on this point. A minister who met him in Boston in 1740 wrote, 'he appears to me to be full of the love of God, and to be fired with an extraordinary zeal for the cause of Christ.'[5] Sarah Edwards told her brother, 'He speaks from a heart all aglow with love.'[6] Others spoke of his being lost 'in tender and intense love to souls'.[7] A

---

[1] These quotations and other similar ones are given in Philip, *Life of Whitefield*, p. 248. Philip comments: 'He preached not only in dependence on the Holy Spirit, but "in *demonstration* of the Spirit and in power". Thus the holy oil which anointed so many under him, had first been poured on his own head.'

[2] Tyerman, *Whitefield*, vol. 1, p. 386.

[3] 'The Beloved of God', *Sermons on Important Subjects*, G. Whitefield (London, 1825), p. 630.

[4] Whitefield, *Works*, vol. 5, p. 35.

[5] Tyerman, *Whitefield*, vol. 1, p. 422.

[6] Quoted in Murray, *Jonathan Edwards*, p. 162.

[7] Philip, *Life of Whitefield*, p. 553. 'If my heart is in a proper frame, I feel myself ready to lay down my life, to be instrumental only to save one soul' (*Important Subjects*, p. 236). This same spirit was so evident in Robert M'Cheyne. 'A servant-girl, in a house where he stayed, described him as "*deein* to hae folk converted".' *Reminiscences of Andrew A. Bonar*, ed. Marjory Bonar (London: Hodder and Stoughton, 1895), p. 9.

hundred years later this feature of his preaching was still remembered in America.[1] His hearers were often convinced that his love and compassion for the multitudes was the love of the Saviour himself. He resembled the One whom he preached.[2] Perhaps the finest testimony to Whitefield's Christlikeness is in the verses to his memory by William Cowper. It includes the lines:

> *He loved the world that hated him; the tear*
> *That dropped upon his Bible was sincere.*
> *Paul's love of Christ, and steadiness unbribed,*
> *Were copied close in him, and well transcribed;*
> *He follow'd Paul: his zeal a kindred flame,*
> *His apostolic charity the same.*

Lest anyone should think that all this was only a characteristic of English Methodism the words of Jonathan Edwards should also be heard. Largely on the basis of one sermon, which others have entitled 'Sinners in the Hands of an Angry God', Edwards' ministry has been represented as though his subject on that occasion was the staple of his ministry and the very opposite of divine love. But Edwards himself speaks very differently. In explaining how a gospel minister is to be 'a burning light', he points to the Holy Spirit as 'the spring of divine life' and whose energy is likened to fire. The Spirit's presence, he believed, will be seen in a preacher as 'a holy ardour' and he continued: 'divine love or charity is the sum of all true grace, which is a holy flame enkindled in the soul: it is by this therefore especially, that a minister of the gospel is a *burning light*; a minister that is so has his soul enkindled with the heavenly flame; his heart burns with love to Christ, and

---

[1] When J. W. Alexander of Princeton heard Thomas Guthrie preaching in Edinburgh in 1857 he noted that 'the best of all' was his 'effusive gospel beseeching. I cannot think that Whitefield himself surpassed him in *this*. You know while you listen to his mighty voice, broken with sorrow, that he is overwhelmed with "the love of the Spirit".' *Forty Years: Familiar Letters of J. W. Alexander*, ed. John Hall, vol. 2 (New York: Scribner, 1860), p. 267.

[2] Again there is a parallel with M'Cheyne of whom a hearer said, 'It was not his matter nor his manner either that struck me; it was just the *living epistle of Christ*'. *Reminiscences of Andrew Bonar*, p. 29.

fervent desires of the advancement of his kingdom and glory: and also with ardent love to the souls of men, and desires for their salvation.'[1]

It is in Edwards' writings also that we find, drawn from the testimony of his wife, Sarah, one of the most remarkable accounts of the enjoyment of God's love ever set down on paper: 'It seemed,' she wrote, 'to be all that my feeble soul could sustain, of that fulness of joy which is felt by those who behold the face of Christ and share his love in the heavenly world.'[2]

Not surprisingly it was Edwards' written ministry which played such a part in the age of missionary endeavour which dawned in England towards the end of the eighteenth century. At the centre of the English Baptists who led the way was Samuel Pearce of Birmingham of whom J. W. Morris, a contemporary, wrote, 'few were more successful in converting sinners unto God'. It was in terms of the degree to which 'holy love' was 'the governing principle' in Pearce, Morris believed, that his outstanding usefulness was to be explained:

The Gospel can only be imparted by that Spirit which is of God; no zeal, no talents can supply its place; and the enmity of the human heart can only be overcome by the omnipotence of love . . . It is of the utmost importance that more of this spirit be imbibed, in order to any real or extensive usefulness. Those who can impart not the gospel of God only, but their own souls also, because the salvation of men is dear to them, will generally find that their labour is not in vain in the Lord.[3]

It was precisely in terms of that truth that the great missionary expansion into China as well as India took place. Dr and Mrs

[1] Edwards' *Works*, vol. 2, p. 957.
[2] Ibid., vol. 1, p. lxv. See also pp. 376–8. Without disclosing the identity of the person whose experience he records, Edwards says that it 'included the greatest, fullest, longest continued, and most constant assurance of the favour of God and of a title to future glory, that ever I saw any appearance of in any person . . . There was also a sense of the need ministers have of much of the Spirit of God' (p. 378).
[3] J. W. Morris, *Memoirs of the Life and Writings of the Rev. Andrew Fuller* (London, 1816), pp. 80–1. Pearce (1766–99) was a close friend of William Carey and had hoped to go with him to the East.

Howard Taylor explained it as, 'Love first, then suffering, then a deeper love – thus only can God's work be done.'[1] Elisabeth Elliott has interpreted the life of another pioneer missionary, Amy Carmichael, in the same terms, and she quotes the words of Jeremy Taylor: 'Lord, do Thou turn me all into love, and all my love into obedience, and let my obedience be without interruption.'[2]

The reference to Amy Carmichael (and that to Sarah Edwards already quoted) is a reminder that these experiences are by no means confined to ministers. The biography of Alexander Moody Stuart, whose Edinburgh ministry in the last century was attended by many eminent Christians, contains another striking illustration of this fact. During his early ministry on the island of Lindisfarne in the 1830s an incident took place which Moody Stuart was never to forget. At that period he used to meet weekly with another Christian for prayer. This friend was a ploughman, strong, tanned and full of health. But one summer's evening, as they rose from prayer, Moody Stuart noticed that his companion appeared unwell. His face had turned pale, he looked as though he was about to faint and as though he was struggling with some kind of distress which might overcome him. The ploughman then left in haste and with an obvious unwillingness to speak. The explanation came as the two men met two days later and Moody Stuart states it in this way:

I hailed him at some distance in the fields to inquire for his health. 'You seemed unwell when we parted the night before last; were you sick?' 'Oh, no.' 'Were you in distress of mind?' 'No.' 'What then?' Slowly and reluctantly he replied: 'When we were on our knees I was so filled with a sense of the love of God, that the joy was too much for me; it was all that I was able to bear, and it was with a struggle that I did not sink under it.' The fact itself was obvious, although to me it had not excited the least suspicion of the cause . . . For myself it was singularly refreshing to witness the presence and power of the Holy Ghost manifested in a manner so remarkable. It

[1] Dr and Mrs Howard Taylor, *Hudson Taylor*, in *The Early Years: the Growth of a Soul* (London: China Inland Mission, 1962), p. 291.
[2] Elisabeth Elliott, *A Chance to Die* (Grand Rapids: Revell, 1996), p. 151.

was a gracious out-flowing of the love of the Lord Jesus making his servant 'sick of love'.[1]

The same feature was present in Moody Stuart's later ministry at Free St Luke's, Edinburgh. In the words of one of his hearers: 'When he stopped and leaned over the pulpit, looking down at you with so much interest, you felt that the message had come for *you*, and that he loved your soul personally with a great love.' Forty years after the Lindisfarne incident, Moody Stuart welcomed an evangelist to Edinburgh by the name of D. L. Moody. He rejoiced, says his biographer, 'in the wonderful blessing attending his ministry' but he probably did not know how similar Moody's experience had been to that of the ploughman on Lindisfarne.

Three years before Moody first came to Edinburgh he had been on a visit to New York in the hope of raising money to rebuild Christian work in Chicago after a disastrous fire. It was to be a turning point in his ministry, as he later wrote:

My heart was not in the work of begging. I could not appeal. I was crying all the time that God would fill me with His Spirit. Well, one day, in the city of New York – Oh, what a day – I cannot describe it, I seldom refer to it; it is almost too sacred an experience to name. Paul had an experience of which he never spoke for fourteen years. I can only say that God revealed himself to me, and I had such an experience of His love that I had to ask him to stay His hand. I went to preaching again. The sermons were not different: I did not present any new truths; and yet hundreds were converted. I would not now be placed back where I was before that blessed experience if you should give me all the world – it would be as the small dust of the balance. [2]

It was just such experiences that Owen was referring to, two centuries earlier, when he wrote of the Spirit's work in shedding 'the love of God abroad in our hearts': 'To give a poor sinful soul *a comfortable persuasion*, affecting it throughout,

[1] K. M. Stuart, *Alexander Moody Stuart* (London: Hodder and Stoughton, 1899), pp. 61, 230–1.
[2] W. R. Moody, *Life of Dwight L. Moody* (London: Morgan and Scott, n.d.), p. 135. I have discussed Moody's ministry in Britain in *The Forgotten Spurgeon* and *Revival and Revivalism*. 'The best way to revive a church,' said Moody, 'is to build a fire in the pulpit.'

in all its faculties and affections, that God in Jesus Christ loves him, delights in him, is well pleased with him, hath thoughts of tenderness and kindness towards him; to give a soul an overflowing sense hereof, is an inexpressible mercy.'[1]

The inevitable accompaniment of assurance of the love of God is joy in the person who possesses it: 'Restore to me the joy of Your salvation' leads necessarily to, 'Then I will teach transgressors Your ways, and sinners shall be converted to You' (*Psa.* 51:12–13). As Gideon Ousley, a veteran Methodist preacher told a candidate for the ministry: 'While the love of God is burning in your heart you will never want hearers.' Love and joy in the pulpit will need no announcement of their presence and where that same spirit is conveyed to the pew the growth of the church becomes a certainty. 'Assuredly,' wrote C. R. Vaughan, 'if all Christians were as happy as it is their duty to be, there would be no resisting the spread of a faith so visibly rich in power and blessing.'[2]

Conclusions

1. While the experiences given above are not, as noted, confined to preachers of the gospel, there is good reason to believe that, before any new era of church expansion, it is to them that an unusual degree of the Spirit's filling is commonly first given and that it comes to expression in the way they speak about Christ. Referring to the leaders whom God raised up in the sixteenth century, Merle d'Aubigné has said that just as sunrise in the Alps first touches the peaks before it bathes the valleys below so it was these men with whom God first dealt. The same recurring pattern runs through church history. It was seen, for instance, in Scotland in the nineteenth century and in the raising up of evangelists such as John Macdonald and William Burns. Dr John Kennedy, a shrewd observer of the lives of preachers in the Scottish Highlands, has observed the change

[1] Owen, *Works*, vol. 2, p. 240.
[2] Vaughan, *The Gifts of the Spirit*, (repr. Edinburgh: Banner of Truth, 1975) p. 228.

which came to Macdonald when he was settled in Edinburgh and after he had been a minister in Berriedale:

There have been instances of persons becoming 'other men' who were never new creatures in Christ Jesus; but there have been also instances of renewed men becoming other men under a fresh baptism of the Spirit. This was the change which Mr Macdonald underwent in Edinburgh. It was soon apparent in his preaching. Always clear and sound in his statements of objective truth, his preaching now became instinct with life. It was now searching and fervent, as well as sound and lucid . . . His statements of gospel truth were now the warm utterance of one who deeply felt its power . . . So marked was the change which then passed over his preaching that many were led to judge that he had never preached the gospel till then. This is entirely a mistake. He preached the gospel in Berriedale as surely as in Edinburgh, though with far less unction, discrimination, and power.[1]

Horatius Bonar tells us the same thing concerning Burns and his friend, the Rev. John Milne of Perth. It was, he says, at 'the memorable Kilsyth Communion in 1839' that Burns received power, 'the power described by a contemporary writer as possessed by old Henry Venn when "men fell before him as slaked lime".' Before 1839, Bonar adds, Burns 'had not been remarkable as a preacher'. He goes on:

So it was with Mr Milne. His first sermons showed nothing remarkable. But when the great work began in 1839, he himself was brought under its power; he rose up to another level both in life and service. From that time he started on a new course, in which he held on to the last.[2]

---

[1] J. Kennedy, *The 'Apostle of the North', The Life and Labours of the Rev. John M'Donald* (London: Nelson, 1866), pp. 53–4.

[2] H. Bonar, *Life of John Milne of Perth* (London: Nisbet, 1868), pp. 105–6. A. Moody Stuart, however, who probably knew Burns better than H. Bonar, says of Burns: 'While he studied in Glasgow, some years after his conversion, and when the edge of his spirit had been partially blunted, he received under Dr Duncan s ministry a new and far deeper baptism of the Spirit than at first, by which he was specially fitted for the work to which he was to be called.' *Recollections of the Late John Duncan* (Edinburgh, 1872), p. 51. But, as Duncan ministered in Glasgow 1836–40, the time frame is approximately the same. Duncan's words of caution are relevant here: 'I think that no extensive awakening has ever been produced by preaching on the work of the Holy Spirit, but rather by awakening the conscience and setting forth Christ.'

Here is the same fact which we have already considered. Men 'filled with the Spirit' speak in a new way. They have clear vision of the truth. The gospel is a felt reality in a way which it was not before. They have entered more fully into the words of the apostle John, 'That which we have seen and heard we declare to you . . . We have known and believed the love that God has for us. God is love; and he who abides in love abides in God, and God in him' (*1 John* 1:3; 4:16). Referring to the Wesleys, Whitefeld and their friends, William Arthur wrote:

They were the wonders of their age, the seraphim of the earth. But what made them seraphim? They were once no mightier than others as to converting souls. Unbaptized with fire, or but slightly touched, their tongues might have charmed, fascinated, set the world discussing their gifts and extolling their abilities; but they would never have shot fires into the souls of men . . . it was the fire which raised the orator into the apostle and made their words sound as if Christ's first messengers were risen from the dead.[1]

Without more of this anointing how can preachers feel what they speak? They are appointed to speak as representatives of the God who has so loved the world that he gave his Son. Their business is to call others to a feast of love, to a heaven which is a world of love, and all in the name of a Saviour who died of love – how shameful then not to enjoy the very things of which we preach! 'Love,' says an old writer, 'is the sap of the gospel, the secret of lively and effectual preaching, the magic power of eloquence. The purpose of preaching is to reclaim the hearts of men to God, and nothing but love can find out the mysterious avenues which lead to the heart.'[2] Revivals have never come without preachers learning more of this. 'Let him speak of love,' wrote Bunyan, 'that is *taken* with love, that is *captivated* with love, that is *carried away* with love. If this man speaks of it, his speaking signifies something; the powers and bands of love are upon him, and he shews to all that he knows

[1] W. Arthur, *The Tongue of Fire* pp. 327–9.
[2] Abbé Mullois, quoted in *Hints on Preaching: a Cloud of Witnesses*, Anon (Cincinnati, 1879), p. 96.

what he is speaking of . . . These are the men that *sweeten* churches, and that bring glory to God and to religion'.[1]

The absence of this element is too often justified by the idea that the work of preaching has only to do with teaching and instruction. But scriptural preaching is much more than that. It includes exhorting, testifying, entreating, persuading and beseeching. Such was Paul's preaching at Ephesus that he could say, 'Remember that for three years I did not cease to warn everyone night and day with tears' (*Acts* 20:31). The absence of this element of urgency and compassion shows that something fundamental is missing. It was axiomatic for Whitefield that when a preacher only 'informs' his hearers and fails 'to move the affections and warm the heart . . . that preacher, let him be who he will, only deals in the false commerce of unfelt truth.'[2] This in Whitefield's belief was the explanation of the conditions prevailing in the churches at the time of the Evangelical Revival: 'I am persuaded the generality of preachers talk of an unknown and unfelt Christ. The reason why congregations have been dead is, because they had dead men preaching to them. O that the Lord may quicken and revive them!'[3]

Here then is a fundamental reason why ministers of the gospel should believe with Owen that there will not be a brighter day until there is 'a more plentiful effusion of his Spirit from above'. John Willison, a Church of Scotland evangelical leader, confirmed the same truth in the course of a series of sermons in 1741: 'When he is signally to increase his kingdom, he will raise up and qualify ministers for the work; who shall be men of large hearts . . . inspired by a burning

---

[1] *The Saints' Knowledge of Christ's Love*, in *Works of John Bunyan* (Edinburgh: Banner of Truth, 1991), vol. 2, pp. 39, 35. The idea that Puritan preaching was severe ignores this theme in their writings. As William Gurnall says: 'Sinners are not pelted into Christ with stones of hard provoking language; but wooed into Christ by heart-melting exhortations.' *The Christian in Complete Armour* (repr. London: Banner of Truth, 1964), vol. 1, p. 507.

[2] Quoted by J. B. Wakeley, *Anecdotes of George Whitefield* (London: Hodder and Stoughton, 1879), p. 38.

[3] Whitefield, *Journals* (repr. Edinburgh: Banner of Truth, 1985), p. 470.

love to Christ and the souls of men; inclined to prefer the good of Jerusalem above their chiefest joy.'[1]

2. Everything we have said above must lead to the conclusion that it is the duty of all preachers of the word to seek to be filled with the Holy Spirit and to believe that God is willing to hear that petition for the sake of his Son. Living as we do in a day when conditions in the churches are a great deal closer to those once existing in the church of Sardis than they are to biblical normality, there is every reason to believe that we must turn in penitence to him who 'has the seven Spirits of God'. Many times before has the work of preaching fallen into such ineffectiveness as is to be seen at present. Today there is a widespread nominal Christianity bereft of power, and even where churches are more than nominal the condition of their congregations on a Sunday evening is too often indicative of how little heavenly blessing was actually enjoyed by the larger numbers who were present at the morning service. There is a near famine for the word of God as far as its power and freshness is concerned and everything points to the inability of man to redress the situation. The words of William Arthur are a fitting conclusion to this whole theme:

Religion has never, in any period, sustained itself except by the instrumentality of the tongue of fire. Only where some men, more or less imbued with the primitive power, have spoken the words of the Lord, not with 'the words which man's wisdom teacheth, but which the Holy Ghost teacheth', have sinners been converted and saints prompted to a saintlier life. In many periods of the history of the Church, as this gift has waned, every natural advantage has come to replace it – more learning, more system, more calmness, more profoundness of reflection, everything, in fact, which, according to the ordinary rules of thought, would insure to the Christian Church a greater command over the intellect of mankind. Yet it has ever

[1] 'The Balm of Gilead' (1742) in *The Practical Works of John Willison* (Glasgow: Blackie, 1844), p. 433. 'It was the effusion of the Spirit with the gospel that gave the apostles and first preachers such extraordinary resolution, courage and hardiness, to encounter all difficulties and joyfully to sacrifice their all for Christ' (p. 426).

proved that the gain of all this, when accompanied by an abatement of 'fire', has left the Church less efficient; and her elaborate and weighty lessons have transformed few into saints.

In proportion as the power of this one instrument is overlooked, and other means trusted in to supply its place, does the true force of Christian agency decline; and it may without hesitation be said, that when men holding the Christian ministry, habitually and constantly manifest their distrust in the power of the Holy Ghost to give them utterance, they publicly abjure the true theory of Christian preaching.

Better let the Church wait ever so long, – better let the ordinances of God's house be without perfunctory actors, and all, feeling sore need, be forced to cry with special urgency for fresh outpourings and baptisms of the Holy Ghost, to raise up holy ministers, than that substitutes should be furnished, – substitutes no more ministers of God than coals arranged in a grate are a fire. O for men instinct with the Spirit! O for men on whom the silent verdict of the observer would be, 'He is a good man, and full of the Holy Ghost!' [1]

[1] W. Arthur, *The Tongue of Fire*, pp. 102–3, 106, 226, 266. In a review entitled 'Yale Lectures on Preaching' by several ministers, W. R. Nicoll concluded by regretting that 'the spiritual conditions for successful preaching' was 'a subject almost untouched. Praying for the Holy Spirit, and preaching in the power of the Holy Spirit – these are themes of the most vital importance.' He concluded his critical review: 'We apply to preaching what Culverwell says of religion: "It is a certain fiery thing, as Aristotle calls love; it requires the very flame and vigour of the spirit, the strength and sinews of the soul, the prime and top of the affections." We may well ask, "Who is sufficient for these things?" But our hopes revive as we ponder with an anxious, wistful yearning the deep words, "He shall baptize you with the Holy Ghost and with fire."' *The British and Foreign Evangelical Review*, vol. 27, 1878, p. 532. Nicoll was a Presbyterian minister, and it would be a great mistake to think that Arthur's emphasis belonged only to Methodists. 'No man can be a great preacher, without great feeling,' said J. W. Alexander of Princeton; and J. H. Thornwell believed that effective preaching must have 'the constraining influence of heaven-born charity'. Speaking of the primary duties of a minister, another nineteenth-century Southern Presbyterian wrote: 'Let him be baptized with the baptism of the Holy Ghost, and preach Christ, with all his heart, and soul, and mind, and strength.' (Thomas E. Peck, *Miscellanies* (Richmond, Va.: Presbyterian Committee, 1896), p. 299.

5

The Interpretation of Experience

'The Spirit does his work through the truth as his instrument'[1]
C. R. Vaughan

'It is not sufficient to commune with the truth, for truth is impersonal. We must commune with the God of truth. It is not enough to study and ponder the contents of religious books, or even the Bible itself. We must actually address the Author of the Bible, in entreaties and petitions.'[2]
W. G. T. Shedd

The confusion which we considered earlier over the meaning of revival has its parallel in the realm of individual Christian experience. Widely different views exist, for instance, over the significance of being 'filled with the Spirit'. Some have insisted that it means

not our having 'more of the Spirit,' but rather the Spirit having more of us . . . Many who earnestly seek this fulness of the Spirit fail to see this. They are longing, waiting, praying for God to give them something more; when, in order to be 'filled with the Spirit,' they must *give Him* something more than they have given already.[3]

Contrary to such words, others teach that all Christians are

---

[1] *The Gifts of the Holy Spirit*, p. 366.
[2] *Homiletics and Pastoral Theology* (repr. London: Banner of Truth, 1965), p. 291.
[3] Ernest Boys, *Be Filled With the Spirit*, p. 29, quoted by Andrew Murray, *The Spirit of Christ*, p. 316.

filled with the Spirit at regeneration and that subsequent 'failure and poor performance' is due to the loss of this fullness 'through sin or unbelief'.[1]

One thing is clear: which of these, or other views yet to be considered, is true cannot be decided by an appeal to experience. For the fact is that Christians, on the apparent basis of the same kind of spiritual experience, may formulate very different teaching. Therein lies a danger in quoting such testimonies as we have given in the last chapter. From such accounts one can too easily proceed to set down a pattern of experience which it is the duty of all Christians to seek. But something else needs to intervene before that conclusion is reached.

There is reason to believe that much of the confusion over the work of the Spirit in an individual arises out of wrong starting-points.

The Bible First

We have to start with Scripture, not with experience. Our own consciousness is no safe guide even to understanding our own experiences. We can be very imperfect interpreters of what happens to us or others; Scripture alone is dependable. There is much that is hidden from our awareness even in our own lives. Thus a young Christian, when he begins to confess Christ, may suppose that this is the first step in his salvation. Only from Scripture does he later learn that there was Another present, unannounced, whose work of new-creation went before and enabled him to 'say that Jesus is Lord' (*1 Cor.* 12:3). Similarly, unless more information had been supplied to him, the resurrected son of the widow of Nain would have remained ignorant of what had to occur *before* he 'sat up and began to speak' while being carried to his funeral (*Luke* 7:15). John Bunyan gives another illustration of the same point when

---

[1] John R. W. Stott, *Baptism and Fullness: The Work of the Holy Spirit Today* (Leicester: Inter-Varsity Press, 1987), p. 66.

he gives us a picture of what was shown to Christian in the Interpreter's house. Christian, he says, saw 'a fire burning against a wall, and one standing by it, always casting much water upon it to quench it; yet did the fire burn higher and hotter.' The fire was the work of grace in the believer's heart, and the one who cast water the devil, but the explanation for the myster-ious outcome was not visible: 'So he had him about to the back side of the wall, where he saw a Man with a vessel of oil in his hand, of which he did also continually cast (but secretly) into the fire.'[1] If Christians did not have Scripture they could never see 'behind the wall'.

Many mistakes have arisen from good men drawing wrong conclusions from experience. For even true experience, when misinterpreted, becomes the source of wrong teaching. This has sometimes happened in revivals. For instance, in times of awakening, when there has been strong conviction of sin, the public confession of wrong-doing has sometimes followed. Seeing the one following the other, some have concluded that confession of sin *causes* revival to take place and they have proceeded to insist on public confession as the way to further revival. But there is no scriptural justification for such a view, indeed the public confession of sin may well contravene express scriptural injunctions (e.g., *Eph.* 5:12) and is certainly not required by the words of James 5:16.

The original teaching of the Keswick movement which arose in the 1870s provides another illustration of the same danger. About that time some Christians in England appeared to enter into a greater blessing in their Christian lives and their new experience became the basis for the teaching which said that a 'full surrender' of one's life, and the putting away of every known sin, is the way to be 'filled with the Spirit'. This was tantamount to saying that every Christian needs a second conversion, or a crisis experience which secures 'the higher Christian life'. Andrew Bonar, biographer of M'Cheyne and a

[1] John Bunyan, *The Pilgrim's Progress* (Edinburgh: Banner of Truth, 1977), p. 29.

man personally experienced in revival, attended one of these Keswick-type meetings in 1884 and made the following wise observation:

The meetings held here by some of the brethren for 'deepening holiness' have led me to consider what it is that they think they have got beyond others. I am persuaded that what most of them mean is this, viz., that acquaintance with the personal Saviour and constant fellowship with Him which imparts fresh life and unction to prayer, conversation, preaching, etc. All this, however, is not any second conversion, but it is the Spirit's breathings through the heart *in a new degree*. The Kilsyth awakening was a time when many ministers were remarkably blessed in this manner.[1] Others of us had this from the beginning of our ministry, more or less. And if any make this something *by itself*, instead of just the Spirit bringing in more of Christ, they are in great danger of mysticism. One of my brethren got such a 'stirring up of the gift that was in him' in the early days of his ministry. And often this occurs again and again in the course of our Christian life.[2]

All teaching has to *begin* with Scripture and be *proved* by Scripture if it is to be safe to follow. Especially is this so with our present subject. Experience must not be the starting point, for even on the basis of just such quotations as I have already given from Christian biography, very different views of the work of the Holy Spirit have been formulated and popularised. J. W. Laycock, a Methodist author who has written much of great value on Christian experience in revival, is right to warn that there is no substitute for the duty of being 'constantly inspired by the study and exposition of Holy Scripture.'[3] Where the Bible ceases to have this priority there is no possibility of accurate discrimination between the true and the false. 'Our only security from the fallible or perverting influence of man, is entire, unquestioning submission to the infallible Word of God.'[4]

[1] The reference is to the revival of 1839. See above, p. 100.
[2] Andrew A. Bonar, *Diary and Letters*, pp. 353–4. Italics added.
[3] J. W. Laycock, *Methodist Heroes*, p. 133.
[4] C. Hodge, *Systematic Theology*, vol. 3, p. 485.

The Work of Christ

There is a second starting point for the study of Christian experience: we have to be clear about the work of Christ before we proceed to the Holy Spirit. It is all-too-possible to assume that in thinking of Christian experience our concentration has to be on the work of the Spirit. We are liable to suppose that Christ's work for us ended with his death and resurrection, and that now it remains for the Holy Spirit to do all that we need. This is certainly not the New Testament perspective. There we are directed not only to what Christ has done but to what *he is doing*. He is the Mediator whose intercession is now availing for us (*Rom.* 8:34; *Heb.* 7:24–5; *1 John* 2:1). He lives to rule all as 'head over all things to the church, which is His body, the fullness of Him who fills all in all' (*Eph.* 1:22–23). It is from Christ's fullness, and upon the basis of his merit, that the Holy Spirit brings all grace to the believer.[1]

What Christ's ascension and exaltation means for the continuance and final perfection of the church Paul further states in Ephesians 4:10–16. Yet we suffer from a strange proneness to neglect Christ's present work and this failure is evidently not peculiar to our generation. Over three hundred years ago John Owen observed : 'That Christ died for us, all who own the gospel profess in words; that he lived for us here in this world . . . all men will grant . . . but that Christ now lives a life of glory in heaven, *that* most men think is for himself alone.'[2] Charles Vaughan in the nineteenth century makes a similar comment:

---

[1] 'We say, there is a real communication of grace from the person of Christ, as the head of the church, unto all the members of his mystical body by his Spirit, whereby they are quickened, sanctified, and enabled unto all holy obedience . . . We say not, that we receive it as "water out of a conduit," which is of a limited, determined capacity; whereas the person of Christ, by reason of his Deity, is an immense, eternal, living spring or fountain of all grace.' Owen, *Works*, vol. 2, p. 334. As all the Puritans emphasised, the Holy Spirit 'takes reasons from Christ'.

[2] Owen, *Exposition of Hebrews*, vol. 5 (Edinburgh: Banner of Truth, 1991), p. 535.

We are apt to regard the love of Christ as having done its work when he passed out of sight into the blue vault over Olivet, having made a wonderful display on a brief theatre which closed up with its closing scenes. But that same great love which led him from the manger to the cross is still beating in his bosom. It is as keen in the administration as it was in the achievement of redemption. The appeal of the living sinner is not merely to a great by-gone and finished work of a dead Redeemer, but also to a living love and a living power in a living Saviour; to a love as much more tender and vehement than the warmest of mere human and Christian sympathies as his infinite heart is more capacious of the generous affection.[1]

We have already touched on the relationship between the mediatorial reign of Christ and the giving of larger measures of the Spirit in revival. Although the Holy Spirit as God is co-equal and co-eternal, in the economy of redemption he acts as the property of Christ. This is the scriptural teaching. As Bavinck writes: 'This taking possession of the Holy Spirit by Christ is so absolute an appropriation that the apostle Paul can say of it in 2 Corinthians 3:17 that the Lord (that is, Christ as the exalted Lord) is the Spirit . . . (or, as another translation has it, of the Lord of the Spirit) . . . He is now in possession of the seven Spirits (that is, the Spirit in His fulness), even as He is in possession of the seven stars (*Rev.* 3:1).'[2]

How the ministry of the Spirit is related to the present work of Christ is taken up by Owen in his exposition of Hebrews 7: 24–25: 'But He, because He continues forever, has an unchangeable priesthood. Therefore He is also able to save to the uttermost those who come to God through Him, since he always lives to make intercession for them.' Owen explains Christ's 'immediate actings towards the church' in terms of 'his sending and giving the Holy Ghost.' 'He lives for ever to send the Holy Spirit unto his disciples. Without this constant effect of the present mediatory life of Christ the being of the

---

[1] C. R. Vaughan, *The Gifts of the Holy Spirit*, p. 358.
[2] Herman Bavinck, *Our Reasonable Faith* (Grand Rapids: Eerdmans, 1956), p. 387.

church would fail, it could not subsist one moment.' It is from Christ, he writes, by the Spirit, that we receive:

1. All *saving light* to understand the word of God.
2. All *habitual grace*, whereby the souls of the elect are quickened and regenerated.
3. All *supplies of actual grace*; which the whole church has from him every moment, and without which it could yield no obedience to God.
4. All *spiritual gifts*, the sole foundation and means of the church's edification.
5. All *comfort and all consolations*, which in all variety of occurrences the church doth stand in need of.[1]

We believe then that it can be argued that all study of revival and Christian experience which does not begin with the work of Christ is bound to deviate from Scripture. The supreme issue has always to be whether men and women are savingly related to the Son of God. Nothing compares with that in importance. For the New Testament, regeneration and union with Christ is always *the* definitive event, distinguishing the Christian from all other people. John Stott is surely right in saying: 'Some Christians talk of their further experiences in exaggerated language, as if previously they were in bondage, now they are free, formerly everything was watery, now the water has turned into wine. But they must be mistaking subjective feelings for objective reality. For when we become united to Christ by faith, something so tremendous happens that the New Testament cannot find language adequate to describe it.'[2]

To begin to think of assurance of salvation, experiences or spiritual gifts, apart from the redemptive work of Christ is to invert biblical priorities and to forget that the great purpose of the Spirit's coming is to glorify Christ (*John* 16:14). As Octavius Winslow says: 'It is to Christ obeying and suffering, bleeding

[1] Owen, *Hebrews,* vol. 5, p. 536.
[2] Stott, *Baptism and Fullness,* p. 71.

and dying for us, that we are to look for our evidences, fruitfulness, and hope, and not to the work of the Holy Spirit wrought in our souls. Essential as is the work of the Spirit, He is not our Saviour.'[1]

Diversity of Teaching on 'Christ Baptizing with the Spirit'

Before we proceed to this subject another caution is needed. Our attention to the work of the Holy Spirit should not be narrowed down to only one part of his work. The New Testament says much on the comprehensiveness of his ministry. To affirm that the Holy Spirit teaches, comforts, brings to remembrance, sanctifies and strengthens, is only to begin to list what we find in Scripture. In a few verses of Romans chapter 8 alone we are given seven activities of the Spirit in believers: he indwells us and will finally raise our bodies from the grave (9–11); he subdues corruption (13); he leads (14); he witnesses and assures (15–16); he prompts us to wait for glory (23); and he enables prayer (26). The very breadth of the Spirit's work has therefore to be a warning against reducing his divine and mysterious operations to only one or two ideas. His work is multi-dimensional and to be preoccupied with any single aspect is not to follow Scripture.

The issue around which much controversy has centred in recent years has to do with what is fixed and permanent in the Spirit's work in the Christian and what is occasional, new or repeated. Fundamental to this discussion has to be the fact that the Spirit's indwelling is once-and-for-all at regeneration. The promise 'abide with you forever' (*John* 14:16) remains true for every Christian: 'the water that I shall give him will become in him a fountain of water springing up into everlasting life' (*John* 4:14). And because this indwelling is an eternal relationship it is necessarily of greater importance than

---

[1] O. Winslow, *Soul-Depths & Soul Heights; an Exposition of the Hundred and Thirtieth Psalm* (London: Shaw, 1874), p. 22.

particular blessings which flow from it. Much error has resulted from a belittling of what happens at regeneration as though some subsequent work of the Spirit is of greater necessity or significance.

Further, it should be agreed that something integral to Pentecost happens to every individual at the time when he or she becomes a Christian, and it is not subsequently repeated. At Pentecost believers, indwelt by one Spirit, became united as one body with the risen Christ. The church entered an existence independent of any land or nation and received a supernatural resource to fulfil a world-wide mandate. Into the unity of that church every individual is brought at conversion. Thus the unity of the body of Christ is declared in the New Testament as an accomplished fact, 'For by [or with] one Spirit we were all baptized into one body . . . and have all been made to drink into one Spirit' (*1 Cor.* 12:13).

Agreement, however, ends at this point and the main point of difference is whether or not every Christian is necessarily at conversion as 'filled with the Spirit' as believers were at Pentecost. Or to put the same question in another way, is the phrase 'baptized into one body,' which we have just quoted from 1 Corinthians with reference to regeneration, the *only* fulfilment to be expected of the words of John the Baptist concerning Christ: 'He will baptize you with the Holy Spirit and fire' (recorded with slight variations in *Matt.* 3:11; *Mark* 1:8; *Luke* 3:16; *John* 1:33; *Acts* 1:5 and *Acts* 11:16)?

I have already sought to argue above that, leaving aside the question of miraculous gifts, we cannot suppose that *everything* which marked the church at Pentecost is a permanent part of all Christian experience. The high degree of boldness (*parrhesia*), joy and assurance which then and later marked disciples is not duplicated in every regenerate person today. Christian ministers may be very deficient in the authority which marked the preachers of the early church. But how can this be explained if what happened to the church at Pentecost now happens to every person when they become a Christian? Can being filled with the Spirit really be the *same* as being a

Christian? Rather, is it not apparent that an individual may genuinely belong to Christ and yet have little assurance? And that a preacher may be orthodox and lack unction? It is hardly convincing to say in reply that such Christians did possess the same pentecostal fullness at regeneration but that they lost it subsequently. After long pastoral experience Charles Vaughan came to a more probable conclusion: 'Many a truly regenerate and painfully sanctified child of God never reaches, – apparently, at least, – the sweet blessing of the Spirit's unction.'[1] In other words, we may be regenerate and yet not resemble Spirit-filled preachers and Christians of the apostolic era.

From the conclusion reached in our last paragraph a school of teaching has advanced the view that every Christian needs 'the baptism of the Spirit' and that this is an experience which generally occurs after conversion. According to this teaching Christians receive the Spirit in two stages: first, in a limited manner at their conversion; second, when they obtain 'the baptism of the Spirit' and the Spirit is known in his fullness. This reasoning sounds plausible but there are important considerations which show that it should not be accepted. They may be stated as follows:

1. The New Testament nowhere presents a two-stage doctrine of Christian experience. What we have is teaching on the Spirit's work, and records of experiences which he gives, but no suggestion anywhere that all is to be understood in a two-stage framework.

---

[1] Vaughan, *Gifts of the Holy Spirit*, pp. 280–1. See also p. 215: 'The bulk of modern Christians are living far below the grade of both character and comfort to which they are not only authorized, but required, to aspire and attain.' Thomas E. Peck, in commenting on what happened in Acts 2, observed: 'Ministers of the gospel too generally lack this *parrhesia* and tongue of fire, both in preaching and praying. One reason, and the chief, perhaps, is that in spirit they are rather of the law than of the gospel; the dispensation of bondage rather than that of liberty.' *Miscellanies of Rev. Thomas E. Peck*, vol. 3 (Richmond, Va.: Presbyterian Board, 1897), pp. 58–9. Both these authors, let it be noted, spoke for Southern Presbyterian orthodoxy.

2. In the six texts in the Gospels and the book of Acts which refer to Christ 'baptizing' with the Spirit his activity is described by a verb. This teaching with which we are disagreeing constantly changes the verb 'baptizing' into a noun, 'baptism with the Spirit'. The difference may seem slight but when the definite article is constantly added to the noun so that it becomes '*the* baptism with the Spirit,' the impression is conveyed of *one* event, one defining moment, which should be normative for every Christian. No such conclusion can be drawn if the actual language of Scripture is retained.

3. This same teaching holds that it is the duty of all Christians to fulfil the conditions which will secure this vital 'second-stage' experience. But if there is a single experience as important as this set down in Scripture, one would assume that the conditions necessary to obtain it would also be clear. Yet when exponents of the teaching come to giving directions how 'the baptism' is to be obtained there is neither unanimity nor clarity. They agree that the blessing is conditional but there is no agreement on the texts which supposedly indicate the conditions.

Some teach that 'the baptism' is most likely to be received through prayer and the laying on of hands, and they point to Acts 8:17 and 19:6. But these 'laying-on-of-hands' passages have to do with the fact that in the early church God commissioned men, almost exclusively apostles, to be the means of communicating extraordinary gifts by the laying on of hands. It is the power of the Spirit in connection with gifts which is primarily in view. No such order of men was appointed to be a permanent part of the church's ministry.[1] Further, teaching which requires the laying on of hands for the baptism or fullness of the Spirit is contradicted by all the testimonies from Christian biography quoted above. In none of the experiences to which we referred was a filling with the Spirit preceded by the laying on of hands. Rather, as in Acts 4:

[1] For a full discussion, see Dabney, *Discussions,* vol. 2, pp. 222–60.

31, these Christians knew a sudden enduement of the Spirit's unction and power without human instrumentality.

Others teach that it is by a 'full surrender' and trust in God's word that the baptism or fullness of the Spirit is obtained. Pioneered in Britain by the Keswick movement, this was once a very prevalent opinion and R. A. Torrey became one of its clearest advocates. Torrey listed six steps to be followed, including putting away every known sin and 'absolute surrender to God'. He concluded his directions with these words:

Our Lord Jesus says, 'All things whatsoever ye pray and ask for, believe that ye have received them, and ye shall have them' (*Mark* 11:24, R.V.). When you pray for the Holy Spirit you have prayed for something according to God's will and therefore you may know that your prayer is heard and that you have what you asked of Him (*1 John* 5:14,15). You may feel no different, but do not look at your feelings but at God's promise . . . you will afterwards have in actual experience what you have received in simple faith.[1]

Starting from the position that all Christians are to be told how they may have what the believers at Pentecost possessed, Torrey here finishes up offering something different. If there is one thing clear in the book of Acts it is that when people were suddenly filled with the Spirit something *happened* to them of which they, and other people, were conscious. There was no question of accepting 'in simple faith the bare promise of God's Word,' and no teaching about how to 'appro-priate Him'.[2] It is hard to avoid the impression that such teachers as Torrey, observing from experience that the fulfilment of

[1] R. A. Torrey, *How to Succeed in the Christian Life*, (London: Nisbet:, 1906), p. 33. Or see his larger book, *How to Work for Christ* (London: Nisbet, 1901), pp. 169–73.

[2] 'It has been well said', writes Torrey, 'that God has already given Christ to the world (*John* 3:16), but that each individual must appropriate Him by a personal act to get the personal advantage of the gift, and so must each individual personally appropriate God's gift of the Holy Spirit to get the personal advantage of it' [*The Baptism of the Holy Spirit* (Belfast: Revival Movement Association, n.d., p. 14)]. This form of thinking can only exist where the Calvinistic understanding of both revival and conversion is either not understood or rejected.

conditions cannot in fact reproduce what is to be found in the book of Acts, have accordingly lowered expectations over what is to be expected.

On the basis of the above considerations we conclude that it is an error to make *one* experience of the Spirit normative for every Christian. To teach a single baptism, as something which every believer could obtain if only he knew how, is to deny that the time and measure in which the Spirit is given is in Christ's hands. With some justification F. D. Bruner goes further and argues that the whole teaching of a second experience of the Spirit involves a denial of the principle of grace, teaching, as Bruner says it does, 'that the gospel is sufficient for the beginning but not for the continuing of the Christian life, for bringing the Holy Spirit initially but not fully. Faith suffices for a start but keys, secrets, steps, and conditions must bring the Christian into a higher, deeper, fuller or more victorious life.'[1]

Bruner's words throw light on why advocates of the two-stage teaching are not to be found among those who hold a Calvinistic understanding of salvation.[2] The idea that we only receive 'the baptism' when we 'appropriate Him' originates in the same theology which teaches that God has put the Spirit and revival at our disposal.

The Older Evangelical Teaching

From such arguments as the above a number have concluded that what we said earlier on Pentecost must be wrong and that

---

[1] Bruner, *Theology of the Holy Spirit,* p. 240.
[2] The idea that Martyn Lloyd-Jones should be regarded as an exception is without real justification. For a good summary of his position see his *Preaching and Preachers* (London: Hodder and Stoughton, 1971), chapter 16. He believed in 'a baptism of power,' of which he says, it 'is not something "once for all"; it can be repeated, and repeated many times' (p. 308). His language and exegesis are not always precise but, taken as a whole, it should be very clear that he was not promoting (as some have claimed) a two-staged Christian experience. I comment further in *D. M. Lloyd-Jones: The Fight of Faith* (Edinburgh: Banner of Truth, 1990), pp. 484–91.

the only 'power' now to be expected is what all Christians receive at their regeneration. There should therefore be no talk of any baptizing work of the Spirit other than that which occurs at the very outset of the Christian life. Those who advocate this conclusion often write as though there is no other position to be considered. As we have already sought to indicate, however, there is another position. It can be stated briefly as follows:

Scripture commonly employs the figure of water poured out as a picture of communications of the Spirit of God. The language 'pouring out' and 'baptizing with the Spirit' mean one and the same thing. The terms are synonymous. Both speak of enlarged, abundant supplies of the Spirit to 'drench' the church. The primary idea is of copiousness. Christ used the idea of baptism in this sense when he spoke of the *largeness* of the flood of sufferings he was to endure on Calvary: 'I have a baptism to be baptized with, and how distressed I am till it is accomplished!' (*Luke* 12:50). As James Dunn points out, 'In the Old Testament the river and floods are used as metaphors for being overwhelmed with calamities'.[1] At Pentecost it was the copiousness (i.e., the baptism) of the Spirit which explains 'they were all filled with the Holy Spirit,' and so when we find the same experience of Christians being 'filled' repeated elsewhere, as in Acts 4:31, why should this not also be understood in terms of the Spirit's baptizing work? If Christ's promise, 'You shall receive power when the Holy Spirit has come upon you' (*Acts* 1:8) was exhaustively fulfilled at Pentecost, how is what happened in Acts 4 to be explained?[2]

Given what has already been said on the relation of the Spirit's work to the on-going mediatorial work of Christ it is therefore appropriate to believe that the promise, 'He will baptize you with the Holy Spirit and fire' is not to be confined to the first Pentecostal fulfilment. If the life of the church springs from its union with Christ by the Spirit; if there is a

[1] J. Dunn, *Baptism in the Holy Spirit* (London: S.C.M., 1970), p. 43.
[2] It is important to note that Acts 1:8 supplies our Lord's own interpretation of the promise, 'You shall be baptized with the Holy Spirit.'

continuing communication of the Spirit to the church – larger at some times than at others – why should the metaphor of baptism, referring to copiousness, be disallowed?[1] Is it not in this very sense that Luke uses it to explain what happened in Caesarea (*Acts* 11:15,16)?

It was on the basis of just such thinking that an older evangelicalism used the language of 'baptism of the Spirit'. Such authors as Kennedy of Dingwall, whom we saw using the words with reference to John MacDonald, were in no way supporters of a two-staged Christian experience. The same language was commonplace among evangelical leaders of the eighteenth and nineteenth centuries.

Whitefield uses 'baptism' and 'effusion' of the Spirit as synonymous. Thus, for instance, he can say, 'Whilst I was baptizing a child, the Holy Spirit was pleased to baptize several, one in particular with holy fire'.[2] His friend, James Hervey, describes two of his ministerial colleagues as 'like men baptized with the Holy Ghost and with fire – fervent in spirit, and setting their faces as a flint.'[3] Thomas Charles, the Welsh leader, believed: 'The baptism of fire, the touching of the live coal, the constraining love of Christ – these make ministers a flame of fire.'[4]

One of the best historians of the first Great Awakening in America asked: 'Was it not significant that the infant church

---

[1] It is common enough in the New Testament for the same word to carry more than one sense. We know of no justification for confining the meaning of baptism simply to initiation, nor for making the sense of the word in 1 Corinthians 12:13 or Romans 6:3 regulate its meaning in every other context. But Charles Hodge would seem to be going too far in writing: 'Any communication of the Holy Spirit is called a baptism, because the Spirit is said to be poured out, and those upon whom he is said to be poured out, whether in his regenerating, sanctifying, or inspiring influences, are said to be baptized.' *Exposition of the First Epistle to the Corinthians* (repr. London: Banner of Truth, 1958), p. 254.

[2] Whitefield, *Works*, vol. 3, p. 21.

[3] Letter to J. Ryland, Sr., quoted in A. C. H. Seymour, *Life and Times of the Countess of Huntingdon*, vol. 2 (London: Painter, 1844), p. 396.

[4] *Thomas Charles' Spiritual Counsels* (repr. Edinburgh: Banner of Truth, 1993), p. 467.

should then have a wonderful baptism of the Holy Ghost?'[1] Similarly, William Gibson, the senior Presbyterian who wrote the fullest account of the 1859 revival in Ulster, affirmed: 'Let the baptism of the Holy Ghost be given, and what before was a pleasing theory, becomes without an effort an actual reality.'[2] Spurgeon often used the same language: 'O God the Holy Ghost, work mightily, we pray Thee; flood the world with a baptism of Thy power.'[3]

It will be apparent that this use of 'baptizing', in the sense of enlarged giving, harmonises with the older understanding of revival. Just as there are larger givings of the Spirit to numbers at once (to which the name 'revival' properly belongs), so there may be a special anointing of the Spirit given to an individual. But too often the difference between the belief that Christ still baptizes with the Holy Spirit in this way is confused with the more modern teaching which we have criticised above. The difference may be stated as follows:

1. *There is no one post-conversion experience of being 'filled with the Spirit' to be sought by Christians.*
The old-school emphasis on the work of the Spirit in a believer was on the progressive and on-going nature of that work and not on any single experience. 'The history of the apostles shows that not once, but on many occasions, they were made partakers of the baptism of the Spirit and fire.'[4]

On the basis of Luke 11:13 ('how much more will your heavenly Father give the Holy Spirit to those who ask Him'), Torrey asserted that all who ask for 'the baptism of the Holy Spirit' must obtain it. But the older evangelicalism did not think in terms of 'it'. Instead of seeing that verse as a reference to one experience they regarded it as a promise for the believer's whole life. Luke 11:13 warrants continuing prayer

---

[1] T. Murphy, *The Presbytery of the Log College* (Philadelphia: Presbyterian Board, 1889), p. 445.
[2] Gibson, *Year of Grace*, p. 379.
[3] *C. H. Spurgeon's Prayers*, p. 109.
[4] Smeaton, *Doctrine of the Holy Spirit*, p. 52.

for the Holy Spirit. 'This is the daily work of believers,' writes Owen. 'If, therefore, our life to God, or the joy of that life, be considerable [i.e., large], in this we are to abound, – to ask him of the Father, as children do of their parents daily bread.'[1] Or again, referring to the anointing of the Spirit, Owen says: 'It is their duty to pray continually for its increase and farther manifestation of its power in them: yea, it is their duty to labour that their prayers for it may be both fervent and effectual; for the more express and eminent the teachings of this anointing in them are, the more fresh and plentiful is their unction.'[2]

In the last chapter we considered the work of the Spirit in giving knowledge and in imparting love. For both aspects the illustration of 'anointing' is used in the New Testament. The Holy Spirit gives us spiritual vision: 'You have an anointing from the Holy One, and you know all things' (*1 John* 2:20). He is the 'eye salve' with which our eyes need to be anointed that we may see (*Rev.* 3:18). At the same time, the sense of God's love which comes from what the Spirit teaches is so invigorating and refreshing that his anointing is like the perfumed oils of the East which refresh and restore strength to the weary. The enjoyment of God's love, says Sibbes, makes the Christian 'fit to do and to suffer anything'. 'Take a man that hath the "earnest" of the Spirit, you shall have him defy death, the world, Satan, and all temptations. Take a man that is negligent in labouring to increase his earnest, you shall have him weak.'[3] Such experiences of the Spirit are obviously to be understood in terms of a heightened assurance of salvation and they are supported by many New Testament references. 'The Spirit Himself bears witness with our spirit that we are children of God' (*Rom.* 8:16).

---

[1] Owen, *Works*, vol. 2, p. 272.

[2] Owen, *Works*, vol. 4, p. 398.

[3] Sibbes, *Complete Works*, vol. 5, p. 402; vol. 3, p. 482. Similarly Thomas Goodwin writes: 'When . . . the love of God is shed abroad in a man's heart, it makes a man work for God ten times more than before, or else more kindly.' *Works*, vol. 1, p. 251.

Now if in relation to the Spirit anointing and witnessing the question is asked, Are such blessings all received by *one* 'baptism'?, the answer surely has to be in the negative. The New Testament shows not two levels but many degrees of Christian experience and many continued and repeated operations of the Spirit of God. Robert Haldane, along with other commentators on Romans 8:16, is surely right in not treating the witness of the Spirit as *one* experience. On the words, 'The Spirit Himself bears witness with our spirit that we are children of God,' he wrote: 'This testimony, although it cannot be explained, is nevertheless felt by the believer: it is felt· by him, too, in its variations, as sometimes stronger and more palpable, and at other times more feeble and less discernible.'[1]

The same thing can be seen with regard to another enduement of the Spirit. One chief consequence of the filling of the Spirit, as recorded in Acts, was the presence of power and authority in speech. The common word, as already noted, is *parrhesia*, 'boldness' or 'freedom of speech', and it is integral to what Paul meant by 'preaching in demonstration of the Spirit and of power.' But while enduement with *parrhesia* could indeed be sudden, as at Pentecost, it was clearly not a once-for-all experience. Rather in this respect also the apostles needed fresh supplies of the Spirit (*Phil.* 2:19; *Acts* 4:31), and accordingly Paul sought for prayer and 'supplication in the Spirit . . . that utterance may be given to me, that I may open my mouth *boldly*, to make known the mystery of the gospel' (*Eph.* 6:18–19).

2. *There is no one experience to be seen as a standard for all because the Spirit's work is varied according to the many differing conditions of Christians and according to the purposes of Christ.*

Understanding this, the older evangelicalism had nothing to

[1] R. Haldane, *Exposition of the Epistle to the Romans* (repr. Edinburgh: Banner of Truth, 1996), p. 363. Similarly Owen, commenting on Paul's prayer for the 'spirit of wisdom and revelation' (*Eph.* 1:17), wrote: 'The degrees of this knowledge, which are exceeding various, both with respect unto the clearness and evidence of conception and the extent of the things known, depend on the various measures whereby the Spirit acteth.' *Works*, vol. 4, p. 396.

say about 'how to obtain the baptism of the Spirit'. They certainly believed in sudden and extraordinary manifestations of God's presence and love but saw them under Christ's sovereign hand. Sometimes, says Sibbes, a Christian's 'apprehension of God's fatherly love' may be so clear that it amounts to knowing 'immediately by way of presence'.[1] 'Sometimes,' he writes again, 'God doth add an excellent portion of his Spirit, a seal extraordinary,' and this gives 'such spiritual ravishings which are as the very beginnings of heaven, so that a man may say of a Christian at such times that he is in heaven before his time.'[2] But on the same theme he cautions:

Much must be left to God's fatherly wisdom in this, who knows whom to cheer up, and when and in what degree, and to what purpose and service; and remember always that these enlargements of spirit are as occasional refreshings in the way, not daily food to live upon. We maintain our life by faith, not by sight or feeling. Feasting is not for every day, except that feast of a good conscience, which is continual; but I speak of grand days and high feasts. These are disposed as God sees cause.[3]

John Owen speaks similarly. He did not doubt that God may work by 'unexpected surprisals,'[4] and that we may receive such persuasions of his love that we have 'heaven in this world'. But he is careful to say, 'the Spirit distributes as he will . . . in the whole business of consolation:– it depends upon the sovereign will of the Holy Ghost; and so is not tied unto any rules or course of procedure.'[5] William Guthrie, referring to experiences of 'a glorious manifestation of God unto the soul, shedding abroad God's love in the heart,' speaks in the same way: 'This is the thing that doth best deserve the title of *sensible presence*; and is not given unto all believers . . . This is so absolutely let out upon the Master's pleasure, and so transient

[1] Sibbes, *Works*, vol. 5, p. 440.
[2] Ibid., vol. 3, pp. 457–8.
[3] Ibid., vol. 5, p. 443.
[4] Owen, *Works*, vol. 3, p. 113.
[5] Ibid., vol. 2, p. 238.

or passing, or quickly gone when it is, that no man may bring his gracious state into debate for want of it.'[1]

This belief that there is no uniformity in the measure of the Spirit's work stands related to the intended differences in the body of Christ: 'To each one of us grace was given according to the measure of Christ's gift' (*Eph.* 4:7). Not all Christians have the same duties or callings. All do not have the same warrant or need to ask for the *parrhesia* which marked the public ministry of the word in Acts. And while all believers need assurance, it is clear that there are occasions when a large measure of the Holy Spirit's aid is especially needed. Thus men called to lead in the recovery of the churches after a period of long deadness or apostasy, have need of such grace in a high degree. Extraordinary encouragement is given for extraordinary service, as is indicated in Luke 21:12–15. Drawing attention to this in the lives of the Protestant Reformers, A. A. Hodge wrote: 'It is a matter of fact that at that period of Church history there were men in whom this grace of assurance of salvation was very prominent. They did have it; and God gave it to them, because he gave them a Herculean work to do which demanded heroes for its performance.'[2]

The same may be said of the preachers raised up amidst much opposition in the eighteenth century and of evangelists and missionaries raised up in the nineteenth. Or again, it is noticeable that special communications of the Spirit are often given to martyrs and sometimes to other Christians as death approaches[3]. Not all Christians are called to suffer as Stephen, or to do the work of a Whitefield, or an Amy Carmichael.

---

[1] W. Guthrie, *The Christian's Great Interest* (1658, repr. London: Banner of Truth, 1969), pp. 108–9.

[2] *Evangelical Theology* (1890, repr. Edinburgh: Banner of Truth, 1976), p. 303.

[3] Words written by the Puritan leader John Howe on a blank page of his Bible and dated October 22, 1704 (the year before his death), read: 'I experienced an inexpressibly pleasant tenderness of soul, tears gushed out for joy, because the love of God was shed abroad through my soul, and to that end on me especially his Spirit was bestowed. *Rom.* 5:5.' R. F. Horton, *John Howe* (London: Methuen, 1895), p. 186.

Nothing, then, is stereotyped in Christian life and experience. There are no formulas. The biblical principle is well stated by James M'Lagan of Aberdeen:

Whether we view the outgoings of His power, as regulated by God's eternal decree, or as adjusted to the character and actions of men, – the Holy Ghost is obstructed by no barrier, is subject to no bondage; but as the wind bloweth where it listeth, even so does this heavenly Breath of Omnipotence apply or refrain His spiritual impulses, when, and how, and to whom, and in what measure, and with what results, he pleases.[1]

Practical Consequences of Wrong Views

It appears to us that there are practical consequences resulting from error on this subject similar to those we have already considered in relation to revival. The view which says that the 'outpouring' or 'baptism' which fills Christians with the Spirit only occurs at conversion, is prone to minimise the on-going experimental dimension of his work in the Christian. It is perhaps significant that Kuyper's large volume on *The Work of the Holy Spirit* has no teaching on assurance or on the necessity of unction for powerful preaching. His book has the appearance of being over-concerned to answer what he conceived to be the dangers of 'Methodism', 'with its individualism and subjectivity'.[2] The same mistake would seem to have been made by other writers of the twentieth century who, in their anxiety to counter Pentecostalism, leave no room for larger communications of the Spirit. These authors too often write as though they were unaware of the older evangelical position. But in so far as they leave out, or give little space to the experimental dimension found in authors from the Puritans down to George Smeaton, they are unlikely to win those whom they are concerned to help.

But the view which would explain all in terms of '*one*

[1] James M'Lagan, *Lectures and Sermons* (Aberdeen: Davidson, 1853), p. 89.
[2] Kuyper, *Holy Spirit*, pp. xii–xiii.

baptism of the Spirit', to be received by all Christians at a
certain point, has consequences no less undesirable:

1. *By building on the experiences of some Christians, and making these
normative for all, an unrealistic model of the Christian life is created.*
This happens when every 'feast day' experience to be found in
Christian biography is quoted as though it ought to be a
pattern and standard for all. This is calculated to lead
Christians either to depression or to the adoption of a
profession beyond the reality they know. Henry Venn, one of
the wisest of the evangelical leaders of the eighteenth century,
has some valuable remarks on how Christian biography may
unintentionally induce discouragement. In writing to a friend
he commended the value of biographies but warned against
allowing the experiences of others to dishearten us. He
referred, in particular, to a recently published biography of
his eminent contemporary, John Fletcher of Madeley, and of
the danger of treating Fletcher as a model. When we do the
latter, he said:

We feel much uneasiness and vexation and are apt to conclude we
are unfit to die, and ought not even to be called Christians, till we are
exactly, or nearly, such as the blessed saint whose history is before us.
Herein we greatly err: we seem not to know that a very great
disparity prevails through all the works of God. In heaven there are
many degrees of excellency; and, no doubt, a vast distance between
the powers and excellencies of the highest and the lowest angels. In
our own bodies, how does the head and eye, and the tongue, surpass
in excellency many other parts! In the Church, it is the same:
according to the ability God gives, and according to the measure of
grace given unto us, *we are what we are.* Some bring forth a
hundredfold – more than three times as much as others ever will
do; according as the same Spirit divideth 'to every man as he will'.
And though the last lines of Mr Fletcher's Life affirm that *every one*
may be exactly like him if he will, I beg leave, on the contrary, to say
that a fowl in a barn-yard, which mounts with great difficulty so high
in the air as the top of the barn, or into a lofty tree, might as
reasonably be expected to accompany an eagle in its flight, as myself
and the bulk of Christians can be just what dear Mr Fletcher was in
his spirit and manner of life. No; a natural cast, a great capacity, a

vivid impression from every object, a very quick sensibility of affections, and a very uncommon measure of grace, must all concur, and be all diligently improved, before a vessel of honour, of such magnitude and brilliance as he was, can come forth from the Great Maker's hand.[1]

The lives of others provide no rule for us.[2] At the same time Venn went on to encourage his friend with the truth that the difference between all Christians is one of degree:

Great grace was then upon this blessed servant of Christ; – yet a measure of the same is in our souls though it be but very little . . . *Love to man*, displayed in Mr Fletcher a noble imitation of his Incarnate God. He indeed thought the day lost, and could find no rest in his soul, unless he was doing good to the bodies and the souls of men. The whole family of Christ are of the same gracious temper, in some degree – they are merciful, loving, and righteous . . . God has given them the spirit of love, and to be kindly affectioned towards their fellow sinners.[3]

2. *The teaching of one Holy Spirit baptism, leading to two kinds of Christian, endangers the New Testament teaching on the nature of progress in the Christian life.*

By putting emphasis on receiving *the* baptism of the Spirit, the tendency of the teaching is to present one experience as though it was a goal, and the more so when this 'second experience' is identified (as it often has been) with sanctification and living 'the victorious Christian life'. But, as already said, the New Testament knows no concentration of attention on any post-conversion experience, rather the spirit of the believer is always to be forward-looking and his language has

[1] *Letters of Henry Venn* (1835, repr. Edinburgh: Banner of Truth, 1993), p. 581. See also on Fletcher, pp. 240, 376, 450.
[2] John Newton understood this and reflected on it to Wesley who had urged him to follow Grimshaw's example and become an itinerant preacher. He was not a Grimshaw, he told Wesley: 'I have not strength of body or mind sufficient for an itinerant preacher . . . To ride a horse in the rain, or more than above thirty miles in a day, usually discomposes and unfits me for anything.' *Life and Times of Selina, Countess of Huntingdon*, vol. 1, pp. 270–1.
[3] *Letters of Venn*, pp. 582–3.

ever to be that of imperfect attainment (*Phil.* 3:12).[1] The more a
Christian advances, the more he knows of Christ, the less he
sees himself to possess and the less will be his inclination to
suppose he has arrived. Indeed, the more experience he has of
the Spirit who has come to glorify Christ the less will he be
disposed to think of himself at all.

A. A. Hodge, referring to a time when he was a pastor in
Virginia, speaks of two very different women to whom he
ministered. One, he writes, 'told me she wanted the witness of
the Spirit, and she talked about it everlastingly; she wanted to
tell her own experience and feelings always.' 'I told her,' he
continued, 'to forget herself. The man who is talking about his
love unceasingly has no love; the man who is talking about his
faith unceasingly has no faith: the two things cannot go
together. When you love, what are you thinking about? Are
you not thinking about the object of your love?' The other
woman whom he knew through six years was of a very
different kind and 'seemed always to walk upon the verge of
heaven. I never heard her speak of any one particular of her
character or of her own graces.' Sometimes when a service was
over, and the congregation dispersed, she would still be found
sitting absorbed in her pew. Then, startled by her pastor's
voice near at hand, 'she cried instantly, "Is He not holy? is He
not glorious? is He not beautiful? is He not infinite?" She did
not speak of her own love or of her own feelings.'[2]

Profound humility has always been the mark of those

---

[1] It seems probable that the nineteenth-century teaching of a two-staged
Christian experience was a development from John Wesley's teaching of the
possibility of a believer attaining to 'Christian perfection' by a single
experience. At a time in Wesley's life when this teaching was leading to an
unhealthy emphasis in his Societies, he countered it with the better advice
not to seek anything 'new, beside *new degrees of love* to God and man . . .
Higher degrees: this is all we have to expect.' 'A thousand mistakes,' he
continued, 'is the not considering deeply that love is the highest gift of God –
humble, gentle, patient, love – that all visions, revelations, manifestations
whatever, are little things compared to love.' 'Cautions and Directions
Given to the Greatest Professors in the Methodist Societies' (1762), reprinted
in *John Wesley*, ed. Albert C. Outler (New York: O.U.P., 1980), p. 301.
[2] A. A. Hodge, *Evangelical Theology*, pp. 306–7.

nearest to Christ. The apostle John would not so much as name himself in his Gospel. 'O, what a drone I have been,' was Whitefield's language as his life drew to its bright close and he lamented, 'O my ignorance! my ignorance!' At the age of fifty-two, five years before his death, he can only see himself as a mere beginner. He writes on his birthday: 'O loving, ever-loving, altogether lovely Jesus, how little, yea how very little have I done and suffered for thee! I am ashamed of myself: I blush and am confounded. Tomorrow, God willing, I intend to take a sacrament upon it, that I will begin to begin to be a Christian.'[1]

The diary of Andrew Bonar is marked by the same characteristic. He too was a partaker in the blessings of the time of awakening which was seen in Scotland in 1839, but over forty years later this is how he could write as an old Christian:

Two things I long to be full of before my ministry ends, viz., fervent zeal for the glory of God in Christ, and tender compassion for souls . . . My cry is, that every visit I pay, every sermon I preach, every tract I write, may be like a spark from a seven-times-heated furnace; that furnace being my heart, filled with the Spirit, and ever burning within me. It has not been so in the past [2]. . . Time for prayer till the afternoon. I sought specially to know the *love of God* of which I am persuaded I scarcely feel anything; and I sought the presence of the Spirit in prayer in our congregations, as in the days of old revival.[3]

For the Christian in this world the goal is always beyond him. No experience here is complete; all is imperfect, which is why 'hunger and thirst' are to be lifelong (*Matt.* 5:6). 'They shall neither hunger anymore nor thirst anymore' (*Rev.* 7:16) is not for this world. 'Such Christians as are resolved to lie down in sorrow, till they have attained to a perfect assurance, must

---

[1] *Works of Whitefield*, vol. 3, p. 343.
[2] Andrew Bonar, *Diary and Letters*, pp. 345–6.
[3] Ibid., p. 349. In an earlier entry he says: 'O my Lord! send me zeal, love to souls, pity, compassion. I felt a sort of fear to dedicate myself to the Lord, to give up myself wholly to him, till in a moment I saw that the Lord is love itself, and cannot but require me to do what is best' (pp. 152–3).

resolve to lie down in sorrow till they come to lay down their heads in the dust.'[1] Thus all teaching must be wrong which minimises the paradox of Christian experience: the Christian is both contented and discontented; satisfied and dissatisfied; rejoicing and yet still groaning (*Rom.* 8:23).[2] The 'filling' which Paul prays for the Ephesian Christians is both a present need and duty (*Eph.* 5:18), and a future prospect. As John Eadie writes on Ephesians 3:19, the full realisation of the words 'that ye might be filled with all the fulness of God' (*Eph.* 3:19) shall be reached in heaven, 'where the spirit shall be sated with "all the fulness of God".'[3]

Conclusions

1. The teaching of Scripture on the Holy Spirit's work in bringing all Christians into progressive conformity to Christ has to be of first concern for every believer. The Christian's character and godliness is given higher priority in Scripture than his service. Therefore all seeking of spiritual enjoyment or of public usefulness *apart from* personal holiness is delusive: 'If anyone loves Me, he will keep My word: and My Father will love him, and We will come to him and make Our home with him' (*John* 14:23). It was said of John Howe, 'He took care to wash the vessel, that it might be receptive of Divine communications.'

2. All Christians are to pray for the Holy Spirit. We are to seek more of his grace and power than we presently know. 'It

---

[1] T. Brooks, *Works*, vol. 3, p. 480.

[2] 'We are elected, not to "earnest," not to "first-fruits," but to be "unblameable"; we are elected to perfection'. Sibbes, *Works*, vol. 3, p. 472. In Bunyan's phrase, 'The milk and honey lie beyond this wilderness world.'

[3] J. Eadie, *Commentary on the Greek Text of the Epistle to the Ephesians*, 3rd ed. (Edinburgh: T. & T. Clark, 1883), p. 260. The 'fulness', writes the same author on Ephesians 3:19, appears to be 'the entire moral excellence of God', in so far as it is communicable. 'The difference between God and the saint will be not in kind, but in degree and extent. His fulness is infinite; theirs is limited by the essential conditions of a created nature.'

becomes us,' wrote Calvin, 'to be instant in prayer, and to beg at God's hands that he will increase in us his Holy Spirit: increase, I say, because before we can conceive any prayer we must needs have the first-fruits of the Spirit.'[1] 'Such as already enjoy the baptism of repentance for the remission of sins may obtain supplies of the Spirit a thousand-fold greater than any they have ever known.'[2]

3. We are not to prescribe the way and measure in which the Spirit's aid and grace be given. Nor are we to judge the extent of his aid by our own feelings as though 'feast days' and the felt presence of Christ are always what is best for us. Even those who have known not a little of felt blessing have said with Rutherford, 'our best fare here is hunger'; and with Edwards, 'Perpetual sunshine is not usual in this world, even to God's true saints'.[3] In the words of another writer:

Some things that *we* might think desirable we may not have. Before Christ was brought face to face with the tempter, he was fitted for his service by being kept hungry for forty days; and it may be that some things that we desire may in like manner be kept back. But faith should always claim that that which God has given us, and is giving us, *is sufficient for present needs*. If faith is only in lively exercise we shall know this, That no single thing we do not possess would be a help to us to-day. What does the Word say? 'No good thing will he withhold' (*Psa.* 84:11). 'My God shall supply *all* your need according to his riches in glory by Christ Jesus' (*Phil.* 4:19).[4]

4. Those who serve Christ in the public teaching and evangelistic ministry of the church have the most urgent obligations to be filled with the Spirit. In the words of Edwards, 'The state of the times extremely requires a fulness of the divine Spirit in ministers, and we ought to give ourselves

---

[1] Calvin, *Commentary upon the Acts of the Apostles* (Edinburgh: Calvin Translation Society, 1844), pp. 57–8.

[2] George Smeaton, 'A Witnessing Church – A Church Baptized with the Holy Ghost', in *Free Church Pulpit*, vol. 3 (Perth: Dewar, 1847), p. 27.

[3] 'Letter to Mrs Esther Burr', in *Jonathan Edwards, Representative Selections*, C. H. Faust and T. H. Johnson (New York: Hill and Wang, 1962), p. 414.

[4] *Days of Blessing*, p. 45 (further details unknown).

no rest till we have obtained it . . . Ministers should be much in seeking God, and conversing with him by prayer, who is the fountain of light and love.'[1]

5. While special experiences of the Spirit's effusions, with a 'sensible' enjoyment of God's presence and love, are not permanent or normal in the Christian ministry they are greatly to be desired. As Sibbes writes, although 'feelings ebb and flow . . . the extraordinary feeling of the Spirit' has long-term influence upon a Christian even though it is not continuing.[2] In the case of ministers, such experiences add largely to a man's usefulness. He will preach with more unction, tenderness and authority. He may well leave behind a fragrance for generations following. As late as 1767 White-field could write of Puritan authors of the previous century: 'Though dead, by their writings they yet speak: a peculiar unction attends them to this very hour.'[3]

6. In times of revival, as in the apostolic age, it would appear that many Christians are unusually filled with the Spirit. Sarah Edwards at such a time in 1741 could write, 'My soul was filled and overwhelmed with light, and love, and joy in the Holy Ghost.' A Christian of the next century who was shown the record of Mrs Edwards' experience commented that, 'instead of being surprised or thinking her experience uncommon, he had seen the day when Mrs Edwards' experience was a common experience with some who turned to the Lord in Skye.'[4] Such a statement would never have been possible if the island of Skye in Scotland had not been visited

[1] Edwards, *Works*, vol. 2, pp. 865, 960.
[2] Sibbes, *Works*, vol. 3, p. 459.
[3] Whitefield, 'A Recommendatory Preface to the Works of Mr. John Bunyan', *Works*, vol. 4, p. 306. A later writer says of the Puritans that in their works 'we have massive theology baptized with all the unction of rich Christian experience'. John Miller in General Preface to Nichol's reprints of the Puritans, *Works of Thomas Goodwin*, vol. 1, p. xxii.
[4] James Ross, *Brief Sketch of Donald M'Queen* (London: Nisbet, 1891), p. 6.

with the same outpouring of the Spirit as was seen first in Jerusalem and again in New England in the 1740s.

Roderick Macleod, one of the leading preachers in the nineteenth century revival in Skye believed that God's purpose in 'such wonderful display of his power' was 'for the awakening of the church of God, so long settled on her lees, to a new realising sense of the necessity and power of the work of the Spirit.'

6

Hindering Revival: Evangelical Fanaticism

'Half the people of God hardly know their head from their heels at this time. They are gaping after wonders . . . We are only at the beginning of an era of mingled unbelief and fanaticism.'[1]

C. H. Spurgeon, 1883

We have already considered what place is left for human responsibility if revivals come by the sovereign will of God. We saw that the Bible teaches both man's total dependence upon God *and* the voluntary nature of his own actions. In a manner hidden from us, the divine and human agencies are conjoined in events in such a way that the will of God comes to pass while men remain fully accountable for all sin and failure. Not a single success in the kingdom of God is ever achieved without the predetermining purpose of God (*Acts* 15:18), yet we are confronted in Scripture with the real danger that we may hinder the gospel of Christ (*1 Cor.* 9:12). This is true in general and it must remain true with regard to revival. If the definition of revival which we have sought to establish is correct – if revival is the heightening of normal Christianity – then it follows that everything which hinders the spiritual life of the churches may also be a potential hindrance to revival: unbelief, pride, impurity, moral laxity, prayerlessness, unfaithfulness to Scripture, erroneous beliefs, contention

[1] *C. H. Spurgeon, Metropolitan Tabernacle Pulpit, 1883, p. 214.*

between brethren – all such things are grieving to the Holy Spirit of God.

In this chapter I want to concentrate on one danger at the present time which has a very close connection with our main subject. It is a danger which can both hinder revival and also cause serious damage when a true revival occurs. But here again we face the problem of terminology. There is no modern word which is suitable to describe the issue to which I am referring. It used to be called 'enthusiasm'. 'Enthusiasm' came into the English language from the Greek word *enthousiasmos*. *Enthousiastes* was a person indwelt or possessed by a god. So enthusiasm, as the word became popularly used in the seventeenth century, was descriptive of the unbalanced religious emotion of those who supposed they had some special nearness to God. Today, however, enthusiasm has entirely lost its original derogatory connotation and it would be very confusing to re-introduce it in that sense. The word 'fanaticism' is equally old, and it also arose in England out of seventeenth-century controversies, but it has held its meaning better. I shall therefore term what I am discussing as fanaticism, although this term too has a defect. It is commonly used in such a broad and ugly sense that it scarcely seems applicable to any who profess evangelical Christianity. But I do not know a more suitable alternative. It is important to explain what I mean by it.

Fanaticism is the opposite of a cold intellectualism. Fanaticism usually pays little attention to books, its great interest is in experiences. Fanaticism may be orthodox in belief but it is more concerned with emotion and with results than it is with objective truth and teaching. While fanaticism may believe what the Bible says about the Holy Spirit, it talks chiefly about the Holy Spirit speaking *within us* – revealing things to us in ways which people who only have the Bible cannot enjoy. Fanaticism thinks it has a blessedness above anything known by ordinary Christians. Fanaticism is zealous for a kind of ultra-supernatural Christianity to which it wants to make everyone a proselyte. Fanaticism is often proclaiming that a revival has begun or is about to begin. But there are things which fanaticism cannot do: it cannot distinguish between fire and wildfire and it cannot see the danger of confusing imagination with truth.

The subject before us is not an uplifting one. On the contrary, it is sad and distressing; yet there are urgent reasons why it needs to be addressed.

The Dangers of Fanaticism

1. *Fanaticism is dangerous because history shows that it is constantly liable to reappear among orthodox and evangelical churches.*

Fanaticism was a major problem to the reformers of the sixteenth century. It emerged again at the time of the Puritan ascendancy in England in the following century. Just at the point in history when it seemed possible that the Protestant churches would be established in a much more biblical form, new voices were heard – 'persons affected by excessive and mistaken enthusiasm' – and all kinds of setbacks and controversies were the result. The very same thing happened again on both sides of the Atlantic in the eighteenth century. John Wesley had repeatedly to warn his Methodist societies of the influence of fanatics arising in their midst. One of them was a man called James Kershaw who prophesied that 'all the Methodists are to go over to America in the belly of a whale'. Wesley called him 'stark staring mad', but others who were not mad fell into similar things. One by the name of George Bell was a class leader of whom Wesley could say, 'No man was more profitable to me'. But Bell, supported by others, came to believe he had special revelations and prophesied that the world would end on 28 February 1763. Recording how he dealt with this claim, Wesley wrote:

I largely showed the utter absurdity of the supposition that the world was to end that night. But notwithstanding all I could say, many were afraid to go to bed, and some wandered about in fields, being persuaded that, if the world did not end, at least London would be swallowed up by an earthquake. I went to bed at my usual time and was fast asleep about ten-o'clock.[1]

Exactly the same kind of thing happened in Calvinistic New England at the time of the Great Awakening. Overreacting against the formality and deadness which had previously prevailed, people such as the Rev. James Davenport began to act as though emotionalism and excitement were of the very essence of true Christianity. 'He not only gave an unrestrained liberty to noise and outcry, both in distress and joy, in time of divine service, but promoted both with all his might.' The result was that many fell into a false zeal which had a devastating influence. Jonathan Edwards lamented how this happened and wrote:

The cry was, 'O, there is no danger, if we are but lively in religion, and full of God's Spirit, and live by faith, of being misled! If we do but follow God, there is no danger of being led wrong!' . . . This was the language of many, till they ran on deep into the wilderness, and were taught by the briers and thorns of the wilderness.[2]

Fifty years later the same kind of thing reappeared in some of the revivals at the time of the Second Great Awakening although it sometimes took different forms. There were, for instance, those who began to teach that it was a mark of the special favour of the Holy Spirit to be able to pray what was called 'the prayer of faith'. By this it was meant that if we pray 'in faith', God cannot be true to his word unless he gives us whatever we have asked. But Scripture says, 'If we ask anything *according to His will,* he hears us' (*1 John* 5:14) and Christians are given no assurance that they can infallibly identify the will of God. Dr Gardiner Spring, one of the leaders at the time of the Second Great Awakening, warned that this was a fanatical view of prayer which 'would sanction every species of wildness and enthusiasm'. It led people to suppose that if they prayed in faith for fifty converts, they must

[1] *Journal of John Wesley*, vol. 5, p. 9. See also *Letters of John Wesley*, vol. 4, ed. John Telford (Epworth Press, 1931), p. 245.

[2] Letter of 23 November 1752, in Edwards, *Works*, vol. 1, p. *cl.* I discuss this more fully in *Jonathan Edwards, A New Biography*, pp. 223–9.

have fifty converts; or, if they prayed for healing, they must have healing. On this idea Gardiner Spring wrote:

I have known some persons in our own city . . . who acted under the influence of this delusion. There are men and women still alive and among us, who remember the circumstances of the death of Mrs Pearson, around whose lifeless body her husband assembled a company of *believers*, with the assurance that if they prayed in faith, she would be restored to life. Their feelings were greatly excited, their impressions of their success peculiar and strong. They prayed *in faith*. But they were disappointed. There was none to answer, neither was there any that regarded. She slept the sleep of death; they were constrained to follow her to the grave.[1]

In opposition to such teaching, Spring laid down that true prayer is always submissive prayer: 'The prayer that God's will may be done, and not our own, is always answered.'

Many more instances of fanaticism could be given but all that I am concerned with here is to show that the frequency with which it recurs is a plain proof that it is a real and continuing danger. Ronald Knox, writing on the subject in 1950, supposed that the phenomenon had probably passed away.[2] He was wrong. Albert Dod of Princeton had a better understanding when he wrote in 1835, 'The elements of fanaticism exist in the breast of every community, and may be easily called into action by causes which we might be disposed to overlook as contemptible.'[3] Fanaticism

---

[1] *Personal Reminiscences of the Life and Times of Gardiner Spring,* vol. 1 (New York: Scribner, 1866), p. 229. When Edward Irving died in 1834, at the age of forty two, Dr Black of the Barony Church, Glasgow, who was at the funeral, 'said that when the mourners retired, they still left standing at his grave a number of young women clothed in white, who confidently expected he would rise again.' Their hopes were consistent with Irving's own teaching for if 'apostolic methods' belong to the church permanently why should some of the dead not be raised now? (A. L. Drummond, *Edward Irving and his Circle,* (London: James Clarke, n.d.), pp. 227–8.

[2] 'It is clear that our fellow countrymen are less susceptible, in these days, to the emotional appeal. Perhaps it is a closed chapter, this chapter in the history of religion.' R. A. Knox, *Enthusiasm: A Chapter in the History of Religion,* 1950 (repr. London: Collins, 1987), p. 578. The fact that Knox calls Wesley an 'enthusiast' (i.e., a fanatic) illustrates how cautiously these terms should be defined.

[3] *Princeton Essays,* p. 151.

is alive in our own day and it is those who are ignorant of its history who are most likely to repeat it.[1]

2. Fanaticism is dangerous because it often occurs where it might be least expected, namely, among earnest Christians.

Of course, there is much which can be called fanaticism which has nothing to do with Christianity and it can generally be easily recognised. It is not likely to deceive evangelical Christians. But the fanaticism which we are considering arises from within the church and is far less easily discerned. It may indeed operate in our own hearts without our ever suspecting it. There is a mixture of grace and fallen nature in all believers and it is a dangerous error to suppose that only non-Christians are susceptible to carnal zeal. There is no reason to think that men such as James Davenport and George Bell were not Christians; on the contrary, a number of the figures who have done most damage by wildfire and unbalanced zeal may well be considered to have been eminent Christians. Spirituality and fanatical zeal may coexist so closely to each other that there is no immediately obvious difference and so no danger is suspected. The best friends of revival may sometimes prove to be its worst enemies.

Fanaticism may appear as nothing more than an excess of what is good. Zeal is good. If we are true Christians we want more zeal; we are opposed to deadness, indifference and apathy. We deplore religious stagnation. We are shocked that we can be so cold and unmoved in a lost and unbelieving world. Conse-quently we are prone to regard anything as an ally which brings excitement and warmth into the situation. We are so convinced of the danger of coldness that we suppose any kind of fire is to be welcomed. So again we may suspect no danger until it is too late.

[1] Samuel Miller of Princeton, writing in 1832, said that the record of such 'mischievous disorders' as I have mentioned above, 'would be sufficient to instruct and warn the Church in all succeeding times. But unhappily, this is by no means found to be the case . . . One generation forgets the experience of that which preceded it. Few read the record of that experience, and fewer still are qualified to profit by it. The consequence is that every few years the same occurrences take place.' Appendix to Sprague, *Lectures on Revivals*, p. 25.

Once a revival has begun history shows that Christians are even less likely to be apprehensive of fanaticism. When they see all round them the evidence of the Holy Spirit's presence and power; when they witness many lives being wonderfully changed; when preaching is marked by the authority of heaven; it is easy to suppose that the Holy Spirit must be the author of everything which is happening in the churches. Too often in a time of awakening, or in writing about it afterwards, Christians have argued that any exercise of caution is unnecessary and grieving to the Spirit of God. They think that no criticism of any kind should be allowed. This is a serious mistake. In revivals, as at every other time, we are still fallen, fallible human beings, prone to faults and errors. Despite all the blessings of true revival, a time of revival is never a time of unmixed good.

In days of high excitement Christians can readily confuse their own strong feelings with the guidance of the Holy Spirit and this can lead to the entrance of practices or beliefs which, lacking the support of Scripture, may prove very damaging to the churches for years to come. Because some new practice was introduced in a time of revival blessing it by no means proves that it must be right.

W. B. Sprague has written well on this point in his *Lectures on Revivals of Religion*. From his own experience in the Second Great Awakening, he writes of those 'who speak of everything that may happen to be connected with a revival as the immediate effect of divine influence'. The Holy Spirit, he continues, 'may be familiarly spoken of as being present in particular scenes, and as prompting to particular actions, which he could not fail to disown . . . Brethren, we honour the Holy Spirit most, when we give him precisely the place which he claims; when we recognise him as the efficient author of conviction, conversion, and sanctification; but he is offended when we undertake to palm upon him what we ought to take with shame to ourselves.'[1]

[1] W. B. Sprague, *Lectures on Revivals of Religion* (1832, repr. London: Banner of Truth, 1959), pp. 111–2.

Opposing the argument that no criticism should be expressed in a time of revival, Sprague writes, 'you may be assured that the cause of revivals is far more likely to suffer by an attempt on the part of its friends to pass off everything for gold, than by giving to that which is really dross its proper name.' Good men, he affirms, are only sanctified in part and may fall into excesses, 'but nothing is more certain than that to tolerate evil in good men because they *are* good men, is directly contrary both to the spirit and letter of the gospel.'[1]

This can be illustrated in the life of Whitefield. Certainly no man was more greatly used of God at the time of the Great Awakening of 1740 – 'Whitefield of Everywhere', as Spurgeon called him. But even Whitefield was for a time misled by the error that if we have strong subjective impressions and impulses we can attribute them to the Holy Spirit. In 1740 Edwards warned his friend of the danger of that idea but three years were to pass before Whitefield discovered it for himself. He learned it in this way. In October 1743 Whitefield's only son was born. A text of Scripture, which 'came' powerfully to Whitefield at that time, was the promise given to Zacharias at the birth of John the Baptist (*Luke* 1:13–14). On that basis he called his own boy 'John' and 'fondly hoped' that he 'was to be great in the sight of the Lord'. When the baby died four months later Whitefield saw the force of Edwards' warning and, referring to the time of the Great Awakening, he was later to say: 'Many good souls, both among the clergy and laity, for a while, mistook fancy for faith, and imagination for revelation'.[2]

[1] Ibid., pp. 221–3.
[2] Whitefield, *Works*, vol. 2, p. 73. 'Steer a middle course between the two dangerous extremes many of this generation are in danger of running into; I mean, *enthusiasm*, on the one hand, and *deism*, and *downright infidelity*, on the other.' *Works*, vol. 5, p. 30. See also Owen, *Works*, vol. 3, p. 13; Edwards, *Works*, vol. 1, pp. 404–5, and my *Jonathan Edwards*, pp. 241–3. Edwards wrote: 'Many godly persons have undoubtedly, in this and other ages, exposed themselves to woeful delusions by an aptness to lay too much weight on impulses and impressions'.

If sincere and earnest Christians can err in this way it shows how exposed we all are to the same danger.

3. Fanaticism is dangerous because it gives occasion for the opponents of revival to dismiss evangelical Christianity and the work of the Holy Spirit as emotionalism.

A constant tendency towards wildfire is explainable, as we have said, in terms of the weakness of human nature. But this is not the whole explanation. If revivals are among the most glorious of God's works then it must be that Satan has a special interest in discrediting them. One of his principal ways of doing this is to drive Christians to extremes of excitement and unthinking emotion. In so doing he comes to Christians as 'an angel of light' while his purpose is to confuse the work of the Spirit with what is merely carnal enthusiasm. He well understands the truth that 'overdoing is undoing'. This is what the Puritans meant by saying that nothing is more dangerous for the chariot of the gospel than when Satan becomes the driver. The outcome will be that people become prejudiced against revivals, all emotion will become suspect, and the public at large can be turned against biblical Christianity. It has ever been the practice of all critics of revivals to seize on factors or incidents which display human weakness and to represent and magnify them so successfully that for years to come the churches become afraid of all emotion and spiritual power.[1]

There has been such a repeating pattern of this in church history that it is impossible to avoid the conclusion that the adverse outcome was the demonic intention. When foolish claims are made for the Holy Spirit, and when things are asserted to be the work of God which can easily be explained in psychological terms, an opportunity is given for true

[1] For examples of this method of writing on revivals see such books as Charles Chauncy's *Seasonable Thoughts on the State of Religion in New England* (Boston, 1743) and William Hamilton's *Inquiry into the Scriptural Character of the Revival of 1859* (1866, repr. Hudsonville, Michigan: Reformed Book Outlet, 1993). Such authors specialise in the negative.

Christianity to be dismissed.[1] Joseph Milner, the church historian, has demonstrated this in terms of the errorists of the second century who claimed special guidance from the Spirit and who 'gloried in their own supposed superior sanctity and happiness.' 'Delusions have ever been raised by Satan to disgrace the work of God.'[2]

Monsignor Ronald Knox, blind to this principle, used the phenomena of fanaticism to fuel an oblique criticism of the Reformation and Protestantism. 'In the long run,' he concluded in his work *Enthusiasm*, 'the issue is between some kind of authority and unrestrained private judgement.' So 'the Church' must provide the authority, and evangelicalism by what it had done to 'imperil' the unity of the Church, and by its insistence that the Bible is the only authority for Christians, brought about the situation in which 'enthusiasm was certain of a hearing'.[3]

[1] On this point Miller observes that when people see a genuine revival 'tarnished by extravagancies', they 'are apt hastily to conclude, that vital piety, and revivals of religion are all a dream. I fear that this fatal delusion is often adopted; and cannot but also fear that the disorders which often attend revivals frequently minister to it. But it *is* a delusion. The very existence of counterfeits, show that there is true coin.' Appendix to Sprague, p. 43.

[2] Joseph Milner, *The History of the Church of Christ*, vol. 1 (London, 1812), pp. 260–1, 444. Jonathan Edwards believed that 'the great Christian apostacy, that masterpiece of the devil's works' was brought on by 'the indiscreet zeal of Christians' whom he drove to 'those three extremes of *enthusiasm, superstition, and severity towards opposers*'. *Works*, vol. 1, pp. 397–8.

[3] Knox, *Enthusiasm*, pp. 5, 577. 'The evangelical (illogically, perhaps, but by habit) regards the Bible, not the inner light, as the ultimate source of theological certainty. But in so far as he is true to type, he will reject the interpretations offered to him by scholars . . . What dangerous results may flow from such an attitude we have considered already' (pp. 586–7). Knox, who became a Roman Catholic in 1917, had no excuse for his parody of evangelicals for his own father, E. A. Knox (1847–1937), Bishop of Manchester, was one and met the old charge that evangelicals 'attach no value to the Church' in his book, *The Tractarian Movement* (London: Putnam, 1933). Another evangelical turned Roman Catholic has argued more recently that 'we must see that we were meant to be one church united under one Head,' and that 'dynamic revival will not happen in a fragmented Christian community.' Keith A. Fournier, *Evangelical Catholics* (Nashville: Nelson, 1990), p. 65.

At the same time it should be noted in passing that even where there is no evidence of fanaticism, observers who are hostile to true Christianity are very capable of misrepresenting the work of the Holy Spirit. The spirit which led Festus to call Paul 'beside himself' and 'mad' has not disappeared. This means that where we depend upon non-Christians for information on a revival we should be very cautious lest we dismiss the genuine along with the false. A striking illustration of confusing information on revival occurs in the case of the work of W. C. Burns in Aberdeen, Scotland, in 1840. If one were dependent on the reports of the secular newspapers alone a very adverse impression of Burns' preaching would be gained. But there are also the eyewitness accounts of Christians and these present a different picture.[1] The disagreement between newspaper reporters and Christian believers was almost total. Worldly men are always incapable of recognising the presence of the Holy Spirit – 'whom the world cannot receive, because it neither sees Him nor knows Him' (*John* 14:17). So it should be no surprise that unbelievers thought the apostles were 'drunk' at Pentecost and that the true work of the Spirit can be condemned. This fact does not, however, lessen the responsibility of churches to avoid everything which would provide just grounds for criticism.

Recognition of Fanaticism

If this danger is as subtle and deceptive as the evidence suggests then it is of paramount importance that Christians should be aware of its most common features. In this respect we are helped by the fact that although fanaticism has appeared in different countries, in different cultures and at different times, its features are remarkably similar. As Samuel Miller wrote in 1832: 'There is a *striking similarity* in the

[1] *Evidence on the Subject of the Revivals, Taken Before a Committee of the Presbytery of Aberdeen* (Aberdeen: Gray and Davidson, 1841).

disorders which have attended and marred revivals of religion in all ages.'[1] These similarities may be listed as follows:

1. *Fanaticism commonly gains its strength among young, immature, and enthusiastic Christians.*

Older Christians may fall into many grievous sins but generally this is not the sin with which they are most tempted. It is fervent young converts who are most likely to be misled and in a time of awakening, when the young are often added to the churches in great numbers, the danger is all the greater. Testimony on this subject is uniform. Richard Baxter, writing of the upheaval among the churches in London in the early 1640s, attributes a good deal of the difficulties to those who stirred up 'the younger and more inexperienced sort of religious people, to speak too vehemently and intemperately . . . for the young and raw sort of Christians are usually prone to this kind of sin; to be self-conceited, petulant, wilful, censorious and injudicious in all their management of their differences in religion and in all their attempts at reformation.'[2]

William Williams, a leader in the Welsh revivals of the eighteenth century, complained of the 'raw youth whom no one would entrust to shepherd his sheep, who is today riding high in a boldness much superior to old ministers who have borne the burden and heat of the day.'[3] Samuel Miller, who lived at the

---

[1] Appendix to Sprague *Lectures* (repr. 1959), p. 42.

[2] *Reliquiae Baxterianae, Richard Baxter's Life and Times*, ed. Matthew Sylvester (London, 1696), p. 26.

[3] Quoted by Emyr Roberts in *Revival and Its Fruit* (Bridgend: Evangelical Library of Wales, 1981), p. 10. The same author tells of an observation once made to a Welsh minister that the older Christians and preachers were not 'rejoicing in a revival' because they were not displaying the same physical forms of excitement as the young, such as jumping for joy. The wise minister agreed but responded in terms that would not be lost on a farming community: 'It is not the old sheep that are to be seen prancing and jumping, but the lambs. Yet the old sheep has its eye ever on the lamb, although she be grazing; and it is very good for that lamb by nightfall that the sheep was grazing to enable her then to give him some milk.' 'For ignorant young converts to take upon them authoritatively to instruct and exhort publicly, tends to introduce the greatest error and the grossest anarchy' (Gilbert Tennent to Jonathan Edwards, in Edwards' *Works*, vol. 1, p. lxi).

time of the disorders which marked the final years of the Second
Great Awakening in parts of America, wrote of 'the remarkable
fact that in all ages *young, and, of course, inexperienced ministers,* have
commonly taken a lead, and discovered the most headstrong
obstinacy in commencing and pursuing measures of an
innovating character . . . claiming to have a gift, unknown to
others, of promoting genuine revivals.'[1]

The introduction of fanaticism into revivals becomes almost
a certainty when young people are hurried into public
positions contrary to the apostolic injunction, 'Not a novice,
lest being puffed up with pride he fall into the same
condemnation as the devil' (*1 Tim.* 3:6). Few wrong ideas in
the churches today are in greater need of correction than the
belief that we must hold on to our young people by paying
special attention to their wishes and by giving them positions
of leadership. It is for sound reasons that no youth cult can be
found advocated in Scripture.

2. *Fanaticism commonly concentrates interest upon phenomena and
experiences, and treats feeling and excitement as possessing primary
importance.*

I do not mean that fanaticism necessarily does this deliber-
ately. Those who have fallen into this usually deny it
completely and say that their only interest is in 'seeing the
Holy Spirit at work'. They will probably claim that they are
only rejoicing in the supernatural. But the testing question is
this, Is their interest truly God-centred and Bible-centred? Or
has subjective feeling taken control? Is their excitement taken
up with physical phenomena?

It is very possible for a large crowd of people to be swayed by a
common emotion, perhaps by laughter or by distress. It is
possible for people to jump for joy or to be overcome to the point
of fainting. Yet these things *in themselves* provide no proof that the
Holy Spirit is the author of what is happening. It is recorded, for
example, that a woman was seen weeping at the edge of a vast

[1] Appendix to Sprague *Lectures* (repr. 1959), p. 42.

multitude who were listening to Whitefield preaching. She was actually too far away from the speaker to hear anything that was being said. Her tears were simply the natural result of sympathy produced by the sight of the emotion of others.

The recognition of this fact does not mean that we should be suspicious of all joy or of all spiritual distress. But it means we cannot judge anything simply by immediate appearances. We have to look at the context in which such things occur before we can assess the probable cause. The question is, Was it the truth of the word of God, coming with power to the mind, which produced these effects? In all revivals, as at Pentecost, it is the truth arresting the *minds* of men and women which produces an external change. The fear and distress and joy are all rational. The gospel gripped the understandings of those who heard. It is not so with fanaticism. Fanaticism usually puts no stress upon clear, biblical teaching. It largely by-passes the mind, and by means of music, excitement, and the personal magnetism of individuals, it puts pressure directly on the emotions and the wills of hearers. In this way responses of various kinds can be induced and these are then confidently proclaimed to be the work of the Holy Spirit.

Physical responses, however emotional, are never the important thing. They may or they may not have any lasting spiritual significance. As James Robe wrote, 'Bodily agitations considered in themselves are no symptoms of persons being under the influence either of a good or bad spirit.'[1] Those who ignore this fact are most likely to promote or to be swayed by fanaticism. In its most recent form this has been seen in the practice of those who suppose that the laying on of hands, with prayer, when resulting in a falling to the ground, is a sure sign of God's work. Spokesmen for this practice appeal to Jonathan Edwards and to the appearance of such phenomena at the time of the Great Awakening. But they ignore how Edwards stresses what we have just said above. If a congregation is outwardly affected by distress or joy so that there are 'outcries, faintings

---

[1] Robe, *Narratives of the Extraordinary Work*, p. 53.

and other bodily effects', these things were, for Edwards, probable but *not certain* 'tokens of God's presence'. What he looked for was evidence that such feeling followed the preaching of 'the important truths of God's word, urged and enforced by proper arguments and motives'.[1] Referring to this same safeguard, and the danger of it not being recognised, Dr Lloyd-Jones has said:

I have known evil-living men to find false comfort, to their own damnation, in the fact that they could still weep and be moved emotionally at a religious meeting. 'I cannot be all bad or else I would not respond like this', they have argued. But it is a false deduction – their emotional response was produced by themselves. Had it been a response to the truth their lives would have been changed.[2]

No one could accuse John Wesley of being against emotion. But he was equally opposed to what we are now discussing and spoke of it in these terms:

I dislike something that has the appearance of enthusiasm, over-valuing feelings and inward impressions: mistaking the mere work of imagination for the voice of the Spirit; expecting the end without the means; and undervaluing reason, knowledge, and wisdom in general.[3]

3. *Fanaticism generally reveals itself by a spirit of pride.*
Again this may not be immediately apparent but fanaticism invariably induces spiritual pride. It did so in the church at Corinth, a church taken up with its supposed attainments and forgetful that the whole purpose of God in redeeming sinners

[1] 'Thoughts on the Revival of Religion in New England', Part 3, iv, in Edwards, *Works*, vol. 1, p. 394. For an example of what I am criticising see Guy Chevreau, *Catch the Fire: The Toronto Blessing – an experience of renewal and revival* (London: Marshall Pickering, 1994). Chevreau acknowledges Edwards' principle that physical actions of themselves can never provide proof of the power of the Holy Spirit, and yet his book is constructed very largely *around* physical phenomena.
[2] 'Mind, Heart and Will', a sermon on Romans 6:17 in *Spiritual Depression: Its Causes and Cure* (London: Pickering and Inglis, 1965), p. 62.
[3] *Letters*, vol. 4, p. 193.

is 'that no flesh should glory in his presence'. A humble and loving character is more precious in the sight of God than the possession of the greatest gifts.

Fanaticism unconsciously leads people to self-importance. This may take many forms. Edwards noted how ready trouble-makers in the churches at the time of the Great Awakening were to speak about themselves and give their testimonies. Gardiner Spring says that the truer the work of God the less inclined will people be to draw attention to themselves and to give publicity to themselves. He draws this contrast between a convert who is under the influence of fanaticism and one who is not: the former has a spirit which seeks 'observation and wishes to be seen, that obtrudes itself on the notice of others, that talks of its own experience and attainments, that is bold and assuming, that wishes to be put forward, and that unblushingly exclaims with Jehu, "Come, see my zeal for the Lord!".' How different, he goes on, 'the spirit of the modest, retiring young convert, who esteems others better than himself, who looks on Him whom he has pierced, and mourns, and who goes to the communion of saints conscious that he is not worthy of the crumbs that fall from the Master's table.'[1]

The same self-confidence and pride is generally also revealed by an attitude of superiority towards other Christians. Fanatics suppose they are well equipped to instruct and correct others while they are unteachable themselves. Far from having any respect for the wisdom of the churches accumulated through centuries in creeds, confessions of faith and Christian literature in general, they have arrived at a position where they have little need of what they call 'book learning'. Such learning may even be denounced as 'dead orthodoxy'. Who needs books when they have the Holy Spirit![2]

[1] Spring, *Reminiscences*, vol. 1, p. 218. 'Some say that they live very near to Jesus. It is an evil sign when men speak of their own attainments.' C. H. Spurgeon, *Metropolitan Tabernacle Pulpit*, 1888, p. 623.

[2] 'It seems odd, that certain men who talk so much about what the Holy Spirit reveals to themselves, should think so little of what he has revealed to others.' C. H. Spurgeon, *Commenting and Commentaries* (repr. London: Banner of Truth, 1969), p. 1.

The office of the Christian minister and pastor, even when occupied by faithful men, has repeatedly come under attack and denunciation from people of this spirit. This has happened repeatedly in the last three centuries. Fanatics are generally unwilling to recognise any leaders beyond themselves. John Wesley gives us a typical instance of this when he tried to correct the Society in which George Bell was involved and which were now enjoying visions and revelations. He writes:

Enthusiasm, pride, and great uncharitableness appeared in many who once had much grace. I very tenderly reproved them. They would not bear it; one of them, Mrs Coventry, cried out, 'We will not be brow-beaten any longer.' . . . Accordingly, a few days after, she came, and before an hundred persons brought me hers and her husband's tickets, and said, 'Sir, we will have no more to do with you; Mr Maxfield is our teacher'. Soon after, several more left the Society, saying, 'Blind John is not capable of teaching us'.[1]

The reference to visions and revelations points to the way in which unsuspected pride can lead Christians to suppose that they have advanced beyond the ordinary means of grace. Novelties, new understandings, innovations and practices previously unknown in the churches, are all defended as having God's sure approval. 'Immediate inspiration' is supposed to be a much more exciting thing than the mere text of Scripture. Commenting on this spirit as he saw it in the 1740s, Edwards asks:

Why cannot we be contented with the divine oracles, that holy, pure word of God, which we have in such abundance and clearness now since the canon of Scripture is completed? Why should we desire to have anything added? And why should we desire to make Scripture speak more to us than it does? Or why should any desire a higher kind of intercourse with heaven than by having the Holy Spirit given in his sanctifying influences, infusing and exciting grace and holiness, love and joy, which is the highest kind of intercourse which saints and angels in heaven have with God?[2]

Too often the answer to such questions has to do with undiscerned spiritual pride. Edwards names pride as 'the

[1] *Letters*, vol. 4, p. 210.
[2] Edwards, *Works*, vol. 1, p. 404.

main door by which the devil comes into the hearts of those who are zealous for the advancement of religion'.[1]

Consequences of Fanaticism

1. *Fanaticism produces controversy and divisions among Christians.*
The effect of genuine revival is to provoke opposition from the self-satisfied and the unbelieving, nominal Christian. But worse disruption is caused if the devil can distract true Christians into opposing one another and fanaticism is a fertile means of bringing this about. When emotionalism and wrong zeal are being identified with true Christianity it is necessary for discerning leaders to sound a warning against the danger. This will lead the promoters of excesses to defend themselves and their actions. The result will be that instead of a revival going forward, a spirit of strife and debate gains entrance and spreads among the churches. This happened in the two great revival periods in America: it entered into the Great Awakening and it was marked in the closing years of the Second Great Awakening. At the latter date, Asahel Nettleton, along with others, believed that the so-called 'new measures' introduced by Finney and others were the product of a wrong zeal which had to be withstood. But he mourned how the resulting controversy switched attention from evangelism to controversy and wrote in a letter of 1827:

As we now have it, the great contest is among professors of religion – a civil war in Zion – a domestic broil in the household of faith. The friends of brother Finney are certainly doing him and the cause of Christ great harm. They seem more anxious to convert ministers and Christians to their peculiarities, than to convert souls to Christ.[2]

[1] Ibid., pp. 398–9. Edwards puts spiritual pride first in dealing with things which are to be corrected or avoided in a time of revival – this is one of the most important of all his valuable observations.

[2] Tyler and Bonar, *Nettleton and His Labours*, p. 344. One feature which proved the judgment that Finney was fanatical was his constant criticism of the evangelical ministry: 'For *many centuries* but little of the real gospel has been preached.' 'The truth is, that very little of the gospel has come out upon the world, *for these hundreds of years*, without being clogged and obscured by false theology' etc. Uncharitableness towards others is ever a mark of the fanatic.

2. *Fanaticism gives opportunity for large numbers of unconverted people to enter the churches.*

If true Christians can fall into the errors of fanaticism, how much more those who have no saving beliefs. When the unconverted are brought under the preaching of the gospel, let alone into situations of mass excitement where dramatic claims are being made, they are perfectly capable of experiencing religious feelings. If such persons are then told of a public action they must take to become a Christian they may well respond and probably be classed as 'converts'. Sir David Frost, one of the best-known sceptics of our times, once made a 'decision' at an evangelistic crusade. Or if sensational 'blessings' are presented as immediately available there are bound to be results. There are plenty of dissatisfied men and women in the world who, like King Herod, would like to see a miracle (*Luke* 23:8). Such people will readily flock to meetings which promise the unusual. Examples of this kind of thing are all too numerous.

In England in 1995 an Anglican clergyman by the name of the Rev. Chris Brain filled a Leisure Centre in Sheffield with a new presentation of what claimed to be the gospel. All the effects of a 'rave' concert were there – special lighting, dry ice, video screens, plus voices 'in the air' chanting 'God is here' – along with such supposedly evangelical practices as the laying-on of hands. But the extraordinary thing, noted in an article in *The Times,* was the kind of people ready to support Brain's meetings. Under a heading, 'How could people fall for such hokum?' Libby Purves wrote:

The great and comic disgrace is that people with an ancient religious culture should fall for such hokum. Solid, middle-aged suburbanites jived for Jesus below the Dali videos and occult symbols; lawyers and council workers wept when the soupy Irish harps kicked in at communion time, and some left their jobs to help the Rev. Barnum – sorry, Brain – to organise his loony raves.[1]

This may be an extreme example but the lesson is the same.

[1] *The Times,* 24 August 1995.

When means and methods other than the presentation of the truth are used to 'win' people to 'the gospel' it is certain that churches, for a time at least, can be filled with devotees of a worldly and non-life- changing Christianity. The excitement such people feel is not simply valueless, it is positively damaging to them. For they may either accept what they are given as genuine Christianity or, more probably, they will ultimately throw it all aside and think that they have proved evangelicalism is nothing but a fake.[1]

Wales: 1904–5

Many of the things we have been considering can be gathered together in a brief survey of the negative side of the last major revival which occurred in Britain: the Welsh revival of 1904–5. I emphasise that I am here concerned with the negative side. That great good was done to thousands at that date is not in doubt, and the words of many eye-witnesses remain as an abiding record of what happened across the land. The Rev. H. Elvet Lewis, for example, in a book which summarised what had happened, believed that the revival had reshaped 'the entire history of Wales . . . As long as the nation remains, there are trees of this river's blessing in 1904–5, "whose leaf shall not fade, neither shall the fruit thereof be consumed".'[2] While his assessment was probably over-coloured by his nearness to the event, those with close experience of the subsequent scene in the Welsh churches have commented on how much faster the religious decline would have been without 'the children of the revival' (as the converts were

[1] An article, 'Ecstasy in the churchyard,' *The Guardian*, 28 November 1995, argued with some justification that the Brain meetings were not simply a freak occurrence, rather, an emotion-based, anti-intellectual faith was now 'new and widespread'. 'I suspect', the author wrote, 'a Holy Spirit which chooses such obviously consumerist forms of self-religiosity . . . New evangelicalism offers religion as a product that will give you the happiness buzz. But is getting high a good enough reason to entrust ourselves and our moral decisions to those who orchestrate it?'
[2] H. Elvet Lewis, *Christ Among the Miners*, p. 6.

commonly called). It was they who did most to maintain prayer and devotion to Christ in Wales through the first half of the twentieth century.

Were it not that books are currently available which give the positive side of the last Welsh revival it would be misleading to direct attention to the negative. Several such books are, however, currently in print.[1] Little is said in these titles on 'the very unfortunate aspects' of the work,[2] and it is arguable that the omission leaves evangelicals less prepared to face the recurrent dangers. As already noted, the existence of excess and even a measure of fanaticism is common enough in revivals. What proved tragic in Wales was that it was the best-known figure in the revival who was chiefly responsible for what went wrong, and so closely was he identified with the excess in the public mind that no one could be critical of him without seeming to be an opponent of the work of God.

How far the twenty-six-year-old Evan Roberts *ought* to have been the best-known figure it is now impossible to tell. A case can certainly be made out for believing that it was the daily press which presented him in that role to the nation. From November 1904 Welsh newspapers canonised Roberts as 'the revivalist'. The *Western Mail* of Cardiff was certain that the work began with Roberts at Moriah Chapel, Loughor, and took the credit for being the first to announce it on 10 November 1904. In reality, the revival began in places where Roberts had no influence and at least two months before that date. A recent writer has estimated that of those converted throughout the revival period, 'Evan Roberts and all his

[1] See Eifion Evans, *The Welsh Revival of 1904* (Port Talbot: Evangelical Movement of Wales, 1969); Brynmor P. Jones, *Voices from the Welsh Revival : An Anthology of Testimonies, Reports, and Eyewitness Statements from Wales's Year of Blessing, 1904–1905* (Bridgend: Evangelical Press of Wales, 1995); H. Elvet Lewis, G. Campbell Morgan, I. V. Neprash, *Glory Filled the Land, A Trilogy on the Welsh Revival of 1904–1905* (Wheaton, Illinois: International Awakening Press, 1995).
[2] The phrase is that of the Rev. Nantlais Williams, quoted by Jones, *Voices*, p. 272.

associates could not have been present in more than 10%' of cases.[1] No such impression could have been gained from the press of that time. A comparative youth, and scarcely two months into studies as a candidate for the Calvinistic Methodist ministry, Evan Roberts provided more dramatic copy for the press than regular ministers of the churches. In October 1904 he was an unknown student; by December of the same year he was 'in the wide world's view'.

Press interest was heightened by the unusual claims attending Roberts' meetings. Any thought of his lack of training and preparation was overshadowed by his insistence that everything in his meetings must be under the direct control of the Spirit, 'No one is to lead except the Holy Spirit'.[2] God's supervision, he assured the people, included the very words he used in prayer:

On Sunday evening he gave the crowded audience a prayer to repeat: 'Send the Spirit now for Jesu's sake.' 'I had put in three more words,' he explained, 'but the Spirit rejected them. The first form I offered was – "O Lord, send the Holy Spirit now for Jesus' sake. Amen." But I was forced to leave out "Lord", "Holy", "Amen". The Spirit will have no idle words.'[3]

It was also the Spirit's leading, Roberts believed, which accounted for his messages being short and few compared with time given to song, prayer and exhortations. Questioned on this, he would reply: 'Why should I teach when the Spirit is teaching?'[4] He embraced the conviction that God was by-passing the regular teaching ministry without any idea that fanatics had often claimed the same thing before. It was an American 'revivalist' of the nineteenth century who once said, 'God is going to save the masses in his own way. He has told the ministers to stand on one side and let him have a turn.'[5]

---

[1] B. P. Jones, *Voices*, p. 66.
[2] B. P. Jones, *An Instrument of the Spirit: The Complete Life of Evan Roberts (1878–1951)* (South Plainfield, N.J.: Bridge Publishing, 1995), p. 58.
[3] Lewis, *Christ Among the Miners*, pp. 70–1.
[4] Jones, *Life of Roberts*, p. 49.
[5] B. P. Jones, *King's Champions* (Redhill, Surrey: Love and Malcomson, Printers, 1968), p. 55.

Many others now took up the same cry and letters by the 'prophets' soon appeared in the press containing such assertions as the following: 'Preaching has failed as a saving agency for a long time . . . God is now going to save sinners for a while without the pulpit.'[1]

As a result of this popular idea, Elvet Lewis could report, 'Sunday after Sunday, ministers appeared, not in their pulpit, but in the midst of an officiating people, silent, or taking part as one of the others.'[2] Later commentators on the revival have criticised the ministers for accepting this procedure but it has to be said that often they were virtually forced to do so. There were many instances of ministers being interrupted and 'drowned out' by singing or praying as they attempted to speak.[3] Such interruptions were commonly encouraged by Roberts who would tell the people, 'If God calls on you to give out a hymn, or to pray, or to give a testimony, do it.'[4] The exhortation could be innocent enough but once the idea took hold that the revival meetings were under the direct control of the Holy Spirit, then an excited congregation could scarcely be stopped if speaking, singing and praying went on simultaneously. All the participants, it was assumed, were being 'prompted' by God. Thus when some, disturbed by such noise in a service, cried, 'Hush!' Roberts directed: 'No, friends, please don't hush. Go on, God can hear all.'[5] It was in line with this kind of belief in 'Spirit-led' informality that Roberts appears to have made no preparation for services apart from prayer. Only twice had he been disappointed in meetings, he told a Liverpool audience (*Western Mail*, 10 April 1905), 'and those were occasions on which he had planned what he thought ought to

---

[1] *Western Mail*, 2 December 1904, quoted by Jones, *King's Champions*, p. 55.
[2] Lewis, *Christ Among the Miners*, p. 98.
[3] E.g. at Liverpool, 6 April 1905, as reported in *Western Mail*; B. P. Jones, *Voices*, pp. 171, 261. On 15 April 1905, the *Western Mail* reported how Roberts, when himself interrupted by a woman singing, 'gave way with a good-natured laugh'.
[4] Jones, *Voices*, p. 201.
[5] *Western Mail* reporting meeting at Nantymoel, 9 February 1905.

take place.' If some found all this disturbing, the press gives the impression that the majority found such departures from the traditional very welcome: 'The setting aside of formal worship and of the usual preaching modes was the sign that a new age had dawned.'[1]

At first Roberts' unpredictable behaviour drew no public criticism and the supportive press coverage given to his remarkable claims of divine guidance hardly left room for any questioning. 'No one,' it was said, 'is sure where the revivalist will appear because he will only go where the Spirit prompts him.'[2] He withdrew from meetings in Cardiff at God's command; he undertook no meetings and spoke to no one for a week because, as he wrote to a reporter, 'I am forbidden'. During that time in February 1905 he heard God who 'spoke plainly in English and Welsh. It was not an impression, but a voice.' What he 'heard' was fully passed on to the press. On one day, for instance, he recorded this occurrence at 6.25 p.m.:

A Voice: 'The faith of the people is being proved as much as thine own. Did not I sustain thee during four months on the pinnacle, in the sight of the whole world? If I sustained thee in public, is my power less to sustain thee in private? If I sustained thee during four months, can I not sustain thee for seven days?'[3]

In the early months of 1905 this kind of direct guidance from heaven became a very regular part of Roberts' meetings. Sometimes, although in the pulpit, he could not speak at all until the meeting was 'clear', that is to say, until some obstacle to the work of the Spirit was dealt with. For knowledge of that obstacle, and how it was to be dealt with, Roberts alone had the prophetic insight. Frequently the responsibility lay with individuals, occasionally ministers, whom he might identify. Similarly he might suddenly stop individuals in the act of praying or singing, assuring them in doing so that he was obeying the Holy Spirit. 'I know,' he

[1] Jones, *Life of Roberts*, p. 57.
[2] Ibid., p. 56.
[3] Reported by *Western Mail* under the date 2 March 1905.

would say, 'when anyone gets up unmoved by the Spirit.'[1] At times he would make individuals stand while he would question them; and other times he would demand public confession of sins.[2] On one occasion, it is alleged, he recognised '300 hypocrites'. Individuals about to be con- verted he could often detect beforehand and he might announce to the meeting, 'Someone wants to surrender now'. 'People were excited and awe-struck and asked, "How is it possible that each time he makes a prediction, someone is there waiting to yield?" '[3]

On one occasion Roberts wept as he told a congregation at Cwmavon, 'There is a soul lost,' and that it had happened in that very meeting due to disobedience to the promptings of the Holy Spirit. As he repeatedly cried, 'Too late,' he 'explained that he was being prohibited from praying for the soul that was lost'. This, he said, 'was the most terrible message he had ever had to deliver.'[4] An event two months later in a meeting in a Welsh Free Church in Liverpool was scarcely less extraordin- ary. Before this service on 11 April 1905 Roberts knew 'that something awful was going to take place.' After receiving an invitation to speak in one of the churches belonging to this 2,000 strong denomination, he had asked God, 'Is Jesus there?' The answer, as he now told the congregation, 'left him almost too weak to walk in from the vestry . . . It is difficult to obey God always but I must do it . . . The foundations of the Church are not on the rock. That's the message.' The *Western Mail* reported: 'The evangelist's declaration in regard to the Free Church of the Welsh produced a great sensation in the City.' A crisis was at hand in what had been a three weeks' mission in Liverpool and it came just two days later. At a

---

[1] At one Liverpool meeting where Roberts declared, 'The place is not clear,' the *Western Mail* (11 April 1905) reported the following sequence: 'Someone started a prayer, "If there be something weighing on this —" Evan Roberts: "Don't say 'if,' friends; don't say 'if'." Thereupon he sat down moaning loudly and crying, "O Lord, bend them." '

[2] Jones, *Life of Roberts*, p. 100.

[3] Ibid., p. 82.

[4] *Western Mail* report from Cwmavon, 21 February 1905.

service composed entirely of 1,200 men in Chatham Street
Calvinistic Methodist Chapel it seemed that nothing could
'clear' the meeting as Roberts sat silent in the pulpit for two
hours. At 9 p.m. a minister prayed for him that his lips should
'be opened in order that he might deliver a message whatever
it might be.' But another minister rose in a front pew and,
addressing Roberts, asked, 'Why dost thou play and trifle with
sacred things like this?' His further words were drowned out as
the congregation began a hymn. An hour later the meeting
was dismissed in 'a disgraceful scene of hubbub and excitement' and, for the first time, support for Roberts wavered in
the *Western Mail*: 'The strange proceedings were the subject of
general discussion in the street, the general verdict being that
both Evan Roberts and his opponents were such strange
people that it was impossible to understand them or their
methods.'[1]

The next day saw the final mission meeting in Liverpool.
Early in the proceedings, one of Roberts' friends, acting as
chairman, read a medical certificate which had been signed
that day by four doctors. It stated concerning Mr Evan
Roberts, 'We find him mentally and physically quite sound.
He is suffering from the effects of overwork, and we consider
it advisable that he should have a period of rest.' Rest and
further spasmodic meetings in Wales were to follow until his
last mission in the summer of 1906, but something had
happened to Roberts from which he was not to recover fully.
Doctors ultimately advised him never to preach again and
from 1906 until his death, forty-five years later, he passed
into shadows as obscure as his previous fame had been
bright.

There is no reason to doubt that Evan Roberts was a sincere
Christian who came to be borne along by currents beyond his
control or understanding. The press had created expectations
of him which were unsustainable. Brynmor Jones complains
that the 'English press' made the unusual in Evan Roberts'

[1] Ibid., under Liverpool, 14 April 1905.

meetings 'so sensational that people flocked to more of the same'.[1] But it was the Welsh press which did more to turn Roberts into becoming, as the Rev. Ioan Williams feared, 'a public idol'. The fundamental problem, however, was a spiritual one and it lay in the assumption that God was giving powers – especially prophetic ones – which were visible proofs of his presence and work. Roberts believed this so intensely that when the possibility arose that his condition was caused by emotional overload rather than by the Holy Spirit, a nervous breakdown was almost inevitable. It was not that he had 'tricked' others, he had himself been misled.[2]

When Elvet Lewis wrote kindly of the Welsh revival in his book of 1906, he wished, he said, to pass over 'mistakes and delusions'. The faults, he admitted, were 'grievous' but understandably he did not want the reality of the revival to be dismissed on their account and he drew attention to services where there was no excess or disorder but a 'unison of awe, and affection, and tender sorrow'[3]. Yet the sad fact is that if only there had been more knowledge in 1904 of the delusions of earlier times there might not have been the repetition of their occurrence and the results would have been far purer. Instead almost every possible feature of fanaticism was seen again: the supposition of immediate guidance, the claims to supernatural knowledge, the 'prayer of faith', the allowance

---

[1] *Life of Roberts*, p. 83. It is tempting to believe that if Roberts had possessed the counsel of trusted ministers or older Christians at the beginning he might have been kept from many mistakes but he does not seem to have been amenable to guidance: 'They wish to direct me . . . I shall never submit. The only director is the Holy Spirit . . . They want to preside, but God is a far better leader' (Ibid., p. 40).

[2] Elvet Lewis partially defends Roberts in terms of his 'undoubted gift of secondsight,' while conceding that he sometimes erred in 'his own direct spiritual promptings,' and that this led to 'some most unhappy incidents'. *Christ Among the Miners*, pp. 80, 148–51. Dr Lloyd-Jones, who at a later date had occasion to treat Roberts medically, believed that Roberts crossed the line from the spiritual to the psychic and that it was this which led to the breakdown from which he never recovered (Address at 1970 Ministers' Conference of the Evangelical Movement of Wales).

[3] Lewis, *Christ Among the Miners*, pp. 165, 106.

given to women to lead services, and not least, the practice of identifying 'converts' the instant they made a public 'decision'[1] – all these things, and more, had their origins long before they were seen again in Wales at the beginning of the twentieth century.

In 1904–5 the practice of giving leadership to the young and the pushing forward of new converts was adopted with an enthusiasm blind to the fact that the experiment was by no means new. Referring to new and young converts, Vyrnwy Morgan wrote, 'The pulpit was thrown open to them and their presence constituted in the minds of many the high-water mark of the Revival.'[2] The same writer records how a Cwmavon minister 'who had not been allowed to preach for several Sundays approached a group of young men between the ages of sixteen and twenty-three: "Am I," asked he, "to preach to-night?" The answer he received was this: "It depends upon what the Spirit will tell *us*." '[3] Some there were who complained at such a state of things but they had little hearing. A correspondent in the *Llanelly Mercury* (26 January 1905) wrote:

In the present revival, the Bible is ignored, and it is claimed that visions and new revelations are received . . . In the Book of Acts it is said that Paul ordained elders in every church . . . It is clear to all who wish to see that it was the elders who were to rule in

[1] Conversion statistics were instantly published. By February 1905 the *Western Mail* recorded 83,936 (76,566 for South Wales and 7,370 for the North) but the manner in which the figures were gathered scarcely increases confidence. One man 'under the influence of drink' declared himself a convert and was counted in (in Liverpool, 9 April 1905, according to *Western Mail*). B. P. Jones, a writer sympathetic to the revival, believes that 'many of the "converts" quickly relapsed – leaving only a remnant of really born-again people'. *King's Champions*, p. 59. See also p. 79.
[2] J. V. Morgan, *The Welsh Religious Revival, 1904–5, A Retrospect and a Criticism* (London: Chapman & Hall, 1909), p. 140. (Morgan's work is flawed by his liberal theology but he believed in revival and we know no evidence that his factual information is untrustworthy.) Writing in 1906, Lewis said: 'With tact and patience must the converts be told to take their places among the rest of the household; they must give up being wonders, and become ordinary and wise.' *With Christ Among the Miners*, p. 183.
[3] Morgan, *Welsh Religious Revival*, p. 42. Italics added.

the churches . . . In the present revival, the elders are condemned as heretics if they do not yield, and conform to the
methods of the young. The officers of the churches are at present
ignored.[1]

Features of this kind were so similar to what had been seen in
Kentucky a hundred years earlier that it is hard to believe that
the following words were written more than half a century
before 1904:

When some of the elder brethren were inquired of about the
expediency and propriety of correcting some extravagancies
which appeared wild and visionary, their reply was, in substance,
that they knew these things were not right; but should they
interfere by attempting to rectify them at that time, it might
interrupt, if not stop, the revival altogether. Here the ministry,
however good the intention, was much at fault. The surrendering
up the control and management of the religious exercises into the
hands of novices, or such as were unskilful and inexperienced,
was the very inlet or gateway to those errors and extravagancies
that soon followed. There was, if we mistake not, one general,
prevailing, prominent feature attending this revival everywhere; it
was the strange, mistaken disposition, in a very large portion of
the people, to undervalue the public means of religion, and, in the
place thereof, to promote a kind of tumultuous exercise, in which
themselves could take an active part, if not become the principal
leaders.[2]

Because the danger of fanaticism was so little understood in
1904, not a few of the things which had actually marred the
Welsh revival were held up for admiration as though they
were crucial to it. To quote Elvet Lewis again, 'The worst part
of the abuse was that it led the ignorant and the shallow to

[1] Quoted by Jones, *Voices*, p. 262. In a predictable response a correspondent of the following week treated the complaint as proof of the absence of
sympathy with revival.
[2] 'The Bodily Effects of Religious Excitement', *Theological Essays: Reprinted
from the Princeton Review* (New York: Wiley and Putnam, 1846), p. 511. The
author's conclusions include the following: 'In revivals of religion, badly
regulated, there may be much extravagance, and yet the work in the main
may be genuine. The wise will discriminate and not approve or condemn in
the lump . . . Pious men and women are imperfect in knowledge and often
form erroneous opinions which lead them to stray.'

mistake passing forms of revival for the abiding reality.'[1] For this reason it would have been well for others if more attention had been given by writers on the subject to what was wrong. A few years after the revival Evan Roberts came to see that 'the bold claims he had made in the past, were enough proof that he had been deceived. From now on he would distrust mystical experiences, and would claim that such things as tongues and prophesyings and visions were not safe until believers had far greater wisdom and experience'.[2] So Brynmor Jones, his sympathetic biographer, tells us in 1995, but this should have been revealed at the time and not ninety years later. Instead, across the English-speaking world evangelicals attempted to reproduce a 'Welsh revival'. Uncritical praise of the revival was spread through many lands and even in China its aberrations were introduced as great claims were made that the public confession of sin would secure the Spirit's power.[3]

I must repeat, in concluding this illustration of fanaticism, that there is much more about the revival of 1904–5 to be read for a balanced picture. It would also appear to be true that there are important aspects, unmentioned here, which do not appear to have been discussed in print, most notably the extent to which the ministry of the Calvinistic Methodist Church – the largest Welsh denomination involved in the revival – was influenced by a theological liberalism which made it basically unsympathetic. Opposition from the ministry has been claimed by some as the chief means by which the revival was arrested and undermined. Others saw the sensationalism and excess as the more influential cause of setback. Vyrnwy Morgan wrote: 'The people craved for

[1] *Christ Among the Miners*, p. 98.
[2] Jones, *Life of Roberts*, p. 173. In the light of these words it is surprising that Jones criticises the advice given to Roberts during the revival: 'If Mr Roberts controlled his emotions to a greater extent than he does at present, and if he endeavoured to know their working reasons more accurately, he would not attribute so many things to the Holy Spirit' (Ibid., p. 101).
[3] See Jonathan Goforth, *By My Spirit*, p. 24: 'Of great inspiration to me were the reports of the Welsh Revival of 1904 and 1905'.

sensationalism, and they had it . . . But the feature was repellent to many, and it helped to arrest the progress of the movement.'[1]

An attempt to adjudicate the extent to which both factors affected the outcome is probably impossible, but it is certain that if more Calvinistic Methodist ministers of 1904 had been familiar with the revival history of their own denomination, and possessed the theology of their forebears, much that was harmful could have been arrested.

Conclusions

1. To discern between genuine zeal and evangelical fanaticism is by no means easy. The temptation to excess is exceedingly subtle and, while all Christians are liable to be deceived, the probability of mistake is increased when leadership in revivals passes out of the hands of the appointed pastors of the churches.

2. It is an important part of preparation for revival that books and authors which show the dangers of fanaticism should be known by Christians. The best preservative against fanaticism is sound biblical teaching, in the church and the home, accompanied by humble dependence on the unction and power of the Holy Spirit. 'The moment that error, superstition, or fanaticism appears, however plausibly veiled in the garb of wisdom or sanctity, its departure from Scripture, a character inseparable from its nature, gives instant proof that its author is another spirit than the Spirit of God.'[2]

3. It should be remembered that the purpose of Satan in promoting evangelical fanaticism is to discredit true revival. As had happened before, reaction to excesses brought in a deadening distrust of all emotion in the aftermath to the Welsh

[1] Morgan, *Welsh Religious Revival*, p. 191.
[2] James M'Lagan, *Lectures and Sermons*, p. 82.

Revival of 1904–5. Further, those who embrace a distortion of evangelicalism may end up rejecting it altogether. Brynmor Jones records how, back home in Loughor in 1906, 'Evan Roberts grew more and more discouraged as he saw some groups of converts following after cults in which they barked at the devil, danced and swooned, or followed healers and prophetesses.'[1] Robert and Hannah Pearsall Smith, ardent exponents of 'higher life' and 'baptism with the Spirit' teaching in the 1870s, eventually came to believe very little that was Christian at all.[2] Ronald Knox's misjudgment of evangelicalism led him to join the Church of Rome and, more recently, a one-time evangelical leader of the charismatic movement in England has acted similarly in joining the Greek Orthodox Church.[3]

4. The extent to which revivals remain pure and free from excess is directly related to the degree of sound scriptural knowledge preserved in the churches and maintained from the pulpits. Before the 1904 revival in Wales the drift of the Calvinistic Methodist Church into liberalism on one hand and an Arminian evangelicalism on the other, meant a general absence of doctrinal strength. No one has disputed the statement of Vyrnwy Morgan that, 'One of the most striking things about the Revival of 1904–5 was the comparative absence of teaching', and he contrasted this with an earlier time 'when the theological interest was uppermost in the pulpit, in the Sunday School, and in the societies for religious experiences.'[4] In April 1905 Evan Roberts said that he had 'not heard a sermon for many months' (i.e., through the whole

---

[1] Jones, *Life of Roberts*, p. 158.
[2] See Hannah Smith's later rejection of fanaticism in her posthumous book, *Religious Fanaticism: Extracts from the Papers of Hannah Whitall Smith*, ed. Ray Strachey (London: Faber and Gwyer, 1928); and, for biography, Marie Henry, *The Secret Life of Hannah Whitall Smith* (Grand Rapids: Zondervan, 1984).
[3] Michael Harper, *The True Light: an Evangelical's Journey to Orthodoxy* (London: Hodder, 1997).
[4] Morgan, *Welsh Revival*, pp. 81–2.

period when the revival was at its height).[1] Another Welsh minister of the 1904 period who was able to remember the awakening of 1859, observed, 'it was for the Atonement they gave thanks in '59; but now they give thanks for their own pleasant feeling.'[2]

Evan Roberts, Morgan claimed, 'had no fundamental doctrine, no system of theology, no distinctive ideal.'[3] But this is not wholly true for Roberts was clearly influenced by the Arminian and Pelagian thought which Finney had done much to popularise in Wales from about 1840.[4] Instead of being a check to fanaticism, Arminianism, with its emphasis on what man is to do, is generally unsuspecting of the danger.

5. The belief that a Christian can discern *with certainty* between his own inclinations and the voice of the Holy Spirit is almost invariably a cause of fanaticism. The Holy Spirit guides through our human faculties, not apart from them, and, unlike

---

[1] From *Western Mail* reporter at Ffestiniog, 23 April 1905. It should be noted that Brynmor Jones considers that 'Awstin', the *Mail's* chief reporter on the revival, enjoyed the confidence of Roberts more than any other journalist, and that 'we can trust him to discern that which is of lasting worth' (*Voices*, p. 39. See also p. 51). The newspaper itself supplied Awstin's photograph with the caption, 'Chief Historian of the Revival in Wales'. The present writer believes that there is a serious question how far the published reports of the *Western Mail* did not in fact damage the revival and how it was understood. Much of the paper's material on the revival was reprinted at the time in a series of seven 32 page pamphlets, covering November 1904 to April 1905. This material is so centred around Roberts that it is understandable that some spoke of the 'Evan Roberts Revival'. The reader is given no knowledge of powerful preaching, without any disorder, that was going on in other places, as, for example, at Rhos, Wrexham, where the awakening 'had been directly caused by the Spirit's taking hold of the traditional preaching' (Jones, *Voices*, p. 116).

[2] Quoted by Emyr Roberts in *Revival & Its Fruit*, pp. 17–8.

[3] Morgan, *Welsh Religious Revival*, p. 55.

[4] His understanding of revival was also the same as Finney's. B. P. Jones tells us that 'he loved to recite' 2 Chronicles 7:14, and believed that 'Revival can only be given by the Holy Spirit when the conditions are fulfilled.' *Life of Roberts*, pp. 16, 34, 168. The *Western Mail* reporter in Liverpool on 6 April 1905, wrote that 2 Chronicles 7:14 'gives in a nutshell the secret of the Welsh Revival'.

the revelation of his will in Scripture, the element of human fallibility is always there. As W. G. T. Shedd wrote: 'The human spirit is not conscious of the Divine Spirit, as of an agent other than and distinct from itself. [To believe the contrary] is enthusiasm, in the bad sense. The Holy Ghost is indeed an agent distinct from and other than the human soul; but . . . [the believer's] own mind makes no report of two agents or persons.'[1] The recognition of this fact warrants the warning which Whitefield came to give his hearers: 'Watch the motions of God's blessed Spirit in your souls, and always try the suggestions or impressions that you at any time feel, by the unerring rule of God's most holy word: and if they are not found to be agreeable to that, reject them as diabolical and delusive.'[2] 'If you look for the Holy Ghost in any other way than through the power of Bible doctrine, seen to be real and felt,' wrote Thomas Chalmers, 'you will have no more success than if you looked for a spectre or some airy phantom of superstition.'[3]

6. 'Remember that the time of revival, however genuine the work, is especially the time for watchfulness. The most prosperous season in a Church is one of dangerous exposure. The mount is the place to become giddy. Beware of all efforts to kindle excitement. Be animated, be diligent, be filled with the spirit of prayer; but be sober-minded. Sobriety of spirit and humility of mind are inseparable. Let all noise and all endeavours to promote mere animal feeling be shunned. You can no more advance the growth of religion in the soul by excitement, than you can promote health in the body by throwing it into fever. Religion is principle. It is the peaceful love of God, and can only be promoted by the *truth* and prayer, united with a diligent waiting upon all duty.'[4]

[1] Shedd, *Commentary on Romans* (repr. Grand Rapids: Zondervan, 1967), p. 248.
[2] Whitefield, *Works*, vol. 5, p. 30.
[3] On Romans 8:16 in *The Works of Thomas Chalmers*, vol. 24 (Glasgow: Collins, n.d.), pp. 60–61.
[4] *Memorials of Charles Pettit McIlvaine, Late Bishop of Ohio*, ed. W. Carus (London: Elliot Stock, 1882), p.82.

7. Should revival be granted in our day the following lessons are vital:

(i) Everything possible should be done to avoid mere excitement and to maintain normal routines. Late night church meetings and near-sleepless nights commonly lead to a loss of judgment as well as to exhaustion. If people are in a state of audible distress during a service, or in a physical condition disturbing to others, it is possible for their condition to be reproduced in others simply by the operation of sympathy or hysteria. Ministers need to discountenance any such spread of emotion both by giving no credence to the idea that these cases are special instances of God's work and by arranging for the removal from the service of any whose feelings cannot be restrained.

(ii) Unpopular though it may be, the first appearances of wildfire need to be resisted. Fear of doing this lest it should be 'opposing the Spirit' has often prepared the way for situations which pass beyond control and bring great discredit upon the gospel.

(iii) Great care and caution is needed in any co-operation between churches and the news-media.[1] To welcome publicity from any and every source is contrary to Scripture (*Luke* 4:41); the introduction of television cameras belonging to outside agencies is particularly likely to be damaging. Even when supportive, undiscerning media may do much harm. The desire to spread news which is to the glory of God needs to be balanced against the danger of premature assessments and of creating a spirit of pride in a congregation which has suddenly become a centre of interest. More than a year elapsed between the event and Jonathan Edwards' published account of the revival in Northampton in 1735 but he came to believe that even that had been too short a time.

(iv) The Bible as our only infallible means of knowing the mind of God has to control both practice and spirit. In the

---

[1] See the words of Kenneth MacRae on this subject during a time of revival in Lewis: *Diary of Kenneth A. MacRae*, ed. Iain H. Murray (Edinburgh: Banner of Truth, 1980), p. 369.

words of Theodore Cuyler, 'A revival that is not founded on Bible truth is a blaze of pine shavings, and will end in smoke.'[1]

---

[1] *How To Be a Pastor*, pp. 92–3.

7

Six Things Revival Will Bring

'A more copious out-pouring of the Spirit is wanted to set all things in order. Errors in doctrine, licentiousness in conduct, deadness and formality in profession, will not stand before the strong influences of the Spirit. O that there should appear an evident difference between his work and everything human, and between those ordinances in and through which he works, and those ordinances wherein he hides his face and leaves men to themselves.' [1]

John Elias

W inston Churchill once wrote to his schoolboy grandson urging him to be a student of history because, he argued, history provides the best means for making intelligent guesses about the future. By reading Scripture Christians can do more than guess the nature of a future awakening. We know it will be in accord with all that we are told about the character and work of God. We may know this without reading church history, but, as I want to show in this closing chapter, the testimony of the past provides strong confirmation of what will yet be. This is not to say that revivals are identical; we have already noted that they may differ in several respects, yet history shows that certain main features are always present and it is not speculation to believe that these will be present again in the future. [2]

[1] Edward Morgan, *John Elias*, pp. 267–8, 259.
[2] In *The Puritan Hope* I sought to address the question, 'How do we know whether the world has not already seen its last major revival?' That book proposes reasons from unfulfilled scriptural prophecy why, while living in the expectation of Christ's advent, we may still believe that 'the end is not yet'.

Revival Restores Faith in the Word of God

I have argued earlier that the giving of revival does not necessarily imply the existence of a previous declension. Yet it is true that the most widespread revivals in the last four centuries have followed eras when unbelief was dominant both in society and in the church. This was the case before the Reformation of the sixteenth century and again before the Evangelical Revival two centuries later. Bishop Butler could lament of England in 1736: 'It has come to be taken for granted that Christianity is no longer a subject of inquiry; but that it is now at length discovered to be fictitious.'[1] Unbelief was established in the pulpits of Geneva before the revival which began in 1816. Jean Jacques Rousseau had mocked the Swiss pastors of that city with the words: 'It is asked of the ministers of the Church of Geneva, if Jesus Christ be God? They dare not answer. It is asked, if he were a mere man. They are embarrassed, and will not say they think so . . . They do not know what they believe, or what they do not believe.'[2]

The twentieth century has seen a more widespread and enduring defection from historic Christianity in the English-speaking world than has been witnessed in any period since the Reformation. This defection has occurred through the removal of the foundation to all Christian teaching, namely that the words of Scripture are so given of God that the teaching they contain is entirely trustworthy and authoritative. The Bible stands supreme above all human wisdom and religious tradition. It alone is *the* Book which God has given for the salvation of men. If, therefore, Scripture loses its true place in the church nothing remains certain.

Protestant churches came to depart from belief in Scripture not so much by outright denial as by acceptance of the claim, made in the name of scholarship, that 'theories' about the

---

[1] Butler in Preface to his *Analogy of Religion.*
[2] Quoted in *The Lives of Robert and James Haldane,* 1852 (repr. Edinburgh: Banner of Truth, 1990), p. 422.

divine inspiration of the Bible are unnecessary. Further, it was argued that Christianity would gain wider acceptance if it ceased to require submission to *all* that Scripture teaches. In the words of the Rev. Maurice H. Fitzgerald, one of the many exponents of this idea and the biographer of H. E. Ryle, Dean of Westminster: 'The new learning could afford a firm foundation for Christian belief to which the old theory of verbal inspiration, irretrievably shattered by the advance of human knowledge, could never make good its claim again.'[1] Against this claim Dean Ryle's own father, Bishop J. C. Ryle, had argued that the whole of Christianity must sooner or later fall where the verbal inspiration of Scripture is denied. For that belief 'is the very keel and foundation of Christianity. If Christians have no divine book to turn to as the warrant of their doctrine and practice, they have no right to claim the attention of mankind. They are building on a quicksand , and their faith is vain.'[2]

But in 1900 the spirit of the age was with the son and not the father whose beliefs were now regarded as 'narrow, old-fashioned, obsolete'.[3] Some there were, however, who, while accepting the Higher Critical view of Scripture, could see that a massive change was bound to follow if man himself was to determine what he would believe. In a letter to a friend dated 8 January 1902, Professor Marcus Dods wrote, 'The churches won't know themselves fifty years hence. It is to be hoped some little rag of faith may be left when all's done.'[4]

In confronting the consequences of this rejection of biblical authority, which occurred on both sides of the Atlantic, there have been those who have laboured to defend Christianity

---

[1] Maurice H. Fitzgerald, *A Memoir of Herbert Edward Ryle* (London: Macmillan, 1928), p. 77.

[2] J. C. Ryle, 'Inspiration' in *Old Paths* (London: Thynne, 1898), pp. 1–2.

[3] This representation, 'as some may be pleased to call that way,' is given by J. C. Ryle in an article, 'Evangelical Religion' where he argues that 'the first leading feature in Evangelical Religion is the absolute supremacy it assigns to Holy Scripture as the only rule of faith and practice'. *Knots Untied* (London: Thynne, 1896), pp. 4, 24.

[4] *Later Letters of Marcus Dods* (London: Hodder and Stoughton, 1911), p. 67.

with apologetics and other forms of scholarship. Bishop Butler and others did the same thing in their day. But while accepting a measure of value in such endeavours, it has to be said that neither in the eighteenth century nor in the twentieth could the tide be turned by these means. Unbelief is primarily a moral rather than an intellectual problem, and apostasy comes from a sinful bias against God, not merely from mistaken thinking. Accordingly the only effective means for the restoration of reverence has to be the action of God in changing man's moral nature. It is the same age-old issue with which Christ confronted Nicodemus – Israel's teacher who did not know that rebirth is necessary for spiritual sight and that it is the work of the Holy Spirit which produces faith in the minds of men. God himself must authenticate the truth to make it real to us. In the words of Owen: 'There is a sacred light in the Word: but there is a covering and veil on the eyes of men, so that they cannot behold it aright. Now, the removal of this veil is the peculiar work of the Holy Spirit.'[1]

This being true, it inevitably follows that every period which has seen a widespread restoration of faith has always been a period when the convicting and regenerating work of the Holy Spirit has been manifest. Apologetics may modify conditions for the better but it is only under the powerful preaching of the gospel that unbelief is scattered as mist before the sun. In this respect, as in others, revivals have brought a repetition of what happened when the gospel confronted the wisdom of men in the apostolic age. 'Learned men scorn to submit their reason to divine revelation,' Jonathan Edwards noted, but his confidence was that Christianity had overcome exactly the same problem long before:

God was pleased to suffer human learning to come to such a height before he sent forth the gospel into the world, that the world might

[1] Quoted by Ryle, *Old Paths*, pp. 33–4. He writes: 'Say always, when you open your Bible, "O God, for Christ's sake, give me the teaching of the Holy Spirit".' As Calvin has shown so forcefully, this dependence on the Holy Spirit follows from the truth that we are by nature 'void of all power of spiritual intelligence'. *Institutes*, Book 2, ch. 2.

see the insufficiency of all their own wisdom for the obtaining the knowledge of God, without the gospel of Christ, and the teaching of the Spirit. When in the wisdom of God, the world by wisdom knew not God, it pleased God by the foolishness of preaching, to save them that believe.[1]

When William Tyndale reasserted this same principle at the outset of the Reformation in England the response he encountered was precisely the same as the one with which the unbelieving Jews rejected Christ. When he confronted church dignitaries in Gloucestershire with Scripture, his employer's wife asked him: 'Were it reason that we should believe you before them so great, learned and beneficed men?' But while unbelief always sets itself against Scripture the Holy Spirit owns his own truth and uses it to bring thousands to faith. Too often in times of declension churches have acted as though there must be some meeting of minds with the accepted scholarship of the day if unbelief is to be countered; and many attempts are made to gain respectability for biblical belief. But revivals follow a different course as preachers take up a new agenda based on the conviction that 'faith should not be in the wisdom of men but in the power of God' (*1 Cor.* 2:5). Speaking of this point with reference to the preachers of the Evangelical Revival of the eighteenth century, J. Fordyce has written:

These preachers did not care much to argue much about the existence of God, the probabilities connected with a future life, or the reasonableness of Christianity. To them Christ was a real Being, and His Gospel a real salvation; to them this salvation was not a future prospect, but a present and conscious possession; to them the Bible did not merely contain things of high value – it was the word of the living God, the full and final word on all matters connected with man's highest life here and hereafter. Believing all this with intensity of faith, they spoke out of full hearts, and their word was with power; their gospel became the 'power of God unto salvation' to many thousands. Hence the new life and quickening experienced far and wide; hence the crowds that gathered round these new preachers, wherever they stood up to speak. Men who could see

[1] Edwards, *Works*, vol. 1, p. 601.

nothing in the logic of Berkeley or the ethics of Butler, for whom Paley's twelve men had no message, saw before them, felt within them, new manifestations of Divine power. God not only lived somewhere and somehow: *He was actually present among them.* The triumphs of Christianity and the living power of Christ were not merely found in the records of early history, in the thousands of Pentecost, or the heroes and martyrs of a later age; they were to be seen and felt in every city, town, and village of old England. Thus without any reasoning, with but little argument, the Deistic position was completely undermined, and the walls of the proud Jericho of eighteenth-century unbelief fell flat before the blasts of the new evangel.[1]

Revival Restores Definiteness to the Meaning of 'Christian'

The purpose of Scripture is to make men 'wise for salvation through faith which is in Christ Jesus' *(2 Tim.* 3:15). It is therefore not surprising that when Scripture becomes the absorbing interest of men and women that interest centres upon how they receive salvation and eternal life. This was the subject upon which the apostolic churches were in controversy with the world without and false teachers within. In periods of spiritual decline the reverse is the case. What Scripture treats as paramount becomes marginalised and a nominal Christianity comes to prevail in which there is no clear distinction between church and world, between external morality and the power of godliness. Experience of the living Christ and of the Holy Spirit is no longer regarded as essential. Assurance of salvation and personal holiness likewise cease to be urged and a vague impression prevails that all churchgoers, and perhaps others as well, are 'good Christians'. In such situations the truth that certain things have to be *believed* in order to the possession of salvation virtually disappears.[2]

[1] 'Unbelief in the Eighteenth Century,' in *British and Foreign Evangelical Review,* vol. 31, pp. 32–3.
[2] There is no uncertainty in Scripture on this fact, e.g., John 8:24; Rom. 10:9; 1 Tim. 4:16 etc.

The powerful preaching of the gospel in a time of revival always follows Scripture in making the meaning of being a Christian *the* great issue. The periods of the Reformation and the Evangelical Revival differed in many respects but at both times 'what is a Christian?' was the supreme subject and the fundamental cause of the collision between a restored Christianity and an unfaithful clergy. This fact is plain in the lives of both Whitefield and John Wesley. Preaching about 'those who imagine themselves Christians, and are not,' Wesley continued:

These abound, not only in all parts of our land, but in most parts of the habitable earth . . . they are no more Christians than they are archangels. Yet they imagine themselves so to be; and they can give several reasons for it: for they have been *called so* ever since they can remember; they were *christened* many years ago; they embrace *Christian opinions*, vulgarly called the Christian or catholic faith; they use the *Christian modes of worship*, as their fathers did before them; they live what is called a good *Christian life*, as the rest of their neighbours do. And who shall presume to think or say that these men are not Christians? – though without one grain of true faith in Christ, or of real, inward holiness; without ever having tasted the love of God, or been 'made partakers of the Holy Ghost'![1]

It was for preaching in this vein that Wesley was banned from the pulpit of St Mary's, Oxford. It was too much for the clergy and others among his hearers to be asked, 'is this city of Oxford a *Christian* city? Is *Christianity, scriptural Christianity*, found here?'[2] Whitefield's experience was parallel. 'In our days,' he declared, 'to be a true Christian is really to become a scandal.'[3]

The revival in Geneva of 1816–17 was much more local yet it saw this same pattern. Robert Haldane, the instrument of that awakening, reported how after the pastors of the city and the professors of the school of theology heard his teaching, 'They began to preach openly against what I taught. They

---

[1] John Wesley, *Sermons on Several Occasions*, First Series (repr. London: Epworth Press, 1948), xxxii pp. 420–1.

[2] See Tyerman, *Life and Times of John Wesley*, vol. 1, p. 450.

[3] Whitefield, *Works*, vol. 4, p. 32. For a typical example of a clash between Whitefield and a clergyman over the meaning of being a Christian see his *Journals*, p. 356.

insisted that men are born pure . . . They taught that the Gospel was useful, but not indispensable, to salvation.'¹ But a new day had dawned with the conversion of sixteen students in the theological school. At a later date Haldane reminded M. Cheneviere, the professor of theology and one of his opponents, of what had happened:

Towards the end of the session, and when the time arrived that the students were to be ordained, it became sufficiently apparent that they knew something else besides the morality recommended by heathen philosophers and nominal Christians. You found they could do more than deliver a smooth harangue, inculcating the observance of a scanty morality. They had begun to take him for their model whose speech and preaching were not in enticing words of man's wisdom, but in demonstration of the Spirit and of power. They could address their hearers in a style different from the smooth language of the Geneva pulpit, as if all were Christians – all a very good sort of people, who needed only to be reminded to go on as they were doing in the performance of their duties, or who, at most, required some little reformation.²

When the line between the church and the world has been blurred, and ideas of salvation have become vague and inclusivist, a revival always reasserts the real meaning of being a Christian. A Christian is one who has received the free pardon of sin and a new life solely through faith in Jesus Christ and his redemptive work. This is a *new gospel* for those accustomed to other beliefs and the clarity with which it breaks upon men and women in a time of awakening enforces the meaning of Christian to a degree which nothing else can do. And 'corrupt reasonings of men are silenced by the strong light of divine truth.'

¹ *Lives of Robert and James Haldane*, p. 433.
² Ibid., p. 451. Haldane was here replying in 1824 to an attack by M. Cheneviere. Haldane's *Exposition of Romans* (repr. Edinburgh: Banner of Truth, 1996) shows how fundamental the issue of how a sinner becomes a Christian was to him, as it was to Paul himself. It was the same for J. Gresham Machen as his book *Christianity and Liberalism* (1923) demonstrated.

Revival Advances the Gospel with Amazing Swiftness

In his sermon on 'A Witnessing Church – a Church Baptized with the Holy Ghost', George Smeaton wrote:

It is the nature of fire to spread abroad. I am come, said Jesus, to send fire upon the earth, and what will I if it be already kindled? And when the Spirit comes in this fiery baptism, the words of Jesus spread like a conflagration from mouth to mouth. In the early days, when the apostles were under this fresh baptism, and also in the days of the Reformers, the burning words spread from home to home, from land to land.[1]

It is not generally the will of God that large numbers of men and women are converted suddenly but it happened in the apostolic era and it has been seen again in every awakening. After long years, perhaps, in which conversions have been comparatively few in number, success occurs with a speed that astonishes all who see it. The Rev. William Cooper of Boston declared that more souls had come to him in deep spiritual concern in one week in 1740 than he had witnessed in the whole twenty-four years of his preceding ministry. When John Wesley formed his first Methodist Society in London in 1740 it had seventy-five members: by 1743 the number stood at 2,020. In 1767 the Association Meeting of the Calvinistic Methodists at Bala, in North Wales, was attended by 200 persons; by 1814 some 15,000 to 20,000 were present.

At a time when the population of the New England Colonies was only around 340,000, it is estimated that from 25,000 to 50,000 were added to her churches in the early 1740s and perhaps 300,000 in all thirteen Colonies. That First Great Awakening in the Middle Colonies, wrote W. H. Foote, 'laid broad and deep foundations for the spiritual church to arise in the wilderness,' while that of 1802, 'spread over the Southern, and Western, and portions of the Middle States, with a power almost terrific'; it 'lighted up the fires of the sanctuary in the

[1] *Free Church Pulpit*, vol. 3, p. 25.

South and West like a pioneer chain of forts, both a refuge and a temple for the adventurous emigrants.'[1]

When revival returned to the churches on both sides of the Atlantic in the years 1857–59, it was estimated that half a million joined the Protestant churches of America; 100,000 the churches in Ulster; and 50,000 the churches in Wales.

The speed with which the gospel achieves success has thus always been a mark of revival. The words of Henri Pyt, one of the converted Genevan students of 1817 who became an evangelist in France, could have been written by many others who lived in similar days: 'What joy to see the kingdom of the Lord advance with such rapidity! Is it possible to remain idle in the midst of that devouring zeal which burns for the cause of Jesus in so many thousands of our brethren?'[2]

Connected with this kind of spread of the Christian faith is always the fact that in such days there is no shortage of men and women ready to witness and serve Christ at home or overseas. In times when church work and missionary endeavours have dwindled for lack of support, it has been from revivals that a new supply of manpower has arisen. The Second Great Awakening in the United States brought thousands into Christian service. Exactly the same has been true in all parts of the world where revivals have occurred. In Worcester, South Africa, there was an awakening under the ministry of Andrew Murray in 1860. Describing that event forty-three years later, an eye-witness wrote:

The fruits of that revival were seen in the congregation for many years. They consisted, among others, in this, that fifty young men offered themselves for the ministry, and this happened in days when it was a difficult matter to find young men for the work of the ministry.[3]

[1] W. H. Foote, *Sketches of Virginia*, 1850 (repr. Richmond, Va.: John Knox Press, 1966), p. 164.

[2] *Lives of Haldanes*, p. 455.

[3] J. Du Plessis, *The Life of Andrew Murray* (London: Marshall Brothers, 1919), p. 196. Andrew Murray, and his brother, John, were influenced by the ministry of W. C. Burns in Aberdeen in 1841. His teaching on the Holy Spirit developed somewhat along the lines of Keswick teaching, valuable though it remains in some respects.

In 1887 after a systematic visitation was carried out in the congregations of the Free Church of Scotland, by deputies for the General Assembly, the following information was reported:

Our deputies have often noted the fact that they have found ministers all over the country, who thank God for faithful fellow-workers in office, who were brought to the knowledge of Jesus Christ during the revival and evangelistic labours of the years 1859–1860.[1]

Still more remarkable in this connection was what happened in parts of the Pacific in the last century. In Tonga, for instance, a remarkable revival was witnessed under Methodist preaching in 1834. 'Missionaries,' Robert Evans writes, 'were careful only to receive into the membership those who received instruction and demonstrated a change of conduct;' even so, nine thousand people became full church members in six years, and from that number many evangelists and teachers went out all over the Pacific, often at the risk of their lives.[2] Evans reports that the same concern for outreach appeared in the Solomon Islands during the 1980s when converts asked, 'What can we do to serve and contribute to the countries which surround us?'

The lesson is plain: the more living experience there is of Christ, and the stronger the faith of believers in the truth of his word, the greater will be their concern for the conversion of others. It is when sense of debt to Christ and awareness of his love are at their height that the church has ever made the swiftest advances in the world.

Revival Always Has Moral Impact upon Communities

One of the strongest claims of unbelief has always been that matters of faith are only questions of opinion which make no real difference to the character of men. It is for this reason that every inconsistency of conduct in *professing* Christians is seized upon by the world as evidence that the reception of Christianity

---

[1] *Free Church General Assembly Proceedings*, 1887, p. 75. Quoted by Ian A. Muirhead, *Scottish Church History Society Records*, vol. 20, part 3, 1980, p. 195.

[2] Robert Evans, *Evangelical Revivals in the Pacific* (Ark Angles, P.O. Box 190, Hazelbrook, NSW, 1997), p. 11.

makes no basic difference to human nature. The possibility that the author of the unbelief is able to sow 'tares' among 'wheat', and even to disguise himself as 'Christ' does not come within the consideration of those who advance this argument.

When the devil merges the world with the church in times of declension, it is true that no moral distinction between the 'religious' and the non-Christian may remain readily apparent. But when a revival occurs there is a disruption of this amalgam. Men and women, alive with a life which is so contrary to what they once were, are proof that the gospel is able to make all things new. The world may not like the change but it becomes very hard to deny the difference and, albeit secretly, the world comes to respect it. Thus it was written of the early church, 'None of the rest dared join them, but the people esteemed them highly' (*Acts* 5:13).

Thus people who embraced the Bible at the time of the Reformation became known not simply for a Protestant 'work ethic' but, more importantly, they stood for honesty, for faithfulness to God and man, for the elevation of womanhood, and for liberty from tyranny. The Puritan movement carried this forward in England, 'building up a kingdom of righteousness in the hearts and consciences of men' who were 'serious, earnest, sober in life and conduct, firm in their love of Protestantism and freedom'. And as the same historian wrote of how, after all the corruption of the Restoration period and the early years of the eighteenth century, it was the Evangelical Revival which brought back the same characteristics: 'Slowly but steadily it introduced its own seriousness and purity into English society, English literature, English politics.'[1]

[1] John Richard Green, *A Short History of the English People* (London: Macmillan, 1888), p. 604. At the time when he wrote Green could even say, 'The whole history of English progress since the Reformation, on its moral and spiritual sides, has been the history of Puritanism.' J. C. Ryle wrote in 1877: 'I invite any honest-minded reader to look at a map of the world, and see what a story that map tells. Which are the countries on the face of the globe at this moment where there is the greatest amount of idolatry, or cruelty, or tyranny, or impurity, or misgovernment, or disregard of life and truth and liberty? Precisely those countries where the Bible is not known.' *Old Paths*, p. 15. The change in Britain since Ryle wrote has not been due to any change in the Bible or Christianity.

American history has been parallel in this regard. The moral change in Boston in the 1740s was characteristic of what happened in other parts of North America. Trumbull wrote of Boston:

There was in the minds of people, a general fear of sin . . . It was the opinion of men of discernment and sound judgment, who had the best opportunities of knowing the feelings and general state of the people at that period, that bags of gold and silver, and other precious things, might, with safety, have been laid in the streets, and no man would have converted them to his own use. Theft, wantonness, intemperance, profaneness, sabbath-breaking, and other gross sins, appeared to be put away.[1]

The national change was still greater in the years 1790–1830 which saw the enlarged population of the United States move decidedly from the toleration and acceptance of infidelity to a general respect for Christian belief and conduct.

The revival of 1859 in Northern Ireland likewise brought an immense change for many in the population. The drunkenness endemic in some sections of society was reversed as the drink trade went into sudden decline. In one district which possessed nine public houses, two were closed by the conversion of their owners, a third for lack of trade and the quantity of alcohol sold in the six which remained open was less in 1860 than had formerly been sold by one.[2] A still more intractable problem before 1859 was the animosity between Protestants and Catholics. In this regard the attitude of nominal Protestants was as bad as that of many on the other side. In the Protestant Sandy Row district of Belfast it had long been the custom on the twelfth of July 'to catch the Papist birds by throwing stones at them'. 'The essence of Protestantism, and the conversion of Romanists in that region, consisted in the abundant use of brickbats and bludgeons; but the old war-cries were now hushed by a higher voice, and in few parts of our beloved

[1] Benjamin Trumbull, *History of Connecticut*, vol. 2 (New London: Utley, 1898), pp. 111–2.
[2] Gibson, *Year of Grace*, p. 29.

land was that short sermon oftener preached, "Believe on the Lord Jesus Christ, and thou shalt be saved," than in this very district.'¹ This same change was widely seen elsewhere. The Rev. J. Geddes of County Tyrone reported how, prior to the revival, sectarian and anti-Catholic feeling was at a height with his neighbourhood 'in a ferment – nightly marchings, law proceedings, &c. Since the movement began, not a drum had been struck in the bounds, and the leading Orangemen meet and pray for the Romanists, whom a little ago they hated.'² In the darkest corners of Ulster men marvelled at the power of the gospel, 'making out of the rudest and most unpromising materials a moral, peaceful, and happy people.'

Volumes could be filled with the same point drawn from the mission fields of the world where the same kind of transformation occurred though not necessarily in revivals. John Paton, pioneer missionary to the New Hebrides (now Vanuatu) in the 1850s could write: 'All the scepticism of Europe would hide its head in foolish shame; and all its doubts would dissolve under one glance of the new light that Jesus, and Jesus alone, pours from the converted Cannibal's eye.'³

Despite such evidence, at the end of the nineteenth century it became fashionable to believe that moral and social progress could occur without the preaching of those biblical truths which had changed the course of history. Indeed that fact was in the process of being forgotten. Appealing to the record of the beliefs of evangelical Christianity, Joseph Parker wrote in 1899:

These may be old-fashioned doctrines, but they created mission-ary societies, Sunday schools, hospitals, orphanages, and refuges for penitence; they gave every child a new value, every father a new

---

¹ Ibid., p. 156.
² Ibid., p. 162.
³ John G. Paton, *An Autobiography* (repr. Edinburgh: Banner of Truth, 1994), p. 107. The former cannibal to whom he refers was 'that noble old soul, Abraham . . . Any trust, however sacred or valuable, could be absolutely placed in him.'

responsibility, every mother a new hope, and constituted human society into a new conscience and a new trust.[1]

The witness of the moral effects of biblical Christianity explains very clearly why the New Testament gives far more space to the necessity of holiness in believers than it does to outreach among non-Christians.

Revival Changes Understanding of the Christian Ministry

This point has already been made in the preceding pages but there is one aspect which warrants particular notice. Genuine Christian scholarship has an important place in the life of the churches and theological seminaries. But history shows that it is all-too-easy for preparation for the ministry to become an intellectual exercise. The danger is increased when the instructors are academics more than preachers, and especially so in eras when there is no academic respectability to be gained from the truths which Scripture makes fundamental to preaching. Where this situation exists, evangelical seminaries have often become part of a downward drift as the teachers succumb to the temptation to show their peers in the academic world (who are not governed by reverence for Scripture) that they are not ignoramuses nor obscurantists.[2] Along with this

[1] Joseph Parker, *A Preacher's Life* (London: Hodder and Stoughton, 1899), p. 99.
[2] This temptation, along with a false charity, probably explains why there was so little resistance to the entrance of unbelief in Christian dress in the last century: 'How many even of God's ministers, when German mysticism, rationalism, and neology come into Christian churches, pulpits, and courts, in the university gown, *dare* not contend against it, for fear of being spoken of as "ignorant and unlearned"; and yet that was one of the conditions of apostolic boldness! Men are too anxious to be ranked with scholars; and so when error, however deadly, wears the glittering serpent-like skin of scholarship no one seems to dare to smite it with a bold blow!' A. T. Pierson, *The Acts of the Holy Spirit* (London: Morgan and Scott, n.d.), pp. 42–3. For important background see, 'The Influence of the German University System on Theological Education', Dabney, *Discussions*, vol. 1. Dabney's analysis remains eminently relevant in the theological world of today.

there may come the desire to prove the status of the institution they serve by the success of their students in degree programmes which give little or no attention to biblical priorities. When, added to this, seminaries face financial pressures to enlarge the student body by the introduction of curricula never intended for a 'school of the prophets', participation in drift becomes almost inevitable.

David F. Wells has written forcefully on how such influences are at work in the evangelical theological education of the present day. He notes how the B.D. degree was upgraded in the States to the M.Div. in the early 1970s, and the Doctor of Ministry degree (D.Min), of which more than ten thousand were issued by 1993, was soon added. But this change, Wells argues, was not prompted by higher views of the Christian ministry:

It was, of course, the old market mechanism at work. In the 1970s, many seminaries were hard-pressed financially, and the D.Min. was a lucrative new product to sell. At the same time, many ministers were hard-pressed psychologically as they sensed the decline of their profession, their growing marginalization in society, and the corresponding loss of power and influence that that entailed. And so the shotgun marriage was consummated.[1]

What we are dealing with here is an inevitable tendency in human nature when it is uncorrected by Scripture. Instead of insisting that men for the ministry need to be trained in a courageous indifference to human opinion, and to show themselves 'approved to God' (*2 Tim.* 2:15), evangelical seminaries which give first attention to increasing their influence will inevitably begin to decline. Over a century ago the Rev. John Kennedy of Dingwall wrote of this same process as it was occurring in the ministerial training of the Free Church of Scotland:

Just as it became easier to acquire credit for being intellectual and learned and evangelical at once, a danger arose . . . The attempt to form an alliance between learning and the gospel, then as always,

[1] D. F. Wells, *No Place for Truth* (Grand Rapids: Eerdmans, 1993), pp. 235–6.

proved to be a dangerous thing. Either is usually given up in order to give place to the other. Paul laid aside his learning that the gospel might occupy the whole sphere of his preaching. But men of another spirit, in these last days, began to lay aside the gospel to give place to the 'excellency of speech and of wisdom'. Gradually the proportion of gospel truth diminished. Those aspects of truth which were least popular, and those modes of presenting it which seemed most to interfere with intellectual display, began to be dropped, and, to a sad extent, speculation took the place of dogma, and the sphere of the subjective was almost ignored, careful dealing with conscience avoided, and the lightnings of Sinai were displaced by flashes of intellect, and its thunders by the power of eloquence . . . Idolatry of intellect found a shrine under the shade of evangelism, and this as it has ever been, proved to be the germ of rationalism.[1]

Kennedy was not alone in his judgement on the effects of theological education in his day. In England the Congregationalist leaders, John Campbell and John Angell James, both warned of the danger inherent in students for the ministry being prepared by the curriculum of London University's recently introduced B.D. degree course. Whatever the gains, they were in James' opinion, 'as dust in the balance compared with sound theology, fervent piety, and preaching power.' 'Our young men are deficient here [i.e., as physicians of souls],' James wrote to a friend in the States in 1855. 'Their sermons are not very well adapted to produce conviction and conversion . . . Much of our preaching just now has little to do with the heart and conscience . . . Revivals are rare with you as with us.'[2] Spurgeon shared the same conviction and argued that what men for the ministry needed was to learn 'to preach efficiently, to get at the heart of the masses, to evangelize the poor'. This could never be, he held, if their instructors had not learned this themselves:

[1] John Kennedy, *The Present Cast and Tendency of Religious Thought and Feeling in Scotland* (repr. Inverness: North Counties, 1955), pp. 14–5.
[2] *The Life and Letters of John Angell James*, ed. R. W. Dale (London: Nisbet, 1861), pp. 552–3. James' idea of the Christian ministry is well-stated in his work, *An Earnest Ministry, The Want of the Times* (repr. Edinburgh: Banner of Truth, 1993), and, on the introduction of University degrees into ministerial training, see *The Works of John Angell James*, vol. 9, pp. 401–6.

Tutors should be what they wish their students to be; and what manner of men should ministers be? They should thunder in preaching, and lighten in conversation; they should be flaming in prayer, shining in life, and burning in spirit. If they be not so, what can they effect?[1]

To the argument that such an outlook is simply idealistic the answer is that revivals in the past have introduced just such ministerial training. The Great Awakening in the Middle Colonies was very closely connected with the school of William Tennent which worldly men sneered at as the 'log college'. But Tennent's little work produced *preachers* and when, in due course, it became the College of New Jersey at Princeton, its influence reached to all parts of the land. When the prestige of Princeton as a centre of learning eventually weakened its value as a training school for ministers, men of the older outlook took steps to form Princeton Theological Seminary in 1812. They believed that 'filling the Church with a learned and able ministry without a corresponding portion of real piety, would be a curse to the world and an offence to

[1] C. H. Spurgeon, *An All-Round Ministry, Addresses to Ministers and Students* (repr. London: Banner of Truth, 1960), p. xvi. The identical view is argued by Gardiner Spring: 'If the deacons must "first be proved", much more the ministers; and if ministers, much more the instructors of ministers. No matter what the talents of a theological instructor may be, it is not possible for him rightly to exhibit the truth of God, and teach others to exhibit it, if he himself has not been in the habit of exhibiting it to the *popular* mind. Books written by these distinguished authors . . . have great excellencies, but they have this one deficiency, that they have no savour of the pastoral office . . . they are wanting in knowledge of the human heart; they are wanting in that which men want to know and feel; they are wanting in that impressive, impulsive, practical exhibition of truth which the popular mind de-mands . . . they savour of scholarship and intellect, while they ought to be imbued with a richer fragrance. We have sought to ascertain if the Scriptures anywhere contemplate a class of theological teachers who have not themselves been the acknowledged and honoured teachers of the people . . . It is one thing to impart theological knowledge, and another to form ministers of Christ . . . The glare of human learning, and the pride of man, are gratified and exalted by concentrating in the schools of the prophets youthful teachers of the highest promise. But the effects of the delusion will, sooner or later, be bitterly bewailed.' *The Power of the Pulpit* (repr. Edinburgh: Banner of Truth, 1986), pp. 202–7.

God and his people.' Instead of that, they wanted the new seminary to be 'a nursery of vital piety as well as of sound theological learning, and to train up persons for the ministry who shall be lovers as well as defenders of the truth as it is in Jesus, friends of revivals of religion, and a blessing to the Church of God.'[1] As an illustration of how this vision worked out in the life of Princeton Seminary the testimony of John B. Adger, one of its early students, is worthy of quotation:

I found myself here in a very different atmosphere from that either of my college or Charleston life. My fellow-students were all devoted to the acquisition of sacred learning, and the cultivation of the spiritual life. Many of them were godly men. Religious truth filled the air. Our conversations were all about the Scriptures. I was thrown into the company and fell under the influence of a number of young men of a deeper Christian experience and a loftier tone of piety than I had ever met. The professors, Drs. Alexander and Miller and Hodge, impressed me as no other Christian ministers had ever done. Not only their profound learning, but the saintliness of their character, filled me with awe. The religious exercises in the Seminary, even those where the professors took no part, were of a sort that I had never previously attended. It was not long before I was led to doubt whether I was any way fit to be there. My distress soon came to be unbearable. I abandoned altogether the hope I had been cherishing that I was a Christian. It was a dreadful experience. I gave up study and betook myself to prayer. After a period of great darkness the Lord revealed himself to me, and I found peace. It was the beginning for me of a new religious life.[2]

What is needed today is major change in the very ethos which currently so largely prevails in the training of men for the preaching ministry. It is in this area that compromise with 'the world spirit about us in our age' is sadly evident.[3] It is

[1] *Life of Alexander*, pp. 225–6. Further on this subject see David C. Calhoun, *Princeton Seminary, Faith and Learning, 1812–1868* (Edinburgh: Banner of Truth, 1994).

[2] John B. Adger, *My Life and Times, 1810–1899* (Richmond, Va.: Presbyterian Committee of Publication, 1899), p. 72.

[3] In this regard one of the most important books of the last half-century has to be Francis Schaeffer's *The Great Evangelical Disaster* (Westchester, Ill.: Crossway, 1984), whose words I quote.

encouraging that the danger is seen by at least a few seminary professors. David Wells writes:

There are, happily, many ministers who have broken the professional mold, although they have done so only against great odds, and, as a consequence, they have often had to work on the fringes of evangelical life. In order to break the mold, most have to turn on its head the kind of training they received in seminary.[1]

It may be that the pressures which have made the present mould so strong will not be effectively challenged this side of a great revival. Then, if not before, the churches will see what a critical mistake was made a century ago in not listening to those who gave warning. Among them was Robert Sample who wrote in 1897: 'The great want of to-day is a holier ministry. We do not need more stalwart polemics, more mighty apologists, or preachers who compass a wider range of natural knowledge, important as these are; but men of God who bring the atmosphere of heaven with them into the pulpit and speak from the borders of another world.'[2]

Revival Will Change the Public Worship of the Churches

It may be thought that if anything needs no further change at the present time it is the worship and praise of God. For the fact is that within the last forty years scarcely anything has been changed so much as modes of worship. The form of worship in many evangelical churches has become almost unrecognisably different from what it was before. But the question is whether amidst this transformation the big thing has been addressed, namely, that worship – as the word itself should remind us – has to do with the worth-ship of God. Fine externals and music, beautiful accompaniments, even the Bible and orthodoxy, may be present where there is no real admiration of God, no giving to him the glory due to his name.

[1] *No Place For Truth*, p. 250.
[2] Robert Sample, 'Effective Preaching', in *The Presbyterian and Reformed Review*, Philadelphia, April 1897, p. 295.

For adoration and worship depend on a living knowledge of
God (*John* 4:22).

There is reason to believe that far too much of contemporary discussion of worship is misdirected. The assumption has been that our problems have to do with changing
the inherited forms and externals: these relics of the past
have been judged largely responsible for the dull services
which have impoverished the churches. Former generations
of Christians, it is supposed, were tradition-bound in the
things from which we have recently been liberated. The
assumption is that before our day little thought was given to
worship. Nothing could be more mistaken. But the truth is
that in the past worship was addressed from a different
standpoint; the first concern was the vision of God and the
response which Scripture requires of man. In the words of
Calvin, 'We ought always to keep before our eyes the majesty
of God, which dwells in the Church.'[1] Isaac Watts summarised the spirit of the whole Reformation and Puritan
tradition when he wrote:

> *Had I a glance of thee, my God*
> *Kingdoms and men would vanish soon;*
> *Vanish as though I saw them not,*
> *As a dim candle dies at noon.*

Our great contemporary need has to do with something far
more fundamental than the outward form of worship. Too
many modern changes in public worship look like attempts to
provide substitutes for the work of the Holy Spirit; and the
emptiness of these substitutes is often apparent. If a sense of
the greatness and majesty of God is not present in a
congregation then nothing else can produce awe and wonder.
Such a spirit has certainly marked Christian worship in its
brightest days and it has ever been present in times of
awakening. 'The death-like awe of silence and solemnity
sometimes seemed as if it was the hem of the robe of his glory

[1] John Calvin, *Commentary on John*, vol. 1 (Edinburgh: Calvin Translation
Society, 1847), p. 93.

waxing all but visible.'¹ So wrote John Bocock of a service in his church in Virginia during a revival in the nineteenth century and such descriptions were commonplace.

Among all our recent changes in worship there is nothing which will make congregations awe-struck. Nor, to be fair, have innovations been intended to aid such a spirit. Interest has centred rather on such things as are calculated to induce brightness and 'liveliness'. That intention is not to be censured. Joyless worship is dishonouring to God as well as deadening to congregations. In Scripture we often read such words as, 'Be glad in the Lord and rejoice, you righteous; And shout for joy' (*Psa.* 32:11). But it is very possible to look to the wrong means for joy. External expressions of 'joy' may exist which have little or no connection with the source from which real joy must flow. Praise has its rise in spiritual knowledge. Joy has its source in truth. Scripture makes that sequence clear: 'Teach me Your way, O Lord; I will walk in Your truth; Unite my heart to fear Your name. I will praise You, O Lord my God, with all my heart, And I will glorify Your name forevermore' (*Psa.* 86:11–12). When people, burdened with a sense of guilt, come to complete deliverance through faith in the atoning sufferings of Christ, and when the love of God fills the hearts of believers, then joy is irresistible. The clearer the knowledge, the higher will be the praise.

At such times, as we have noted in these pages, something of the very happiness of heaven is manifested among the people of God. The words of a Christian businessman who attended a Methodist service in Bristol near the beginning of the Evangelical Revival in 1739 are typical. In its outward form the meeting which he attended differed little from the customary model of hymns, prayers and preaching. But there the similarity ended:

Never did I hear such praying. Never did I see or hear such evident marks of fervency in the service of God. At the close of every

¹ *Selections from the Writings of John Bocock* (Richmond, Va.: Whittet & Shepperson, 1891), p. 402.

petition, a serious Amen, like a gentle, rushing sound of waters, ran through the whole audience. Such evident marks of a lively devotion, I was never witness to before. If there be such a thing as heavenly music upon earth, I heard it then. I do not remember my heart to have been so elevated in Divine love and praise, as it was there and then, for many years past, if ever.[1]

The unction of the Spirit attending the word of God was the explanation of the joy and, as Luke Tyerman said, 'Make a man happy and he is sure to sing.'[2] A. W. Tozer has to be right when he wrote: 'In my study and observations, a revival generally results in a sudden bestowment of a spirit of worship. This is not the result of engineering or manipulation. It is something God bestows on people hungering and thirsting for him.'[3] One of the marks of the genuineness of such worship is that it sees no contradiction between stillness and reverence and joy and fervent praise. Where either is absent we may conclude that there is little evidence that men and women are filled with the Holy Spirit. 'Walking in the fear of the Lord and in the comfort of the Holy Spirit' (*Acts* 9:31) represents the spiritual experience which is genuine.

This brings us to the right point at which to conclude these pages. God means to exalt his name and to be praised for ever. The purpose of the gospel is 'the praise of the glory of His grace' (*Eph.* 1:6), and for that purpose the promise of the Holy Spirit remains sure, 'He will glorify me'. We shall then certainly pray according to the will of God when we ask that his name be hallowed and his kingdom come. Such prayer will gather importunity the more we see dishonour done to him to whom the kingdom and the power and the glory belong. But

[1] Tyerman, *Life and Times of John Wesley*, vol. 1, pp. 253-4. The preacher on this occasion was Charles Wesley.

[2] Ibid., p. 398. It was the same in Calvinistic Wales and New England. 'Our public *praises* were then greatly enlivened,' Edwards wrote of the year 1735. At a time of unusual blessing in Banffshire, Scotland, some visitors once asked, 'Might we have a prayer meeting?' The answer they got took them by surprise: 'Oh, it is all praise here just now. It is all praise.'

[3] *A. W. Tozer on Worship and Entertainment*, ed. J. L. Snyder (Camp Hill, Pa.: Christian Publications, 1997), p. 92.

however great the darkness and the dishonour, we may pray with faith, with thankfulness, and with expectation, knowing that our unworthiness is no obstruction to a divine and almighty Saviour. For it is our Father in heaven who said, 'I had concern for My holy name . . . I do not do this for your sakes, O house of Israel, but for My holy name's sake' (*Ezek.* 36:21–2).

God of Eternity, Lord of the Ages,
Father and Spirit and Saviour of men!
Thine is the glory of time's numbered pages;
Thine is the power to revive us again.

Pardon our sinfulness, God of all pity,
Call to remembrance Thy mercies of old;
Strengthen Thy Church to abide as a city
Set on a hill for a light to Thy fold.

Head of the Church on earth, risen, ascended!
Thine is the honour that dwells in this place:
As Thou hast blessed us through years that have ended,
Still lift upon us the light of Thy face.[1]

---

[1] Ernest N. Merrington, *The Church Hymnary, Revised Ed.* (O.U.P., 1927), no. 642.

Appendices

Appendix 1

Extraordinary Gifts

Much evangelical discussion on the Holy Spirit for over thirty years has centred on the above subject, and particularly on whether the miraculous gifts of the New Testament era were intended for the church in all ages. The issue here is not to be confused. It is not a question of whether God still works supernaturally but whether or not there is any group endowed to exercise *such gifts* as Christ referred to when he commanded: 'Heal the sick, cleanse the lepers, raise the dead' (*Matt.* 10:8). I can only touch on that discussion here. Among recent books the reader will find a full and careful discussion of the subject in Sinclair B. Ferguson, *The Holy Spirit* (IVP, 1996).

What I would point out is the fact that not since the time of the apostolic church has there been any group of Christians whose claim to be in possession of the extraordinary gifts of the New Testament age has deserved credibility. These gifts were unknown in the time of Chrysostom (*c.* 347–407) and Augustine (*c.* 354–430). Nor have they ever been possessed by any evangelical leaders in any of the revivals from the Reformation to the present century. Against the claim of the Roman Church that she is authenticated by the continuance of the miraculous, the reformers appealed solely to Scripture. They claimed apostolic truth, not apostolic gifts. The same was true in the Puritan period, through the Great Awakening in the time of Edwards, Whitefield and the Wesleys, and down to Spurgeon. All agreed with Whitefield that 'the miraculous gifts conferred on the primitive church have long since ceased.'¹ If such leaders were filled with the Spirit, as they were, in order to do such a mighty work, it is strange that they knew no miraculous gifts – supposing they were intended to be permanent. The more so as the Scripture teaches that gifts are sovereignly given by the Holy Spirit 'who works all these things, distributing to each one individually as He wills' (*1 Cor.* 12:11).

This is not to say that miraculous gifts have not been *claimed* among Protestants at any time. They have been repeatedly claimed by those whose ultimate history proved them to be fanatics whose hopes were delusions. This happened at the time of the Reformation and again in the following century when numbers were misled by those claiming to possess the spirit of prophecy. 'This age has had full and sad experience,' wrote John Flavel, of 'how catching and bewitching these things are.'² The same thing happened on the Continent among the French prophets; among the followers of Antoinette Bourignon; and among followers of Philipp Jakob Spener. One of the saddest examples in British history occurred in the 1830s with the influence of Edward Irving, concerning whom, on his death, Robert M'Cheyne wrote: 'A holy man in spite of all his delusions and errors. He is now with his God and Saviour, whom he wronged so much, yet, I am persuaded, loved so sincerely.'³

Theoretical discussion of the possibility of the continuance of miraculous gifts may continue but the historical facts are clear: great revivals have occurred without the presence of any

---

¹ Whitefield, *Works*, vol. 4, p. 9. Edwards is very clear and definite on the same subject. For references see my *Jonathan Edwards: A New Biography*, pp. 242–3. Further on the whole subject, and for documentation on historical references, see Walter J. Chantry, *Signs of the Apostles: Observations on Pentecostalism Old and New* (Edinburgh: Banner of Truth, 1976).

² John Flavel, *Works*, vol. 3 (repr. London: Banner of Truth, 1968), p. 482. For a larger seventeenth-century treatment of the subject, see Samuel Rutherford, *A Survey of the Spiritual Antichrist*, London, 1648.

³ A. Bonar, *Memoir and Remains of R. M. M'Cheyne* (London: Banner of Truth, 1966), p. 27. For a fuller account, see Arnold Dallimore, *The Life of Edward Irving* (Edinburgh: Banner of Truth, 1983).

such gifts, while excitement and interest in them may abound where there is no revival. All the claims for the renewed existence of extraordinary phenomena which have been successively made in the last thirty-five years – tongues, healings, prophecies and 'slaying in the Spirit' – far from preparing for revival, have rather been a distraction from the great truths which the Spirit has always honoured in the heralding of awakenings.

Appendix 2

Co-ordination of Grace and Duty[1]

by Hugh Martin

There is an extraordinary amount of light to be found in Philippians 2:12,13, as to the nature and connection of the Divine and human agencies in the sanctification, perseverance, and final salvation of the people of God. The Divine agency is asserted as a gracious and blessed fact; the human agency is enjoined as a solemn duty; and the one is made the basis of, or the ground or argument for calling forth, the other.

In the *first* place, the Divine agency is asserted as a gracious and blessed fact. 'It is God that worketh in you both to will and to do of his good pleasure'. In the *second* place, the human agency is enjoined, as distinctly as the Divine agency is affirmed. 'Work out your own salvation with fear and trembling.' In the *third* place, the two clauses which thus constitute one text, are so united as to form an argument or step of reasoning. The one is made a ground or basis for the other. The certainty and gracious nature of the agency of God is laid as a foundation for that agency of the Christian's own to which he is here exhorted. The fact that God worketh in his people is assumed as a powerful argument, or call, or motive

[1] Abridged from an article by Hugh Martin (1822–85) in the *British and Foreign Evangelical Review*, vol. 32, 1883. Titles of Hugh Martin's currently published by the Banner of Truth Trust are *Jonah*, in the Geneva Series of Commentaries, *The Shadow of Calvary* and *Christ for Us*.

for them to work. 'Work out your salvation with fear and trembling, for [because] it is God who worketh in you to will and to do of his good pleasure.' The scripture before us affirms that the high place of supremacy which God, by his Spirit, has thus assumed for himself in and over the soul of his own creature, chosen as the object of redeeming love, is not abandoned after this conversion has been effected, but is still maintained by the same God who 'worketh' there 'to will and to do.' Against this, however, it is objected:-

I. In the first place, that, if one being exert over another such a mastery and supremacy as is thus assigned to God over the souls of his people, whereby he certainly and invincibly works out his own purposes in them, then the subject of such an operation is not treated as a free and reasonable agent but as a mere machine, being made the helpless instrument of blindly accomplishing the designs of another.

A variety of answers might be given to show the unfounded and untenable nature of this objection:

(1) It is flagrant contradiction to the *spirit* of the text, which contains a solemn exhortation to Christians to watch over and work out their own salvation, and which supports this exhortation by urging a very solemn motive to obedience. Now, it is not treating a man as a machine to urge him to the performance of a duty, and press on his attention those considerations which ought to determine his line of conduct. It takes for granted that he has an understanding, and appeals to it when his faculty of intelligently comprehending what is said to him is sought to be awakened and informed. It supposes he is possessed by a conscience, and to that spiritual power within it intrusts, or seeks to lay on, a sense of obligation in the thing enjoined.

It is further to be observed, that while this is precisely the way to deal with man regarding him as possessed of reason and of freedom, this style of treatment is so little dispensed with or set aside by the doctrine of the Spirit's agency in

effectually renewing and sanctifying the believer, that, on the
contrary, the consideration of that agency is just the starting
point of the apostle's address in so dealing with his readers.
Instead of the effectual working of God's power superseding or
dispensing with the necessity of an appeal being carried to the
understanding and the will of the Christian, that effectual
working is itself made the topic of exactly such an appeal to the
Christian considered as dealt with and as capable of an
intelligent choice. When we read the first clause of our text, we
can reply to the objection that Scripture deals with believers
not as machines, but as free and reasonable agents, notwithstanding the supremacy and infallible efficiency of the agency
of God within them. But when we read the whole verse, and
find in what connection and on what grounds Scripture thus
exhorts and reasons with its believing readers, we can not only
reply that ALTHOUGH omnipotent grace be within them, they
are not thereby acted on formally and mechanically – but
further, that they are dealt with rationally and spiritually
precisely BECAUSE omnipotent grace worketh in them mightily.
So utterly is this objection in opposition to the whole scope and
spirit of the text.

(2) It is in equally flagrant contradiction to the express
language of the text. It is declared in these words that God
worketh in his people *to will*. He secures that their own free
choice shall be exercised: he renews and reforms their desire:
he guides and directs their inclination. In all to the
performance of which he carries them, he carries their *will*
also along with him. He makes them willing in a day of his
power. If he wrought in them '*to do*', without working in them
'*to will*', then indeed there might be some colour for the
allegation that the doctrine of effectual grace supposes man to
be dealt with as a machine, for a machine has no will. But if
every godly action which God worketh in the Christian is
preceded by a godly desire, inclination, and will to do that
action, this is exactly the condition which prevents the action
from being mechanical.

II. But again: It is further objected against the doctrine of invincible, prevailing, and controlling grace, that it is calculated to relax the diligence and energy of those who believe themselves the subjects of it. If it be true that the Almighty Spirit of God, dwelling in the Christian, infallibly and effectually secures his sanctification, nothing (it is argued) can be more natural than for the man himself to remit all his anxiety and sense of responsibility, and indolently leave to this omnipotent Agent the accomplishment of a work, for the furtherance of which any little energy of his can add nothing to that omnipotence already engaged upon it. The doctrine, it is said, will lead to indolence.

In reply to the assertion that the agency of God makes man a machine, it is enough to say that where God worketh he 'worketh in you *to will.*' And in like manner, in replying to the assertion that the same doctrine of God's certainly successful work of grace in his people is calculated to subdue and dispense with their own activities, it is enough to say that where God worketh he 'worketh in you *to do.*' The very thing which the Divine agency accomplishes is the expulsion of indolence and indifference, the replenishing of all the active powers with spiritual life, and the directing of them in and towards spiritual action. How therefore an operation which, from its very nature, is intended and calculated to result in the production of energy – an operation which is no otherwise and no further exerted than as it gives birth to energy – how this can beget the contrary inactivity it is impossible to comprehend; and hence indeed the objection ought not so much to be styled an objection to the doctrine of Divine agency, as an utter misconception of that doctrine, and a total denial of it in the only sense in which it is affirmed in Scripture, or held by intelligent Christians. The energetic Christian working out his salvation successfully, you are aware, can take no credit to himself, because, according to the doctrine of the text, it is God that worketh in him. But as little can the slumbering Christian, not working out his own salvation, take any warrantable comfort, just because, according to the same doctrine, his inactivity is a proof that God is *not* working in him to will and to do. That God worketh in his people effectually to will what is good and holy, and so as infallibly to secure their salvation, can minister no delight to the man who, by his conscious disinclination to Divine things, must know that the Divine Spirit has been so grieved away as to be no longer 'working in him *to will*.' And in like manner, the fact that God worketh in his people to *do*, to act spiritually, energetically, and successfully, so that they shall ultimately overcome and gain the prize, can afford no comfort to the man whose spiritual indolence tells him that God is not working in him to do.

* * *

The answers which the text thus so obviously affords to the two leading objections, so often urged against the Scripture doctrine of God's converting and sanctifying effectual grace, obviously tend to throw light upon the text itself, and to illustrate that connection between the Divine and human agencies against which, in point of fact, these objections are levelled. 1. Which is first in order of nature? 2. Which is first in point of time? 3. Which is first in point of importance? 4. Which is first in point of extent? It may tend yet further to illustrate this subject if we now reply to this short series of questions which an intelligent and reverential inquirer might be supposed to put.

1. And, first, it may be asked – Whether is the Divine agency or the human agency first in the order of nature, i.e. of cause and effect? If man's agency is closely related to God's, and yet is, as we have seen, voluntary – which is the cause of the other? or are they, though connected, yet not bound together by the tie of cause and effect at all? To this we answer, that the Divine agency is first in action in the order of nature. It is the sole cause of the believer's own agency. The whole of the believer's agency is the issue or effect of God's action. The text, in

asserting that God worketh in you to will and to do, attributes
to him every godly action you perform, and every godly
inclination which prompts you to the performance of it. It
assigns to his agency the work of quickening, strengthening,
controlling, and directing your powers of action, so that you
'do' his commandments or act out his will. And it further
assigns to his agency the work of quickening and spiritually
energising and righteously guiding your power of choice, so
that you 'will' what he wills, and delight yourself in his desires.
The godly deed, and the godly will from which it flows, are
alike the gift, and the in-wrought work of God. His Spirit is the
sole cause of a new heart and the sole cause of a new life.

2. But, secondly, it may be asked – Whether is the Divine
agency or the human agency first in point of time? And to this
I answer, that neither of them precedes the other in point of
time. Though the agency of God precedes the agency of the
believer in the order of nature, yet in respect of time they are
simultaneous. For, consider what it is that the Divine agency
accomplishes as soon as it comes into operation. God worketh
in you to do. He actually works that; not merely proposes and
attempts that; but does it. It is not only the intention of God's
working that you *should* work. But the certain effect of God's
working is that you *do* work. Your working is the immediate
and inevitable product – yea, the very essence or substance –
of God's work. The Divine agency cannot operate for a
moment without operating human energy; for such, by the
very terms of the text, is the nature of effectual grace. It works
in you to will and to do.

Take an instance or two. When the Spirit of supplications
descends on the believer, working according to the meaning of
that name which he hath been graciously pleased to assume,
the immediate result is that the believer prays in the Spirit.
The Spirit maketh intercession for him, and how but by
prompting the desires of his heart, which in their existence and
necessary heavenward tendency constitute the very essence of
prayer? Again, when the Spirit of wisdom and of revelation is

poured out and acts as an enlightening agent, 'shining in the heart,' the very meaning of this act implies that immediately the believer, with open face, beholds the glory of the Lord, and in the Spirit's light doth he see light. When the same gracious Spirit comes in another aspect of his gracious character, even as a Spirit of adoption sent forth into the believer's heart, instantly the Lord hears the cry, 'Abba, Father.' And exactly so with the general relation between the human agency and the Divine: the same thing is true which we behold in these particular cases alluded to. There is no interval of time between them. Their nature is such as to preclude this. If at any moment God is working in you, then at that very moment you are willing and doing. Your present godly will or work is not the result of God's past, but of God's present working in you. And God's present working in you is not the cause of any future godly will and deed, unless God shall work in you then as well as now. Your work and his are simultaneous. Neither of them is first in point of time.[1]

3. But, thirdly, it may further be asked – Whether is the Divine agency or the human agency first in point of importance? If by this be meant, Whether could God's agency or the believer's be more easily dispensed with? I reply that neither of them exceeds the other in importance, but that they are each alike indispensable. The Divine agency is indispensable, for we are not sufficient of ourselves to think anything as of ourselves, but our sufficiency is of God. And evidently also the human agency is equally indispensable, for if we are not thinking, willing, acting after a godly manner, it is clear that nought of God's sufficiency has been communicated to us, and nothing has been accomplished. Keeping in remembrance the answer to our first question, namely, that God's agency is the cause of man's, and hence that the Lord is not obstructed in the sense of needing to wait ere he put forth his power on a soul on the

[1] It is also vital to remember that, while it is God who is setting our spiritual life in motion, the soul is absolutely unconscious of any motions save its own.

ground that it is not yet willing or doing, and that no such idea is meant to be conveyed when we say that the human agency is absolutely necessary, we may now, without any disparagement to that which is the cause of the other, affirm that the one is just as indispensable as the other.

'Without me,' said Jesus, 'ye can do nothing.' And so without irreverence may we suppose him saying, 'Without you I can do nothing.' 'He did not many mighty acts there because of their unbelief.' The fact is – and it is to this that all our thoughts and reasonings on this subject are tending – the fact is that the agency of God in and through the believer, and the unbeliever's own voluntary and energetic godly agency in and under God, are inextricably united and intertwined with each other – so much so, indeed, that in strict propriety they are not to be regarded as two things ultimately distinct, but, when viewed more closely, resolvable into one, called at one time human agency, and at another time Divine agency, according to the point at which we stop in our inquiry into its nature, and especially its origin. In the one case, when I am working out my salvation, and a spectator sees only me working, he traces my work to my will: and attributing the work to me, which is perfectly correct, he denominates the work mine, or the agency human. But if that spectator is a spiritual man, and so is led to trace the matter a step or two further, he would now attribute my spiritual actions, and the very will which prompts them, to the God who gave them by working in me to will and to do. And what he formerly and rightly called human agency, he will now, and as correctly, call the agency of God. And most properly and beneficially may this alternating view be taken of the great work whereby a converted man is ultimately freed from all the power and wiles of Satan, all the vestiges of inward corruptions and all the corruption and temptation that are in the world. At one time, and for certain purposes, he is to look upon the work as his own. And at another time, and for other ends, he must feel and acknowledge that the work is God's.

For deepening my sense of responsibility I must bear in

remembrance that I and not another have to do this work; that I myself, and no other, must work out my salvation with fear and trembling; and then for bearing me up under the overwhelming impression that I have such a work to do, and in order to encourage myself in the Lord, I am to call to mind that it is God who performeth all things for me, and of his gracious pleasure worketh in me to will and to do. For purposes of duty, I must never forget that the work is strictly mine, – my *own* work, as truly as my *own* salvation. For purposes of praise, I must joyfully acknowledge that all the work is his, that no flesh should glory. And is not this the full explanation of those passages in which the apostle appears so often, as it were, to correct himself, and substitute another statement for the one which he apparently condemns and parts from, but to which he again returns as being quite defensible and accurate after all? He is only alternating between two expressions or assertions, both of them true, but which would indeed be contradictory were it not that they are to be resolved into one. 'I live, yet not I, Christ liveth in me; and yet I live a life of faith on the Son of God.' 'By the grace of God I am what I am.' 'I labour, striving according to his working that worketh in me mightily.' 'I laboured more abundantly than they all, - yet not I, but the grace of God that was with me.' 'I can do all things through Christ that strengtheneth me.' It is thus also we are to harmonise those numerous passages in which the very same work is attributed in one to the agency of God, in another to the believer himself. For on this principle it is at one time said that God purifies his people's hearts, and at another that they have purified their own souls by obeying the truth; at one time they give praise to God because he alone has cleansed them, and at another there is laid on them the duty of cleansing themselves from all filthiness of the flesh and spirit; at one time that God keeps every regenerated disciple through his own name, and at another that every one who is begotten of God keepeth himself.

4. There is yet another question which may be put on this

subject, viz., Whether the Divine agency or the human agency is first in point of extent? Whether does God's agency or man's accomplish most in this great undertaking in which they are so intimately united? The answer to this is, that neither of them exceeds the other in extent, but they are co-extensive. Man does as much when he works out his salvation as God does when he works in him to will and to do. They are mutually the measures of each other. This must be obvious from the views already taken of the relation which subsists between them, involving, as that relation does, a deep and ultimate identity. The Spirit of supplication is operating in me, just so far as I pray in the Spirit; the Spirit of wisdom is enlightening me to that extent, and no more, to which in his light I behold light; the Spirit of adoption is given me up to the measure of that filial confidence with which I can say, 'Abba, Father;' the Spirit who worketh all in all is given me so far as I labour according to his working; and the Spirit of the fear of the Lord is mine, so far as, working with fear and trembling, I stand in awe and sin not. It is God alone who energises the Christian; and so God does all. But he energises the Christian for the whole Christian life, and so the Christian himself does all. He cannot take a single step in advance of the efficacious grace of God, for that grace alone is sufficient for him, and Divine strength only can be perfected in his weakness; but to the full extent of that strength he is strong when he is weak, for grace does not take a single step beyond *him*, or without carrying his will and his work along with it.

It is because men have not chosen to observe, or understand, that the Divine and the human agencies in man's sanctification are exactly co-extensive, that the two objections which we formerly noticed were ever raised, or have so often been revived. The one supposes the action of God to go beyond the action of the believer's will; to that extent it would be dealing with him as a machine. The other supposes the Divine agency in like manner to go beyond the quickening and forthputting of the believer's energy, and to that extent leaving and encouraging him to be indolent. But these things are not so; neither let any be deceived, for to what extent God is working in you to will and to do, to that same extent will ye willingly and cordially work out your salvation with fear and trembling. And the conscious reality and measure of *will* with which you are working out your salvation is the only and the sure index of the measure or reality of that grace wherewith ye may infer that God is working in you.

* * *

This is an argument which addresses itself to your sense of awe. Consider what God is; what God hath said; what God hath done; and then think - that God dwelleth and worketh in you; contemplate the character of God as revealed in creation, in providence, in Scripture, and in the cross of Christ; and then think – that this God dwelleth and worketh in you! He who by stupendous power created this globe and hung it upon nothing, and gathered its waters in the hollow of his hand, and weighed its mountains in scales and its hills in a balance - this same God dwelleth within you!

No man ever did humbly and on right grounds realise that God was 'working in him to will and to do,' without feeling that the thought was an inspiring one, and that it nerved with a might and power to quell temptation, to scatter the fanciful allurements of sin, to burst the nets and snares of worldly compromise as cobweb-nets and nothing better, and to rescue him from the contact of that evil which was, perhaps, well nigh obtaining the mastery over him. And so will you find it on every fresh occasion an exhaustless fountain of hope and of encouragement, a perpetual spring of nervous energy and undying perseverance, an endless source of conquest and of triumph. Work, then, believer, while it is called today; whatsoever thy hand findeth to do, do it with thy might. Work the work of him who sent thee into the world, as the Father sent Him into the world, who will never leave you alone, but will be with you himself as the Father was ever with him. Work out your salvation solemnly, yet cheerfully, with awe, yet with hope; with an overpowering sense of a fearful responsibility, yet with the exulting assurance that you are enabled to meet and to discharge it. God *dwelleth* in you - let your soul be filled with holy fear and humble tremblings at his presence. God *worketh* in you - let your soul return unto her rest, convinced that he will perform all things for you most faithfully and well. A great work to do, but a great God to do it. 'And the God of peace make you perfect in every good work to do his will, working in you that which is well-pleasing in his sight, through Jesus Christ, to whom be glory for ever and ever.'

Appendix 3

Presbyterian Doctrine on Regeneration, Inability and Free-Agency[1]

We would observe that certain errors have been lately exhibited, which we think furnish just ground of alarm to the church. We will not undertake to say how much of this error may consist in unusual phraseology, nor how far it may arise from incorrect theological views. The mysticism of words has often been sufficient to raise separatory walls between brethren. Yet whether the error consist principally in words or things, it is not to our churches a matter of indifference. Words are understood to stand for things, and the erroneous phraseology of a writer or speaker is calculated to lead his readers or hearers wrong, and if generally adopted must subvert the faith of the purest churches. The points of error which we think the most dangerous to us, relate to original sin, regeneration, justification by the righteousness of Christ, and the ability of the creature. The doctrine of the Presbyterian Church touching *original sin* has always been, that our first parents, by their first act of disobedience, fell from their original righteousness and communion with God, and so became dead in sin, and wholly defiled in all the faculties of

[1] The following is taken from an Act of the Virginia Synod, adopted at Petersburg, 7 Nov. 1836 and printed in W. H. Foote, *Sketches of Virginia*, Second Series (Philadelphia: Lippincott, 1855), pp. 508–10. The original document, here abridged, was presented to the Synod by five of its members, George A. Baxter, Wiliam Hill, S. B. Wilson, William S. Plumer and James M. Brown.

soul and body; and they being the root of all mankind, the guilt of this sin was imputed, and the same death in sin and corrupted nature conveyed to all descending from them by ordinary generation; and that from this original corruption, whereby we are utterly indisposed, disabled, and made opposite to all good, and inclined to all evil, do proceed all actual transgressions. We deeply regret to see a phraseology used on this subject which is calculated to subvert the doctrine of our confession of faith, and, as we believe, of the Sacred Scriptures. Such as, original sin is no sin, but a mere tendency to sin, which in itself is not sinful; the posterity of Adam are in no sense guilty of, or liable for, his first sin; and that men are born innocent and without any moral character, etc. Whatever explanations may be given of such language by those who use it, we cannot but view it as calculated to introduce ruinous error into our church, if used by Presbyterian ministers.

On the subject of regeneration, Synod must testify against all modes of expression which imply that regeneration consists in a change of the governing purpose by the creature, or in a holy act, or series of acts of the creature, and not in the mighty working of the exceeding greatness of the divine power in new creating the soul, and enabling it to put forth holy exercises – or that regeneration is in any proper sense the work of any creature but of God only.

We are very much grieved by observing a tendency in many modern writings to introduce something like the Unitarian doctrine of justification; a doctrine which supposes that the death of our Saviour made no proper satisfaction to the claims of the divine law, and that the justice of heaven did not require such satisfaction to be made; but that God was always placable, and willing to justify the sinner by a mere act of sovereign pardon as soon as the sinner would turn to him with penitence and submission. We consider this doctrine as one of the most insidious and dangerous errors which has ever corrupted the Church of Christ. It sometimes assumes the plausible, but deceitful phraseology that Christ has made our atonement; has purchased our redemption, and that we are saved through his merits; while it denies, and is intended to deny the imputation of our Saviour's righteousness as the vicarious propitiation for our sins.

The *ability of the sinner* is sometimes rashly and erroneously exhibited, as if he were able to convert himself, and make himself a new heart independently of the sovereign, regenerating and converting grace of God. This doctrine, when carried out, goes to the subversion of our whole creed, and as we believe, to the subversion of the whole system of the gospel. Yet on this point we feel called on to say that there is on the other side an error which leads to an extreme equally dangerous and subversive of the Christian faith. We mean the error of those who assert that the sinner has no power of any kind for the performance of duty. This error strips the sinner of his moral agency and accountableness, and introduces the heresy of either Antinomianism or Fatalism. The true doctrine of our confession, and as we believe of the Scriptures, keeps continually in view the moral agency of man – the contingency of second causes – the use of means, and the utter inexcusableness of the creature; whilst at the same time it places all our dependence for salvation, on the sovereign power and grace of God, in the regeneration and justification of the sinner. Therefore, whilst Synod do constantly affirm that by the fall the human understanding has been greatly darkened, the faculties of the soul greatly impaired, and through the depravity of the heart the human will is entirely deprived of freedom to that which is good, and is free only to that which is evil, and that continually; yet they do assert that they cannot approve of any language which in its fair interpretation deprives man of his moral agency – denying that his enmity is voluntary, or teaching that it is in any wise excusable . . .

In the foregoing sentiments we are unanimous. And now we

solemnly call on all our members, and the friends of Zion within our bounds, in maintaining the unity of the spirit in the bonds of peace, to beware of a liberality which in any wise disregards the distinction between truth and error – to cultivate the spirit of fraternal kindness and confidence – to watch against the spirit of angry controversy – to pray for the peace of Jerusalem – to hold fast the form of sound words – to obey the truth and follow holiness, without which no man shall see the Lord.

Title Index

Biographical works are listed under the name of the person described, not the book title or author's name. Collected writings are listed under the author's name. Where several titles relate to the same person, they are brought together under his name. Commentaries and other expositions are listed together under *Commentary*. Full details of titles will be found on the page where the work is first mentioned.

General Index

Christ's work, comes before that of
the Spirit, 109–12
Christian, meaning of, 175–7
Christian experience
interpretation of, 105–33
of the love of God, 90–9
progress in, 127–30
two-stage, 120–130
unrealistic models of, 126–7
Chrysostom, 197
Churchill, Winston, 170
Colquhoun, John, 78
Comrie, Alexander, 26–7
Congo, 72
Conversion, distinguished from
regeneration, 49 n
Cowper, William, 66, 95
Crossweeksung, N. J., 2
Cuyler, Theodore, 1, 5, 11, 12, 39,
169

Dabney, R. L., 44 n, 51, 115 n, 184 n
Dallimore, Arnold, 198 n
d'Aubigné, J. H. Merle, 99
Davenport, James, 137, 139
Davis, Henry, 67
Dod, Albert B., 37 n, 45, 46 n, 50 n,
52, 138
Dods, Marcus, 172
Dornoch, Scotland, 71
Duncan, John ('Rabbi'), 71, 100 n
Dundee, Scotland, 90
Dunn, James, 118

Eadie, John, 130
Edwards, Jonathan
on Christian experience, 131
on extremes and fanaticism, 137,
141 n, 143 n
on miraculous gifts, 197–8
on physical responses, 147-8
on prayer for the advance of the
gospel, 77
on spiritual pride, 149–50

on nature of revival, 3 n, 23, 24,
32, 33, 73, 173, 192 n
on publicity for revivals, 168
on the ministry, 95, 131–2
on the sufficiency of Scripture,
150
Edwards, Sarah, 96, 132
Elias, John, 52–3, 62 n, 170
Elliott, Elisabeth, 97
Emotionalism (see also Fanaticism),
137, 142, 147–8
Evans, Christmas, 85 n
Evans, Eifion, 154 n
Evans, Robert, 180

Fairchild, J. H., 38
Fanaticism
consequences of, 151–3
dangers of, 136–44
illustrated in Welsh Revival of
1904–5, 153–64
lessons from, 168–9
meaning of, 135–6
ways of recognizing, 144–51
Ferguson, Sinclair B., 14, 197
Filling with the Spirit
and crisis experiences, 107–8,
120–2
and experience of the love of God,
91, 101
and preaching, 70, 81, 84, 101,
103, 122, 131–2
and worship, 192
meaning of, 105–6, 113, 116, 130
repeatable, 18–9, 118
Finney, Charles G., 8, 10, 28–9,
33–53, 62 n, 151, 166
Fitzgerald, Maurice H., 172
Flavel, John, 198
Fleming, Robert, 22
Fletcher, John, 126
Foote, W. H., 178
Fordyce, J., 174
Fournier, K. A., 143 n

set aside in Welsh Revival
(1904–5), 155–6, 165
Presbyterian doctrines (see also
*Larger Catechism, Shorter Catechism,
Westminster Confession*), 39–42, 212–
5
Pride, 148–51
Prime, Samuel I., 5 n, 48 n
Princeton Theological Seminary,
39, 45, 48, 50, 187–8
Public worship, 189–93
Purves, Libby, 152
Pyt, Henry, 179

Reformation, The
appealed to Scripture alone, 143,
174, 197
in relation to worship, 190
moral effects of, 181
preaching in relation to, 81
the Spirit's work in, 21–2, 81
Regeneration, 39, 49–50, 112–3,
212–5
Revival
biblical use of term 'revive', 3, 15
divine sovereignty in relation to,
70–9
excesses in connection with, *see*
Fanaticism
hindrances to, 134–5
human responsibility in relation
to, 54–69
moral impact on communities,
180–4
old-school view, 17–25, 49–53
origin of term, 3
prayer in relation to, 64–9
preaching in relation to, 80–104
recurring effects of, 171–93
schools of interpretation, 7–25
terminology, 2–4
tests of authenticity, 31–2
Robe, James, 22, 32, 67, 74, 147
Roberts, Emyr, 145 n

Roberts, Evan, 154–63
Rousseau, Jean-Jacques, 171
Rowland, Daniel, 85
Rutherford, Samuel, 131, 198 n
Ryle, H. E., 172
Ryle, J. C., 59, 172, 173 n, 181 n

Sample, Robert, 189
Sangster, W. E., 58
Schaeffer, Francis, 188 n
Second Great Awakening, 47, 67,
137, 140, 146, 182
Shedd, W. G. T., 16, 105, 167
Shorter Catechism, 41
Shotts, Scotland, 83
Sibbes, Richard, 88 n, 91, 121, 123,
130 n, 132
Simeon, Charles, 24
Skye, Scotland, 132–3
Slaying in the Spirit, 147, 199
Smeaton, George, 20, 21 n, 23, 125,
131, 178
Smith, Wilbur M., 1
Smith, Hannah Whitall, 165
Sovereignty of God, in relation to
revival, 70–9
Spener, Philipp Jakob, 198
Sperry, William, 2
Sprague, William B., 48 n, 67 n,
139 n, 140–1
Spring, Gardiner, 137–8, 149, 187 n
Spurgeon, C. H., 12, 63, 77, 89, 120,
134, 149 n, 186–7
Stott, John, 106 n, 111

Taylor, Howard, 97
Tarbat, Ross-shire, Scotland, 71
Tennent, Gilbert, 145n
Tennent, William, 187
Thornwell, J. H., 10 n, 104 n
Tonga, 180
Toronto Blessing, 148 n
Torrey, R. A., 116, 120
Tozer, A. W., 51 n, 57, 65, 87, 192

TITLES BY
IAIN H. MURRAY
AVAILABLE FROM
THE BANNER OF TRUTH TRUST

AUSTRALIAN CHRISTIAN LIFE FROM 1788: AN INTRODUCTION AND AN ANTHOLOGY

'Iain Murray's book describes the difficult beginnings of the Christian witness [in Australia], when "most would rather see a tavern, a playhouse, a brothel – anything sooner than a place of worship." He shows how God used faithful men who prayed and preached with dogged determination, undergoing many hardships, to see the church of Jesus Christ gradually established and expanding in this sun-burned land.'

Covenanter Witness

'Thrilling and heart-searching reading.'

Evangelical Times

'We warmly recommend this volume, not just because of its real historical interest, but also because of the encouragement it gives to Christians today to persevere in the face of what seem like insurmountable obstacles.'

Evangelical Presbyterian

D. MARTYN LLOYD-JONES: THE FIRST FORTY YEARS, 1899–1939
(Volume 1 of the Authorised Biography)

'Certain to be one of the major biographies of any Christian leader of the twentieth century.'

Sword and Trowel (Australia)

'If D. Martyn Lloyd-Jones' life were a novel it would be panned by critics as too unrealistic. Because his life is a historical reality we are left to wonder at the providential energy that could have effected such an astonishing career . . . This book is an electrifying apologetic for the powerfully theologized pulpit emphases of the Reformers and Puritans. Such an approach was in eclipse when Lloyd-Jones began his ministry. The renaissance of interest in Reformed theology is due in no small way to this man; he himself would attribute the resurgence to the sovereign grace of God.'

Christianity Today

D. MARTYN LLOYD-JONES:
THE FIGHT OF FAITH, 1939-1981
(Volume 2 of the Authorised Biography)

'This long awaited work is a worthy conclusion to the first volume published in 1982 . . . The life of Martyn Lloyd-Jones, much more than the story of one man's life, is really the story of evangelicalism in general and modern British evangelicalism in particular. Often Lloyd-Jones was the lone foil to many popular tendencies in evangelicalism . . . This biography should be added to the God-called pastor's reading if he wants to understand the times and receive benefit from the life of a man who will probably be viewed in the years ahead as our century's most enduring and doctrinally strong pastoral preacher.'

John Armstrong, *Trinity Journal*

'Splendidly written and passes the litmus test as a good and absorbing read from a biographer completely at home and in tune.'

Methodist Recorder

'Highly recommended, especially for those hungry for "iron rations".'

Christian Renewal (Canada)

JONATHAN EDWARDS:
A NEW BIOGRAPHY

'This is my book of the year for which I have waited a lifetime.'

Graham Miller, *Australian Presbyterian Life*

'Surely Murray's fine biography will gain the audience it deserves.'

William and Mary Quarterly

'A biography giving proper weight to the spiritual life and stature of Jonathan Edwards was needed ... This is what Iain Murray has provided and he has done the job well. He has unique skill in this area.'

J. I. Packer, Vancouver

'Murray provides a standard of excellence among Christian biographers. Edwards' life, especially as he presents it, offers significant challenge to Christians. No one should come away from it without being challenged to a deeper commitment to Jesus Christ, a greater desire for prayer and wholeheartedness, and a stronger resolve to be a doer of the Word as well as a hearer.'

Moody Monthly

REVIVAL AND REVIVALISM: THE MAKING AND MARRING OF AMERICAN EVANGELICALISM, 1750-1858

'It is a rare book that hits both head and heart in a way that turns a life. *Revival and Revivalism* had that effect on me, providing a clear and convincing perspective on the role and importance of revivals in American church history, bringing me to a new stage in my spiritual pilgrimage, and giving me a new hope for the prospects of the gospel in the world.'

Scott McCullough, *Blue Banner* (Pittsburgh)

'This is a book for which I have waited twenty years. It is a treatment of a crucial period in American religious history by one who is thoroughly familiar with the literature of revival and who possesses the theological stance and critical acumen properly to evaluate the events it relates. As a result, the issues raised by Iain Murray's treatment are nothing less than momentous for Southern Baptists as well as for evangelicalism at large.'

Terry A. Chrisope, *Founders Journal*

'*Revival and Revivalism* will be welcomed by evangelicals who reject Arminian theology and its concurrent emphasis on the role of human effort in religious conversion. It certainly will not be welcomed by most contemporary evangelical revivalists who are heirs of the Arminian theological tradition and the "new measures" revivalism of Finney.'

Church History

THE FORGOTTEN SPURGEON

'Iain Murray has written a fascinating book. It should not be read once, but several times, and in addition, certain passages should frequently be meditated upon. It is not a biography of Spurgeon, but it is a study (written in an interesting and absorbing style) of three of the doctrinal controversies through which Spurgeon had to go. To read this book will bring us face to face with some solemn questions. Cannot we abandon some of the frivolities in which we engage, and pray for a revival of preaching? Is it not time that we stop being concerned about *communicating* the gospel and become concerned about *preaching* it?'

Edward J. Young, Westminster Theological Seminary

SPURGEON v. HYPER CALVINISM:
THE BATTLE FOR GOSPEL PREACHING

'This reviewer knows of several pastors and missionaries who first came to the doctrines of grace by reading *The Forgotten Spurgeon*. But Iain Murray says that while his first book was needed thirty years ago to stimulate interest in Spurgeon's doctrinal foundation of Calvinism, the present volume is needed today to correct errors among contemporary Calvinists who have not carefully or fully followed Spurgeon's theology in practice . . . Read and discuss this volume soon. It is significant!'

Steve Martin, *Missionary Update*

For free illustrated catalogue please write to:
THE BANNER OF TRUTH TRUST
3 Murrayfield Road, Edinburgh EH12 6EL
P. O. Box 621, Carlisle, Pennsylvania 17013, U.S.A.